‖‖‖ ‖ ‖‖‖‖‖‖ ‖ ‖ ‖‖‖‖‖‖‖‖‖‖ ‖‖‖
W9-BWP-687

A Guide to Reflective Practice for New and Experienced Teachers

Hope J. Hartman, Ph.D.
The City College of New York

McGraw Hill Higher Education

Boston   Burr Ridge, IL   Dubuque, IA   New York
San Francisco   St. Louis   Bangkok   Bogotá   Caracas   Kuala Lumpur
Lisbon   London   Madrid   Mexico City   Milan   Montreal   New Delhi
Santiago   Seoul   Singapore   Sydney   Taipei   Toronto

The McGraw·Hill Companies

Higher Education

Published by McGraw-Hill, an imprint of The McGraw-Hill Companies, Inc., 1221 Avenue of the Americas, New York, NY 10020. Copyright © 2010. All rights reserved. No part of this publication may be reproduced or distributed in any form or by any means, or stored in a database or retrieval system, without the prior written consent of The McGraw-Hill Companies, Inc., including, but not limited to, in any network or other electronic storage or transmission, or broadcast for distance learning.

This book is printed on acid-free paper.

1 2 3 4 5 6 7 8 9 0 DOC/DOC 0 9

ISBN: 978-0-07-337834-3
MHID: 0-07-337834-8

Editor in Chief: *Michael Ryan*
Editorial Director: *Beth Mejia*
Publisher: *David Patterson*
Sponsoring Editor: *Allison McNamara*
Editorial Coordinator: *Sarah Kiefer*
Developmental Editor: *Jill Eccher*
Marketing Manager: *James Headley*
Project Manager: *Rachel J. Castillo*
Cover Designer: *Mary-Presley Adams*
Design Manager: *Ashley Bedell*
Production Supervisor: *Louis Swaim*
Composition: *Macmillan Publishing Solutions*
Printing: 45# *New Era Matte Plus, R.R. Donnelley*

Library of Congress Cataloging-in-Publication Data

Hartman, Hope J.
  A guide to reflective practice for new and experienced teachers / Hope Hartman. —1st ed.
     p. cm.
  Includes index.
  ISBN-13: 978-0-07-337834-3 (alk. paper)
  ISBN-10: 0-07-337834-8 (alk. paper)
  1. Reflective teaching. I. Title.
  LB1025.3.H379 2009
  371.102—dc22

                                                              2008049015

The Internet addresses listed in the text were accurate at the time of publication. The inclusion of a Web site does not indicate an endorsement by the authors or McGraw-Hill, and McGraw-Hill does not guarantee the accuracy of the information presented at these sites.

www.mhhe.com

JAN 1 1 2011

About *The Practical Guide Series*

New teachers face a seemingly endless set of challenges—classroom management, assessment, motivation, content knowledge, cultural responsiveness, inclusion, technology—just to name a few. Preparing for the profession can at times seem overwhelming. Teacher candidates may begin to see solutions to some of the anticipated challenges as they progress through a program of study but know that there are many that await them in their first classroom. Support by mentors and colleagues is crucial for beginning teachers, and this series is designed to bolster that guidance. *The Practical Guide Series* provides another level of support for these new and future professionals.

The series was conceived in response to concerns about teacher retention, especially among teachers in their first to fourth years in the classroom when mentorship and guidance play a crucial role. These titles offer future and beginning teachers a collection of practical advice that they can refer to in student teaching and in the early teaching years. Instructors of pre-service teachers can use these books to reinforce concepts in their texts with additional applications, use them to foster discussion, and help guide pre-service students in their practice teaching.

Besides addressing issues of basic concern to new teachers, we anticipate generating a level of excitement—one that a traditional textbook is hard-pressed to engender—that will further motivate entrants into this most essential profession with a contagious enthusiasm. A positive start to a teaching career is the best path to becoming a master teacher!

Alfred S. Posamentier, *Series Editor*
Dean, The School of Education,
The City College of New York

This book is dedicated to my parents,
Lillian and Philbert Hartman,
my first and best teachers.

Contents

Preface

This book is designed to help new and experienced teachers teach both **for** and **with** reflective and critical thinking. Teaching for reflective and critical thinking refers to helping your students increase their awareness of their thoughts and knowledge and increase their control over their learning and thinking. Teaching with reflective and critical thinking refers to helping you become more aware of your own thoughts and knowledge about teaching and learning and enhancing your control over your thinking, knowledge, and instructional activities. The overarching goal is for students to become exemplary, independent thinkers and learners with abilities to acquire, use, evaluate, and modify their knowledge and skills in school and in their everyday lives. To accomplish this goal, students need your expert philosophy and practice, characterized by your own reflective and critical thinking.

✴ Background

This book is a culmination of my work of over 30 years with teachers, tutors, professors, and students on how to think reflectively and critically about teaching and learning. My career has been graced with rich, diverse experiences with instructors at all grades and school levels, in all subjects, and in urban, suburban, and rural environments. I am deeply indebted to all of them for helping me understand what really happens in classrooms and how scholarly work on thinking, teaching, learning, and technology can be applied to improve teaching and learning processes. They also helped me appreciate the importance of focusing on subject-specific thinking strategies for teaching and learning in addition to thinking strategies that transcend specific subjects. Finally, they contributed to my understanding of the "big picture" need to teach both for and with critical, reflective thinking. This is a fundamental need for both new and experienced teachers.

✴ Organization

The book is divided into two sections. The first focuses on issues of reflective practice with general importance for new and experienced teachers regardless of the subjects they teach. Topics in this section, Chapters 1–8, include classroom management, teaching strategies, and assessment. The second section, Chapters 9–14, focuses on reflective and critical thinking in each of the major content areas, such as science, English, and history.

Each chapter begins with an overview and ends with a summary and identification of resources, including references to ideas included in the chapter.

⚹ Themes

Themes developed throughout the text are addressing students' prior knowledge, including preconceptions that may inhibit learning; questioning as a strategy to promote reflective and critical thinking; using graphic organizers to improve comprehension and memory and to aid understanding of relationships between ideas; comprehending differences between experts and novices; having a varied repertoire of active learning strategies; meeting the needs of culturally diverse learners; and using technology to enhance teaching and learning.

⚹ Acknowledgments

I am grateful to the four anonymous reviewers who provided me with excellent feedback on an early version of this manuscript. Their advice helped guide my revisions and shape this version of the book, including making the title reflect its value for both new and experienced teachers. My editors, Jill Eccher and Allison McNamara, were the keys to providing this feedback, so I am very grateful to both of them. I also greatly appreciate Cheryl Smith, whose copyediting of the manuscript improved the flow and organization; and Rachel Castillo, my production manager, for ensuring that the text and graphics were faithful to my intent.

The late Howard E. Gruber, my main professional mentor, inspired my interest in improving thinking through a graduate seminar in 1973. In 1974 we co-taught an undergraduate course, "How to Think Better." My career as a professor, tutor trainer, researcher, evaluator, and curriculum and staff developer has emphasized this topic ever since. I am forever indebted to him for his leadership, wisdom, and support.

I am extremely grateful to Zoë Putnam for her outstanding editing of an early version of this manuscript, and for her multifaceted mentoring. She truly has been one of my "super-teachers," influencing my deepest beliefs, values, and behavior.

My daughter, Alicia Volkheimer, and late husband, Michael J. Holub, have provided me with valuable insights into priorities, positive thinking, and persistence.

Finally, I appreciate the continuous support of Bob Wechsler, as we simultaneously worked on our books.

Hope J. Hartman
The City College of New York

Reflecting on Practice

What types of struggles do you encounter in teaching? Why do they occur? To what extent do you think reflectively and critically about your teaching so that you can address such problems most effectively?

What types of struggles do your students have in learning? What are the various causes? To what extent do your students think reflectively and critically about their own learning so that they can overcome their problems?

What strategies can you use to help your students develop their reflective and critical thinking skills so that they can become independent, self-directed learners?

❊ What Is Reflective Practice?

These types of questions about your instruction and your students' thinking and learning epitomize reflective teaching practice. They show your attention to

1. identifying problems or crises that occur in teaching;
2. thinking about causes of classroom events;
3. reflecting on your own actions;
4. making efforts to improve your own success and that of your students.

Reflective teaching practice focuses on "thinking about doing" before, during, and after a lesson. Reflective learning focuses on "thinking about doing" before, during, and after a learning activity. At its most effective, reflective teaching serves as a role model for your students and helps them become reflective learners. Teachers, students, administrators, and even parents can benefit from reflective practice.

Reflective practice is a process of introspection. By analyzing and critically assessing past, current, and/or future thoughts, attitudes, and actions, the teacher strives to attain insight and improve future performance. Reflective practice often occurs as a reaction to a problem that arises, trying to make sense of the problem and how to handle it, but it can also be used proactively to prevent problems from arising. Although becoming a reflective practitioner requires conscious, intensive effort at first, with practice and experience reflection can be automatically applied to everyday life experience both inside and outside the classroom.

Schon introduced two important concepts of reflective practice: "reflection on action" and "reflection in action," both of which are emphasized throughout this book.

Reflection on action generally refers to thinking about how you will perform and how you did perform, reaching both forward and backward. In teaching, this often corresponds to planning a lesson and how you will conduct it, then afterward evaluating the lesson and its success. Evaluating should lead to ideas about how to improve your actions in the future, so backward reaching leads to forward reaching. **Reflection in action** is often characterized as "thinking on your feet," while you are engaged in action. In teaching, this often corresponds to pausing during a lesson to check on students' understanding and learning, and on whether the methods you're using are leading in the right direction or you should try something else.

Observation is an important component of reflective thinking because it enables you to assess various situations. Some observation depends on using your senses, such as seeing and hearing what is taking place. Such observations help you determine what conditions are facilitating teaching and learning and what conditions are impeding teaching and learning. Recollection is another component of reflective thinking because it enables you to use your memory to bring back observations you have made at other points in time. Combining and considering present and past observations helps you develop a clearer picture of factors that affect teaching and learning.

Phases of Reflective Practice

The 1933 edition of Dewey's *How We Think* has an entire chapter on reflective thinking. Dewey identifies five phases or functions of reflective activity.

1. *Suggestion.* Suggestion refers to ideas that arise spontaneously, related to a focused-on thought. It's important to recognize and appreciate suggestion because ideas don't occur in isolation. They occur in a context that contains and automatically conveys related thoughts, if you let them through. In reflective thinking it's important to realize that information presented as facts has potential alternative interpretations.

Suggestion also includes inferences. Inferences go beyond the factual information given in an observation. Reflective thinking involves suspending judgment, seeking out additional observations, and reconsidering the validity of facts and inferences rather than accepting and acting on them with the assumption they are true when first presented.

2. *Intellectualization.* Intellectualization refers to moving beyond the emotional experience of feeling perplexed by an obstacle or problem. It involves the intellectual processes of moving beyond the original, spontaneous reaction to the felt difficulty, recognizing the messiness and complexity of problems, and understanding the situations in which they occur. To solve a problem, first it must be clearly identified and defined in context.

3. *Guiding idea/hypothesis.* After the initial response to a problem has been converted from an emotional to an intellectual reaction, you can exercise more control over the situation and have a better idea about how to solve the problem. Facts, suggestions, and insights become transformed into a tentative hypothesis, which guides problem solving. Further observations, facts, inferences, suggestions, and intellectualization might lead to reformulating the hypothesis.

4. *Reasoning.* Well-informed minds elaborate on ideas generated from hypothesis testing so that they differ from their initial state. Prior knowledge and experience, along with concepts from the current culture, help transform information, to produce related ideas so that eventually there is a chain of extended, related thoughts. Through reasoning, ideas that initially appear to conflict are reconciled or synthesized.

5. *Testing the hypothesis by action.* The final phase of reflection involves conducting a test through observation or experiment to verify an idea. If the idea is true, certain consequences will follow. Both successes (idea is valid) and failures (idea is invalid) are valuable because they provide important information to the reflective thinker. Validation can lead to formulating sound conclusions about the problem situation. Failures can lead to identifying new observations that should be made, generating new hypotheses, defining new problems, and clarifying existing problems. From Dewey's perspective, experience is a teacher because with reflection, it can influence the quality of future practice.

Reflective practice has different implications for different professions. Schon's (1983) book, *The Reflective Practitioner*, which quickly became a modern classic, focuses on the professions of architecture, psychotherapy, science, and town planning. In 1987 he wrote a book focusing specifically on reflective practice in education. His emphasis on reflective practice as "thinking about doing" is very similar to John Dewey's ideas about reflective thinking.

Reflective practice involves integrating aspects of teaching that are often treated as sequential instead of simultaneous. One example is theory, research, and practice. Though often treated separately in teacher education courses, reflective practitioners combine these three forms of knowledge while they are teaching. Another example is thinking and doing. Reflective teachers synthesize thinking and doing while conducting a lesson. A third example is school and everyday life experience. Reflective teachers make explicit connections between what students learn in school and applications of this knowledge to everyday life experience, and they do this while teaching the material, rather than afterward.

✧ Purposes and Themes of This Book

This book is intended to help you achieve the objectives of promoting reflective practice in your teaching and in your students' learning. It is based on current theory and research on how people learn and how to teach in ways that maximize learning. The diverse strategies included are geared toward the needs of new as well as experienced middle and high school teachers.

Questioning

Questioning is a powerful strategy for enhancing reflective thinking. Questions asking you to think about your teaching are incorporated throughout the book to help you develop the habit of questioning yourself and your students so that you can guide your own reflective practice in teaching, and help your students learn to assess and guide their own reflective thinking and learning.

Prior Knowledge

What kinds of assumptions do you make about your students? Are they "empty vessels" with no knowledge about what they are supposed to learn from you? Although this used to be the predominant view of learners, it has been discredited in recent years.

Students come to the classroom with prior knowledge about many of the things they are expected to learn. Some of this knowledge can be used as building blocks to acquiring new information, making their learning more meaningful. However, one of the most common and difficult problems you are likely to encounter is students coming to your class with invalid ideas learned from their everyday life experiences, from books, and even from other classes they have taken over the years.

It may become apparent that a student's learning is contaminated by invalid prior knowledge, some preconception or misconception that inhibits learning. Sometimes it is clear that there was a miscommunication or misunderstanding about something a teacher said or something that was in the book. Consequently, the perspective shift alters teachers' ideas about how to teach particular material to specific students in specific situations.

Naïve theories, preconceptions, and misconceptions are all terms referring to problematic conceptions that can impede learning. Currently, many people prefer the term preconceptions to misconceptions, as a way to distance themselves from "deficit" models of thinking and learning. These types of conceptions occur in all grades and all subjects, and are found in teachers as well as students. One of the purposes of this book is to help you and your students become more aware of preconceptions and implement strategies for developing valid and complete conceptions.

Cultural Diversity

Another purpose of this book is to help you become aware of and challenge assumptions you make about your students and help your students become aware of and challenge the assumptions they make about themselves as learners and the content they study in school. Challenging the assumptions you and others make is part of the essence of critical thinking. A corollary to challenging assumptions is providing solid, well-substantiated evidence to support conclusions. This type of critical thinking is essential for effective teaching and learning, and its development is another major theme of this book.

To what extent do you and your students make assumptions about people on the basis of their cultural or ethnic background? In the United States of America and around the world, many cultures are becoming increasingly diverse. Reflective practice helps culturally different teachers and learners work together more effectively and respectfully. Multicultural learning environments are potentially very rich sources for engendering reflection and critical thinking as multiple and diverse perspectives are likely to abound.

When most of us in the U.S.A. think about learning a foreign language, we might think of Spanish, French, Italian, Chinese, German, or Russian. However, for a significant and increasing number of our students, English is a foreign language because it's not their native tongue. ESL/EFL teachers obviously are well aware of this fact, but teachers of subjects such as science, mathematics, and history often don't think about this issue unless they reflect on what learning is like from their students' points of view.

Our ethnocentrism often inhibits an awareness and appreciation that many of our students have the dual task of learning content, such as science, while simultaneously learning the foreign language of English, which embeds the content. Reflective teachers think about their classroom practices, their actions and communications, and their students' perspectives on what they are learning.

Cultural factors, including students' native language, and family background issues, such as socioeconomic status, can have a major impact on academic success. To what extent are you aware of cultural/family factors affecting your students? For example, how involved are their parents in their school work? Are there other family members, such as siblings, aunts, or grandparents, who contribute to their academic success? To what extent does their family participate in school activities or attend school events? If their parents aren't very involved, what are the reasons? Often parents aren't involved with their children's schooling because of conflicts with work schedules. To what extent is this a problem for your students? How might you find out? How might you overcome this obstacle to communicating with your students' parents and perhaps increase their involvement? Strategies are presented later in this book.

Experts Versus Novices

A characteristic of reflective practice that transcends the various professions is the emphasis on thinking about your professional experiences in order to figure out new and better approaches for achieving your goals. At the end of a day of teaching, both expert and novice teachers often think about their classes and consider what went well and what did not go as well as hoped or expected. The goal of this reflection is to improve teaching.

Novice teachers sometimes think that experts have all the answers. To the contrary! Expert teachers are not always successful reaching their students on their first attempts, but they are willing to identify their failures with attitudes of openness and acceptance and open to taking the risks of trying new approaches or adapting old ones to meet the needs of particular students in particular situations.

Expert teachers recognize that instruction is often a complex, messy enterprise requiring struggle, patience, and persistence. They try to figure out reasons for lack of success by looking at learning experiences from the student's point of view instead of just their own. They appreciate the importance of being sensitive to and recognizing individual differences in students as learners. This perspective shifting from focusing on what makes sense to them to what makes sense to their students often leads to crucial insights about why instruction did not achieve the desired level of success.

Novice learners are much like novice teachers. Novice learners often mistakenly believe that expert students get answers right quickly and easily. They don't realize that expert students are often puzzled when learning and struggle to learn new material so that they understand, remember, and can apply it to new situations. Another theme of this book is the characteristics of expert and novice teachers, and expert and novice learners in general and in specific subjects.

Technology

Finally, education today has numerous, powerful technological resources for promoting reflective practice. However, the best use of technology is to supplement rather than supplant person-to-person teaching and learning. A guideline for using technology effectively is to consider whether you can accomplish the same educational objectives without it. Only if you can't does technology serve education instead of education serving technology. Using technology to promote reflective and critical practice in teaching and learning is another major theme of this book.

✄ Being a Reflective Teacher

Why do you want to be a reflective practitioner? For many teachers it's because they want to do their best to help their students learn and develop to their fullest potential. To accomplish this, you need to observe yourself as a teacher and be open to discovering your own strengths and weaknesses. Being defensive about one's shortcomings, or denying their existence, is the antithesis of reflective teaching. Limitations are growth opportunities! The classroom is best viewed as a laboratory for insight, creativity, and experimentation designed to improve teaching and learning.

Reflecting on your teaching before a lesson is part of the process of planning what to teach, when, why, and how to teach it. This is reflection on action. Reflecting during a lesson is part of the process of checking up on or monitoring students' understanding of the lesson and their progress achieving the targeted goals and objectives. At this stage, reflection enables on-the-spot revision of plans based on students' experiences and needs. Upon discovering a problem in comprehension or mastery, you can invent a new approach or adapt an existing approach to prevent difficulties from continuing and possibly compounding. This is reflection in action.

Reflecting after a lesson helps you evaluate progress, identify strengths and weaknesses, and plan for future lessons based on this experiential analysis and feedback. This is another dimension of reflecting on action. Consequently, reflective practice is a recursive rather than linear management cycle of planning, monitoring, and evaluating your performance by reflecting on and in action. The processes of planning, monitoring, and evaluating teaching (and learning) are recurrent themes in this book, but they are treated most comprehensively in Chapter 2, Managing Teaching Reflectively.

An important component of effective planning for instruction includes knowing what teaching strategies to use, and when, why, and how to use them. These same types of reflections are also essential for students to use learning strategies effectively.

Reflective practice entails adopting the attitude of a careful, thoughtful, self-observer whose attitudes toward teaching and teaching practices are informed by society's purposes and moral values. Activities include slowing down or stopping to notice what is going on, inquiring about instructional events and their specific context, analytically thinking about and critiquing your actions with an open mind, making sense of what is occurring, considering alternative perspectives, contemplating use of a variety of potential actions, and anticipating their consequences.

Reflective practice facilitates modifying on-the-spot actions to enhance effectiveness and learning from your experiences. Compared to non-reflective teachers, reflective teachers have deeper understanding of themselves and their students; their implicit assumptions; instructional goals and strategies; motivation, beliefs, attitudes, behavior, and what constitutes academic success. Additionally, they are better at bridging the gap between theory and practice, appreciating when, why, and how theory can inform practice, and recognizing when theory and practice conflict. Reflective practitioners consider themselves to be ever-evolving works in progress.

Reflective teachers don't get bogged down with stereotypes, overgeneralizations, or past histories of success using a particular approach with other students. They realize there is no single best way to teach anything, that teachers need a repertoire of strategies, and the willingness and skills to make adaptations and create alternatives. This fresh perspective makes teaching a challenging, dynamic, and exciting enterprise.

Reflection on failures in teaching compares to students performing error analyses on the answers they get wrong on tests. When performing an error analysis (discussed most fully in Chapter 7, Reflective Assessment Practices), the learner answers the following self-questions: What did I get wrong? What is the correct information? Why did I make that mistake? How can I prevent future similar mistakes? Learners not only get a second opportunity to master important material, they can also discover patterns in their errors, and develop more effective learning and memory strategies to improve future performance.

One cyclical model of reflective teaching involves asking oneself some variation of these five questions: What did I do as a teacher? What did I intend to accomplish? Why did I arrive at this perspective and approach the lesson this way? How might I teach differently? What and how should I teach now based on my experiences, inquiry, and new insights?

Both reflective teachers and reflective learners are like scientists: They grapple with problems, generate and test hypotheses, collect data, interpret results, draw conclusions, and identify limitations in their own work.

⚔ Strategies for Promoting Reflective Practice

What are some of your thoughts at the end of a work day? It's a good idea to keep a journal to record them so that you can systematically attend to important issues, especially those that recur or become persistent problems. Two strategies specifically designed to promote reflective teaching practice based on your classroom experiences are Guided Reflection and the Critical Incidents Protocol.

Guided Reflection

Guided Reflection involves an individual teacher collecting a set of stories or episodes for reflective analysis and then engaging in a four-step process of reflection about each episode. Each step is guided by a self-question, which is a common strategy for reflective thinking. The questions are:

1. What happened?
2. Why did it happen?
3. What might it mean?
4. What are the implications for my practice?

This protocol was designed to promote deep reflection for improving teaching as a result of rethinking and changing practice. What are some incidents from your teaching experiences that might benefit from Guided Reflection?

Critical Incidents Protocol

The Critical Incidents Protocol is similar to Guided Reflection, but designed for collaborative work with other teachers. It involves teachers sharing their stories with other teachers, receiving and giving each other feedback, for the benefit of both the individual teacher and the group. The groups follow a seven-step process for one hour and ten minutes.

1. Write stories. Everyone in the group writes a story about a problematic classroom event. (10 minutes)
2. Choose a story. The group selects a story to focus on. (5 minutes)
3. What happened? The story author reads the written account of what happened and puts it into a context of professional goals. (10 minutes)
4. Why did it happen? The group asks clarifying questions. (5 minutes)
5. What might it mean? The group asks questions about the incident using the professional context. Group members act as caring professionals who discuss the case while the presenter listens. (15 minutes)

6.   What are the implications for practice? The story author reacts to the discussion and feedback from colleagues and tries to identify new insights for improving teaching practice. (15 minutes)
7.   Debrief the process. The group discusses what happened and how the process worked. (10 minutes)

Your school is likely to have expert teachers who can share ideas on teaching strategies that promote reflective practice and who can mentor novice teachers. How might you identify and get together with other teachers to share and analyze classroom events to support your own and each other's professional development? Build a repertoire of instructional strategies to promote reflective practice that meets your needs and those of your students.

Summary

This book is intended to help you reflect on and critically evaluate your teaching and help your students reflect on and critically evaluate their learning. The goal is to use reflection and critical thinking to improve teaching and learning. Themes developed throughout the book include questioning, activating and addressing prior knowledge, differences between experts and novices, cultural factors affecting thinking and learning, using technology to enhance teaching and learning, and helping your students think critically and reflectively across the curriculum and in everyday life. Various teaching strategies can be used to promote reflective and critical thinking.

Resources

Brookfield, S. *Becoming a Critically Reflective Teacher.* San Francisco: Jossey-Bass, 1995.
Clift, W. R.; and M. C. Pugach. *Encouraging Reflective Practice in Education.* New York: Teachers College Press, 1990.
Cruickshank, D.; and J. Applegate. "Reflective Teaching as a Strategy for Teacher Growth." *Educational Leadership* 38, no. 4 (1981), pp. 553–54.
Dewey, J. *How We Think.* Chicago: Henry Regnery Co., 1933.
Hole, S.; and G. McEntee. "Reflection Is at the Heart of Practice." In *Kaleidoscope: Readings in Education,* ed. K. Ryan and J. Cooper. Boston: Houghton Mifflin Company, 2001, pp. 25–29.
McKernan, J. *Curriculum Action Research: A Handbook of Methods and Resources for the Reflective Practitioner.* London: Kogan Page, 1996.
Pacheco, A. Q. "Reflective Teaching and Its Impact on Foreign Language Teaching," "*Revista Electronica Actualidades Investigatives en Educación*" V. 5 Numero Extraordinario, 2005. Retrieved 7/31/07 from http://revista.inie.ucr.ac.cr/articulos/extra-2005/archivos/reflective.pdf#search=%22Reflective%20Teaching%20and%20Its%20Impact%20on%20Foreign%20Language%20Teaching.%22
Schon, D. A. *Educating the Reflective Practitioner.* San Francisco: Jossey-Bass, 1987.
Schon, D. A. *The Reflective Practitioner: How Professionals Think in Action.* New York: Basic Books, 1983.

Managing Teaching Reflectively

This chapter introduces many of the reflective teaching and learning principles and strategies developed throughout the book. Included are the BACEIS model of improving thinking; goals of teaching; teaching guidelines; principles of critical, reflective teaching; and characteristics of a successful, reflective classroom environment. This chapter also provides several powerful ideas to help you manage the process of teaching, including strategies for effective instruction and for assigning homework. Other chapters have more in-depth discussion of specific teaching strategies, and Chapter 7 has more extensive treatment of assessment. Behavior problems are discussed in Chapter 5, Reflective Classroom Management.

✖ BACEIS Model of Improving Thinking

The BACEIS model of improving thinking is the theoretical framework that underlies the ideas in this book. (See Figures 2.1 and 2.2.) It is a comprehensive framework of factors internal and external to the student that affect academic performance. Internal factors include cognition (thinking and knowing) and affect (emotions); external factors are academic and nonacademic environments. The BACEIS acronym represents these factors as B = behavior, A = affect, C = cognition, E = environment, I = interacting, S = systems.

The model says that internal factors of a student's cognition and emotions are related to each other and are also related to external factors from academic and nonacademic environments. The combination of these reciprocal influences impacts a student's thinking and academic performance.

As Figures 2.1 and 2.2 illustrate, two supersystems interact with each other and behavior. The internal supersystem includes student's cognition and emotions (affect). The external supersystem includes academic and nonacademic environments. The cognitive component involves higher-level (metacognitive) thinking skills and lower-level (cognitive) skills, as well as critical thinking, creativity, and learning strategies. The part of the model focusing on emotions consists of motivation, affective self-regulation, and attitudes. The academic environment includes teacher characteristics, content, instructional techniques, and classroom environment. The nonacademic environment consists of family background, cultural forces, and socioeconomic status. These environmental factors interact with each other and with the rest of the components in the

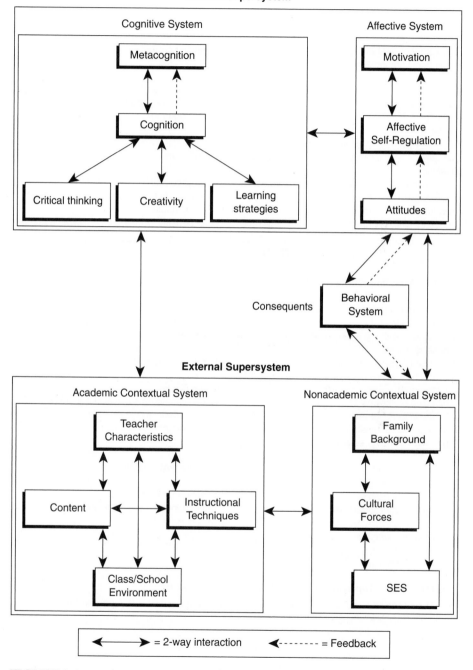

ANTECEDENTS
(Internal & External Supersystems)

Internal Supersystem

Cognitive System

Metacognition

Cognition

Critical thinking   Creativity   Learning strategies

Affective System

Motivation

Affective Self-Regulation

Attitudes

Consequents

Behavioral System

External Supersystem

Academic Contextual System

Teacher Characteristics

Content   Instructional Techniques

Class/School Environment

Nonacademic Contextual System

Family Background

Cultural Forces

SES

← → = 2-way interaction   ←----- = Feedback

FIGURE 2.1 *BACEIS Model Components*

Hope Hartman and Robert J. Sternberg, "A broad BACEIS for improving thinking," *Instructional Science* 21, 1993, pp. 401–25. Reprinted with permission from Springer.

ANTECEDENTS—INTERNAL SUPERSYSTEM

Keisha's Cognitive System

Metacognition
– skim, image
– monitor comprehension
– self question, lookback

Cognition
– encode information
– clarify
– infer

Critical Thinking	*Creativity*	*Learning Strategies*
– evaluates alternative energy sources	– designs new way to purify gasoline	– selective attention

Keisha's Affective System

Motivation
– interested in content and wants to answer questions correctly
– wants to please parents and teachers

Affective Self-Regulation
– expects to be good reader
– values reading

Attitudes

– good reading self concept
– curious about content due to father's occupation
– persists when reading difficult material

EXTERNAL SUPERSYSTEM

Keisha's Academic Contextual System

Teacher Characteristics
– reading specialist
– extensive teaching experience
– positive toward students
– diverse teaching repertoire

Content (text)
– gasoline emissions
– ozone in atmosphere
– cars vs. mass transit
– alternative energy sources

Class Environment
– students challenge authority
– resources accessible
– content at appropriate level

Instructional Techniques
– reciprocal teaching
– imagery formation

Keisha's Nonacademic Contextual System

Family Background
– native speakers of English
– family reads and discusses books at dinner
– brothers/sisters good readers
– father owns gas station

Cultural Forces
– need reading as survival skill in society (signs, labels, job applications)
– television inhibits reading

Socioeconomic Status
– money for books, newspapers,
– leisure time for reading
– father's income crucial to support family

FIGURE 2.2   *Application of BACEIS Model to Reading*

Hope Hartman and Robert J. Sternberg, "A broad BACEIS for improving thinking," *Instructional Science* 21, 1993, pp. 401–25. Reprinted with permission from Springer.

model. The combination of these interacting variables leads to behavioral consequences regarding intellectual and academic performance.

Being aware of these influences can help you understand the big picture of forces affecting students' thinking and academic performance. This understanding can help you design instruction to improve conditions for performance. Using this model to support intellectual development, you can intervene at any point in this complex array.

Instructional implications of the BACEIS Model are represented in a lesson planning approach, the Rich Instruction Model (see Figures 2.3 and 2.4).

Rich Instruction Model

The Rich Instruction Model, summarized in Figures 2.3 and 2.4, is a comprehensive approach to applying the BACEIS model to classroom instruction. It has three sections: Objectives, Lesson Plan Core, and Transfer.

This model is too complex to implement all at once. Teachers have found it best to add components of it to their regular lesson plans *gradually*, until their lessons include the entire model. For example, first you could work on Objectives

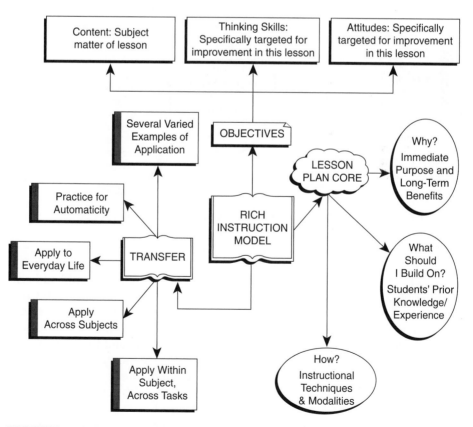

FIGURE 2.3 *Rich Instruction Model*

Adapted from Hartman and Sternberg, 1993, with permission from Springer.

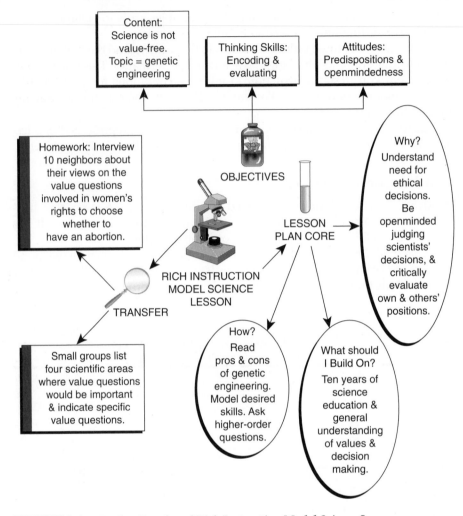

FIGURE 2.4   *Teacher-Developed Rich Instruction Model Science Lesson*
Adapted from Hartman and Sternberg, 1993, with permission from Springer.

and add thinking skills objectives to a content lesson. Then you could add attitudinal objectives. Next you might choose to work on the Lesson Plan Core, identifying the short- and long-term benefits of the lesson. Then you might focus on identifying students' prior knowledge that is important for the lesson. Alternatively, you could begin with the Lesson Plan Core and then start working on the Objectives. There isn't a single "right" way to incorporate all components of the model into your teaching. Do what makes most sense to you.

An example of a history lesson based on this model is in Chapter 14. After examining it, consider how and to what extent your lesson plans are consistent with the Rich Instruction Model. How might you begin incorporating more of the model into your own teaching?

⚔ Teaching Goals

What are your teaching goals? To what extent have you made your students aware of them? To what extent are your goals reflected in your own lesson plans? The following goals are derived from the BACEIS model of improving thinking and incorporated into the Rich Instruction Model.

1. Self-Directed, Reflective Learners and Critical Thinkers. The most important goal of teaching is to develop students who think reflectively, critically, and independently so that they can be life-long independent learners. To what extent do you and your students think about your own thinking?

Reflective teaching practice does not involve simply transmitting information to students, telling them what is wrong, and giving them correct answers, although sometimes these strategies are beneficial. Rather, it's designed to help students become more responsible for their learning and more reflective and critical in their thinking. It should help them manage their own performance in and out of school.

Reflective teaching and learning include both "reflection on action" and "reflection in action." Remember that reflection on action means you and your students think about and carefully consider what actions you might take before engaging in a task (e.g., before conducting a lesson for teachers; before completing an assignment for students) and systematically examine actions you have already taken (e.g., how a lesson was conducted for teachers; how an assignment was graded for students). Reflection in action means that you and your students think about and carefully examine what you are doing in real time, sometimes referred to as "thinking on your feet." You've already encountered these concepts in Chapter 1. You will find them elaborated on later in this chapter, and as a recurring theme in other chapters in this book.

There isn't a single teaching method that will help all students become self-directed, reflective learners and critical thinkers. Differentiated Instruction, defined as matching teaching to the needs, interests, and characteristics of each learner, is a popular approach to addressing individual differences. It includes assessing each student's current levels of performance, identifying their learning preferences, and tailoring teaching methods (personalized scaffolding) to match these features.

Expert teachers have many instructional strategies in their repertoire and know which strategies to use when, as well as why and how to use them. For example, some strategies should be used for only a short time and require little planning whereas others are needed on a long-term basis and require considerable planning. Three strategies recommended to support differentiated instruction are stations, agendas, and orbital studies. Stations are locations in the classroom where students simultaneously work on different tasks. Agendas are lists of tasks tailored for individual students. Orbital studies are individual investigations that revolve around a component of the curriculum. More about these subjects can be found in Crawford, *Differentiation for the Adolescent Learner*.

2. Active Involvement in the Learning Process. To what extent are your students actively engaged in the learning process? Passively watching you solve a problem or listening to your explanation of how to revise a paper will not help them very much in the long run. For learning to be meaningful and long lasting, student participation is essential. Meaningfulness is best constructed through the learner's own actions. Guide students in doing their own work, such as solving their own problems and revising their own papers. Be a coach more often than a lecturer.

3. Content Knowledge. Learning the subject matter is also a primary objective. Research identifies three categories of content learning: adding to it, refining it, and changing it. The concept of adding to knowledge is an important starting point because students often have prior knowledge of material they are learning. Some of it is valid and can be used as building blocks. In many cases, students have content knowledge that is invalid and can inhibit learning.

Building on valid prior knowledge is the essence of meaningful learning. Therefore, regularly elicit students' prior knowledge of a topic before or as you begin teaching it. Systematically make connections between students' prior knowledge and new information. Do this in the subject you are teaching, across other subjects, and in everyday life.

Refining students' existing knowledge involves realizing that students have the basic ideas, but they need to be fine tuned, clarified, or elaborated. For example, a student learning to compute an average may know you have to add all the numbers and divide, but not know what number to divide by.

A third type of work on content is to *change* students' information. Students often have naïve theories, preconceptions, or misconceptions that interfere with learning. For example, students may know they have to multiply sets of numbers separated by parentheses, but may think that they can be multiplied in any order, and not know that the innermost parentheses must be multiplied first. Or, a student might know the terms osmosis and diffusion, but have the definitions confused.

Also, it is common for novice teachers to have preconceptions about some of the content in the curriculum. Become aware of your own as well as your students' naïve theories and use conceptual change strategies to overcome them. (Conceptual change strategies are discussed in Chapter 11 on science.) You are not expected to know everything, but it's important to develop expertise in the subjects you teach. Expertise takes time to develop, so reflect on and critically evaluate your own subject area strengths and weaknesses. There are many professional development resources available online, in schools, and in districts so you can learn new things, just as your students are doing!

Finally, an important goal of content instruction is to help your students learn what it's like to think the way experts do in specific subjects. Students should learn how biologists think, and how that's different from the thinking of historians, which differs from the thinking of mathematicians, which is yet again different from the thinking of specialists in English.

4. Intellectual Skill Development. Help improve students' reflective and critical thinking skills at the same time as you develop their subject-matter knowledge. The better students are at thinking, learning, and studying, the more easily they will grasp and remember content. Students often think that if they just work harder, meaning longer hours and more concentration, they will do much better in their schoolwork. However, if students devote more time to using ineffective strategies, they are likely to learn little and to become very frustrated. More is not necessarily better. Sometimes instead of studying "harder," they need to study "smarter." To do this, students should reflect on and critically evaluate their own thinking and learning strategies, in general and in specific subjects.

5. Attitudes that Foster Thinking and Learning. All the knowledge and well-developed skills in the world will not guarantee success. Attitudes of reflection and carefulness are better for promoting academic success than an attitude of impulsiveness. Cultivate in your students those attitudes that will motivate them to acquire knowledge and skills with understanding, and help them know how to apply them. Help them become confident about themselves as learners, and to persist even when confronted with difficulty, frustration, or boredom. Finally, help students feel responsible for and able to control their own learning.

6. Transfer. Transfer means applying what is learned to situations that differ, at least a little, from the initial learning situation. In positive transfer, earlier learning aids later learning. For example, knowing how to take a bus aids learning to take a subway. Knowing how to add can make it easier to learn to multiply. In negative transfer, earlier learning interferes with later learning. For example, being accustomed to using footbrakes on a bicycle can make it harder to learn to use a handbrake. In zero transfer, earlier learning has no effect on later learning. For example, knowing how to speak Russian has no effect on learning to play the piano.

Try to promote as much positive transfer as possible. Teach students to apply what they learn to the same subject area, to different subjects, to everyday life, and to future professional situations.

7. Learning Environment. Create a learning environment tailored to achieve the preceding six principles. A recent classic on learning, *How People Learn*, has a wonderful chapter devoted to this topic. It identifies four types of learning environments: learner-centered, knowledge-centered, assessment-centered, and community-centered.

Learner-centered environments emphasize paying attention to students' prior knowledge and their skills, attitudes, and beliefs. Knowledge-centered learning environments focus on students becoming knowledgeable, as subject-area experts; meeting content standards; and having well-organized bodies of knowledge. Meaningful learning, teaching for transfer, and understanding the "big picture" are also emphasized.

Assessment-centered learning environments align the curriculum with assessments and use feedback for formative and summative evaluations to promote learning with understanding.

Community-centered environments consider the school and the larger community, such as students' homes and local businesses, in terms of their norms and expectations for student participation and achievement.

To what extent and how is your teaching consistent with these goals? Which are your strengths and weaknesses? How might you make your teaching more consistent with the principles identified in these goals?

⚔ Teaching Guidelines

Following are twelve general teaching principles from research on instruction adapted from McKeachie's classic *Teaching Tips.*

1. Allow students to observe an example of the desired performance, preferably as executed by another student so that it is perceived as an attainable goal. Positive examples usually help more than examples of what not to do, but what not to do examples are useful as supplemental information. When demonstrating how to execute a procedure, direct the students' attention to crucial aspects of the technique. Try to ensure that the examples are culturally relevant to your students. Encourage them to reflect on the differences between your thoughts and actions and their own.

2. Students are helped by verbal cues or labels that identify key features of the skill or concept. Examples might include "Knowing the order of operations is essential for accurate computation" or "Dumping by this chemical company is the most important cause of pollution in our town."

3. Sometimes it's best to start with simplified examples of what you want students to eventually accomplish. Simulations or demonstrations of parts of a complex task often can be more useful as starting points than complex real-life situations, which may overwhelm the student with too many details. Less can be more: Less information may enable more meaningful learning. Because students can't always tell what's important and what's not, they tend to treat all information as equally important. As a result they often try to memorize everything rather than understanding the most important points. Give students information they can really use at the time.

4. Provide opportunities for students to succeed on a task or problem, and don't intervene as soon as you see them going off track. Provide enough guidance so that they don't endlessly continue making errors or going in the wrong direction. Carefully think through the components of an academic task and the sequence of learning activities for successful completion of each component. Structure students' learning experiences from simple to complex, with the steps organized so that each new problem can be successfully solved or each new task can be completed successfully. This sequence can ensure success on the task or problem as a whole.

5. Provide students with practice and feedback. Practice should be both intensive and extensive, as suggested in the Teaching for Transfer section in this chapter, so that students can apply important knowledge and skills with relatively little effort in a variety of situations.

6. Be selective about what feedback you give. Establish priorities and don't try to correct everything at once. Too much negative feedback can overwhelm students and decrease their motivation to improve their performance.

7. Provide some encouraging feedback as well as criticism. If students feel some areas of strength and some degree of success, they are more likely to be motivated to improve their performance than if they feel that everything they do is wrong.

8. Teach students to reflect on their performance and give themselves feedback. Ask students about their perceptions of what and how well they are doing. Model self-evaluation for them by thinking aloud as you go through the process you are using and the basis for your evaluation. Give students feedback *about their evaluation* as well as about the work being evaluated.

9. Feedback that identifies errors won't help if the learner doesn't know what to do to avoid the errors. Give guidance for self-correction so the learner knows what to try next in order to improve performance and prevent future errors.

10. When modeling desired performance for students, deliberately make errors and think aloud so they can see how you recognize and recover from your errors.

11. Encourage peers to help one another. Relinquish some control over monitoring students' performance. Encourage students to seek feedback from their peers, so they're not always dependent on you, and let students know that you expect them to provide constructive feedback for each other.

12. Usually the best teaching involves more coaching or guiding than telling. Coaching includes collaboratively analyzing students' performance with reference to mutually agreed-upon goals.

⚔ Critical, Reflective Teaching Principles

Two fundamental aspects of critical, reflective teaching are emphasized in this book. One aspect focuses on your management processes, the other focuses on your knowledge.

Three management practices associated with successful teaching are planning, monitoring, and evaluating. They can be thought of as considerations before, during, and after teaching. They involve both reflection on action and reflection in action. The information that follows can serve as a guide for refining your teaching by increasing your *awareness and control* over your teaching.

Planning: Before the Lesson—Time for Decision Making

Research has shown that preparation for teaching not only benefits students, but also increases teachers' own learning and motivation. Planning can help ensure the use of effective techniques, such as alternating between listening and summarizing, likely to enhance both learning and motivation. Planning prompts you to reflect on and critically evaluate what you teach and how you teach it. This is one aspect of reflection on action. It can help broaden and deepen your knowledge and understanding of how best to meet your students' needs. New teachers should plan as carefully as possible to meet students' needs. Experienced teachers do not have to plan as much as new teachers, as they can rely more on their intuition. In either case, let the plan be a tentative, general map rather than a rigid agenda etched in stone. Be flexible and prepared to adapt plans to better meet the students' needs.

Planning is the process of deciding not just what you're going to do, but also when, why, and how to do it. It should help you establish the most effective way of meeting the students' needs. Not all dimensions of planning will apply in every situation. Reflect on the five suggestions listed here, adapting/selecting what applies to you.

1. Consider students' background and what the lesson should accomplish. Review the previous lesson in addition to your notes from the last time you taught this lesson to refresh your memory. Reflect on and critically evaluate what went well and how you might be even more effective this time.

2. Reflect on students' prior knowledge, skills, and past errors concerning the topic. Consider what valid and invalid prior knowledge your students may have about the topic, how you will build on valid prior knowledge and how you will help students recognize and replace invalid background knowledge. Break down the task, content, and/or skills to be learned into component parts. Consider what may be the best sequence for approaching them. Also think about the students' attitudes and whether/how to improve them. Some topics are notorious for causing anxiety or boredom. Reflect on them and create new approaches to help develop better attitudes.

3. Set a limited number of specific goals. Avoid overload. Not everything can be accomplished at once, and not everything can be achieved in a single lesson. Figure out how to teach for both immediate and long-term goals. Establish priorities and prepare to discuss them with the students. Decide what homework will best enhance what you cover in this particular lesson.

4. Consider instructional materials and techniques to use in the lesson, including the use of multiple methods and multiple modalities (for example, pictorial as well as written and oral). Be prepared with back-up techniques in case the initial approach does not work.

5. Describe desired outcomes of the lesson in terms of student behavior. What do you want students to be able to do at the end of the lesson that they couldn't do at the beginning of class? Think about the lesson from the student's point of view to imagine how it will be received. Ask yourself planning questions such as those in Table 2.1.

Monitoring: During the Lesson

Monitoring is the process of checking up on yourself and your students while you are teaching. This is reflection in action. Determine how well the lesson is proceeding by reflecting on and critically evaluating students' understanding

TABLE 2.1 Teacher Self-Questions for Managing Instruction		
Planning (Before the Lesson)	**Monitoring (During the Lesson)**	**Evaluating (After the Lesson)**
• What are the content objectives for this lesson?	• How well do students understand this material?	• To what extent were the content objectives achieved?
• How can I elicit students' prior knowledge of this topic?	• Are connections to prior knowledge aiding learning or inhibiting it?	• What was hardest to understand? Why?
• Which methods have been most effective in the past?	• Are students doing what they're supposed to?	• To what extent did students overcome preconceptions that impaired learning?
• What are different ways to represent the material to be learned?	• Are these methods helping students learn or should I try something else?	• Which methods were most successful/ unsuccessful and why?
• How can I best model and stimulate reflective and critical thinking?	• What seems to be working best? Worst? Why?	• Is there anything I should reteach?
• What sequence of activities should I use to achieve these objectives?	• How's the pace? Should I slow down or speed up?	• How can I teach this more effectively next time?
• How much time should I allocate for each activity?	• Am I using their homework most effectively?	• To what extent did students understand when, why, and how to use what they learned?
• What homework should I assign to reinforce what they learn today?	• To what extent are students thinking reflectively and critically?	• How can I be more effective helping students think reflectively and critically?
• How will I help students connect what they learn to other subjects and everyday life?	• Do students understand the connections between what they're learning and other subjects? and everyday life?	• To what extent were students able to apply what they learned to other subjects and everyday life?

of what you're teaching and the extent to which you're accomplishing your objectives. If the lesson is not going as planned, decide how to shift gears and do something in addition or different. Monitoring can lead to on-the-spot planning, and is a key component of effective teaching.

What can you do with students who are capable but unsuccessful? Research has highlighted some behaviors that can stimulate learning. Nonverbal behaviors such as looking at students more and leaning toward the student encourage engagement. Providing information in multiple modalities—orally, in writing, and using pictures or graphic representations—offers more ways to absorb it. Provide students with hints, cues, shortcuts, rules, and a variety of approaches/strategies. Additional suggestions are

1. Revise your plan. Even if you have made a very careful, detailed plan, remember it's a blueprint not a mandate. Use feedback from your students' comments and performance to guide changes.

2. Observe students' body language and listen to what they say as clues regarding their knowledge, understanding, and feelings. Use these clues to help detect problems and guide students in learning the material, performing tasks, and correcting errors.

3. Check up on your own performance and reactions. Restrain any tendencies to be impulsive and emotional. Keep your place in the sequence of learning activities. Recognize when a subgoal has been attained and communicate it to the students. Consider the need for adjustments (shift focus or priorities, change approach, postpone topic).

4. Look ahead. Reflect on the sequence of steps. Critically think about the lesson and anticipate areas where problems or errors are likely. Consider approaches that will prevent or enable students to recover from learning difficulties. Identify different kinds of feedback that you could provide at various points, and evaluate the potential usefulness of each.

5. Look back. Reflect on errors previously made by your current or former students. Examine the types of errors and look for patterns. Help students use awareness of error patterns to self-check and self-correct. Note what has been done and what should come next.

6. Monitor students' comprehension and progress by looking at body language (arms, legs, eyes, and mouth). Give an informal quiz, asking students to use scrap paper. Have students think aloud or listen to students working with each other to identify areas of strength and weakness. Ask monitoring questions such as those in Table 2.1.

Evaluating: After the Session—Time for Assessment

Evaluating is the process of judging what you and your students did in a lesson and how well it was done. It is meant to help you determine what went well, what could have been done better, and how you could improve your teaching next time. When you decide what could have been better and how to improve, devise a plan of action. To get valuable feedback from students, ask them to come to the next class with two or three of their own questions regarding the material.

Experienced teachers mentoring new teachers can be an extremely effective strategy. New teachers may want to have a more experienced teacher sit in and observe a lesson to get constructive feedback. It's also a good idea for new teachers to sit in on classes conducted by recognized "master teachers." This allows the new teacher to actually see and hear what is considered "reflective teaching." Does your school or district have videotapes/DVDs of what it considers reflective or effective teaching? If so, are they available for teachers to view at leisure?

Most teachers are evaluated by their teaching supervisors at some point. You may find it useful to know in advance the criteria by which you will be judged and the method(s) that will be used. Consider videotaping your own class for purposes of self-evaluation. Give your students a questionnaire in which they rate your performance and the overall value of a particular lesson. Assessing a class benefits both the teacher and the students. Your learning is enhanced when you evaluate your own speech and actions during a class, your use of instructional techniques, and your classroom management skills. Consider the following as examples of what to evaluate in a lesson:

1. Compare the actual outcome of the lesson with your intended outcome.
2. Assess the quality of your planning.
3. Assess the quality of your monitoring of yourself and your students.
4. Judge how effectively you and your students communicated.
5. Evaluate the effectiveness of the teaching techniques and materials you used.
6. Reflect on the attitudes demonstrated by you and your students during the lesson.
7. Determine whether or how well you integrated reflective and critical thinking into your content instruction.
8. Use feedback to prepare an action plan for future teaching.
9. Accept responsibility for the outcomes of the class.
10. Ask self-questions such as those in Table 2.1.

✄ Knowledge to Reflect on for Managing Teaching Strategies

Many teachers are likely to have *inert* or inactive knowledge about teaching (and learning). Teacher education commonly provides you with a variety of classroom methods, but doesn't always ensure you understand when, why, and how to use them. As a result, much of what you have learned may remain inert or inactive, due to lack of knowledge of the contexts and procedures for using these methods. Three categories of knowledge are needed for you to reflect on, critically evaluate, and effectively remember and use the instructional principles and techniques already in your repertoire.

Declarative knowledge is facts, definitions, or concepts in a subject area. Declarative information can be elicited by a "What" question, such as What is scaffolding as a teaching strategy?

Contextual or conditional knowledge is information regarding the reason and/or situation in which knowledge or strategies are applied. Contextual or conditional information is often sought by a "When" or "Why" question. This type of knowledge lets you identify conditions and situations in which it is

TABLE 2.2   Knowledge to Aid Reflection on Scaffolding as a Teaching Strategy

What is scaffolding in teaching?	Helping students perform at higher levels by providing them with temporary support. It is based on the concept of the zone of proximal development. The zone of proximal development (ZPD) "is the distance between the actual developmental level as determined by independent problem solving and the level of potential development as determined through problem solving under adult guidance or in collaboration with more capable peers." The ZPD refers to potentialities that have not yet fully developed but are in the process of being developed and can be enhanced by receiving information or temporary support from more competent others, e.g., teachers, parents, siblings, or peers.
Why use scaffolding in teaching?	To enhance students' academic performance by providing them with information and temporary support, which can be gradually decreased as the students' competence increases. Scaffolding can help students to become independent, self-regulated thinkers who are more self-sufficient and less teacher dependent. Like the scaffolding of a building during construction, scaffolds are gradually removed as its structure can support its own weight. Like training wheels on a bicycle they provide temporary support while the rider learns to maintain balance. Once the bike rider is secure, the training wheels are removed and the rider self-balances. Through the support of others, students can perform at higher levels than they could if completely on their own, without help from more competent others. But as they learn, control gradually shifts from other to self-regulation, enabling independent performance.
How can I use scaffolding in teaching?	Bridge the gap between what students can do on their own and what they can do with guidance from others by providing models, cues, prompts, hints, or partial solutions. At the beginning you might need to model or completely guide the student's activity. The student observes you or follows your instructions and does little independent thinking. Next, the student attempts to do the task while you provide supportive cuing, assistance, and additional modeling, as needed. Intervene as necessary. Gradually the student plays a greater role and assumes more responsibility for self-instruction and for teaching peers. Your support is gradually decreased as the student's competence increases. Once fully internalized, the student can apply the knowledge or strategies independently. Research-based scaffolding guidelines: 1. Present the new cognitive strategies, 2. Regulate difficulty during guided practice, 3. Provide varying contexts for student practice, 4. Provide feedback, 5. Increase student responsibility, 6. Provide independent practice.

Hartman, *Metacognition in Learning and Instruction*, 2001. Ch. 8, Teaching Metacognitively. Adapted with permission from Springer.

appropriate to use specific pedagogical principles and techniques. For example, you should know when it is appropriate to use, and why it is beneficial to use, scaffolding.

Procedural knowledge allows you to apply information or strategies you have learned; it includes procedures and techniques. You need this type of information to help you decide which techniques to use in particular contexts and help you think through methods of implementing them in your teaching. For example, you should know how to use scaffolding to help a particular student in a specific situation.

Table 2.2 illustrates these three types of knowledge about scaffolding to show you how it can help you reflect on and critically evaluate the use of scaffolding in your classroom. Similar information on other instructional methods is in Chapter 8, Teaching Strategies to Promote Reflection.

⚔ Teaching for Transfer

Transfer is when prior learning affects later learning or performance. Transfer involves the application of one's prior knowledge. It may be positive, negative, or zero. In positive transfer, the prior learning helps performance of a new task. It is like practice; it helps students learn to learn and is one of the characteristics of intelligent performance. Information learned in one situation carries over and is used in another situation. Learning therefore has a spin-off effect—it leads to learning other things. For example, knowing how to write an essay in English makes it easier to learn to write an essay in History.

In negative transfer, the prior learning interferes with later learning. For example, knowing the pronunciation of vowels in Spanish might make it confusing when learning to pronounce the same vowels in English. Zero transfer is when prior learning has no effect on later learning. For example, knowing the history of World War II is unlikely to have any effect on learning calculus. Usually when educators talk about transfer, they are referring to positive transfer, which facilitates future learning.

Types of Positive Transfer

Transfer may be lateral or vertical. Lateral transfer is applying prior learning to a task at the same level of difficulty. For example, if a teacher helps a student to set up a schedule for reading a text in one course, the student can transfer that scheduling strategy to reading a text in a comparable course. Vertical transfer is when prior learning aids learning something more complicated. For example, if a teacher helps a student learn how to add polynomials, the student can apply or transfer that knowledge when learning to factor polynomials.

Transfer can be "high road" or "low road." High road transfer involves consciously applying information learned in one situation to another situation. It requires reflective thinking. For example, a student may *consciously determine* how to apply test-taking strategies learned to all the different subject areas. Low road transfer is the spontaneous and automatic application of highly practiced skills. For example, once a student knows how to add, the student can add many different combinations of numbers. It does not require reflective thinking. When the student sees numbers and a plus sign, the student automatically knows what to do.

Transfer can also be "near" or "far." Near transfer occurs when the transfer situation is identical or very similar to the initial learning situation. The learner can apply what was learned in the same way as it was used during the initial learning. With far transfer, the new task is substantially different from the original learning situation. What was learned must be adapted for use in the new situation.

To summarize the main points, lateral and vertical transfer refer to the level of difficulty of the new situation compared to the original learning situation. High and low road transfer refer to the degree of consciousness necessary to apply what was learned in the new situation. Near and far transfer refer to the degree of similarity between the original learning and the new situation.

Reasons for Lack of Transfer

What content and strategies do your students need to transfer? Why do your students sometimes fail to transfer what they've learned? Table 2.3 summarizes what research has shown to be reasons for lack of transfer. Some aspects overlap and could fit into multiple categories.

Which of these reasons apply to your students? How might you help your students transfer what they learn?

Transfer Teaching Guidelines

As you read the following guidelines on how to teach for transfer, think about how they relate to the reasons students fail to transfer so you can match transfer

TABLE 2.3   Reasons Students Don't Transfer What They Learn

Category of Reasons	Specific Aspects of Reasons
Inadequate Initial Learning	1. Limited degree of mastery. 2. Too much was covered too quickly. 3. Students didn't understand the organizing principles because of too little meaningful information. 4. Students didn't spend enough time learning outside of class.
Lack of Knowledge about Transfer	1. Students don't see the potential transfer implications of what they're learning, i.e., that they can use it in the future in other situations. 2. They're not clear about how the original learning situation is related to the transfer situation.

Category of Reasons	Specific Aspects of Reasons
Rote versus Meaningful Learning	1. Students memorized the material and didn't understand it. 2. Knowledge consisted of isolated facts instead of connected and organized information. 3. Students learned to perform procedures in specific situations instead of understanding principles that would enable more general use.
Misconceptions	1. Students come to class with an inaccurate understanding of the material (faulty prior knowledge like misconceptions), which inhibits learning and transfer. 2. Students don't understand that transfer is a dynamic, ever-changing process and tend to view it as more rigid, limited, and static.
Inadequate Reflective Thinking	1. Inadequate knowledge of when, where, why, and how to use what they learned. 2. Students don't think about their own thinking and learning. 3. They have insufficient insight into their own learning. 4. Teachers don't provide adequate support to help students think about their own thinking and help them apply what they have learned.
Limited Learning Context	1. Material to be learned was tied to a specific or single context instead of to multiple contexts. 2. Students can apply what they learned to tasks that are identical or similar to the initial learning situation (near transfer) but not to tasks that differ substantially from the initial learning situation (far transfer).
Out-of-Date Pedagogy	Academic tasks used for learning are artificial instead of authentic.
Lack of Motivation	1. Students' motivation is driven more by concern about getting right answers and how others will view them (performance orientation) than by a desire to acquire, understand, and use the material (learning orientation). 2. Students had inadequate opportunities to apply what they learned, which limits their motivation to use it.
Cultural Factors	Cultural knowledge, such as social roles, socioeconomic status, language styles, and stereotypes associated with gender, race, or ethnicity can affect transfer.

problems with potential solutions. Make sure that you don't make the common mistake of confusing the *guideline* itself with the *example*!

Which of these methods of promoting transfer do you use? Which are most/least successful? What does their effectiveness depend on? Which might you use more often?

The Rich Instruction Model, presented earlier in this chapter, the 6PQ Method of Discovery Learning, discussed in the chapter on teaching strategies, and the Learning Cycle Model, discussed in the chapter on science, all have

TABLE 2.4   Teaching for Transfer Guidelines

Concept	Guideline	Example
Similarity	Make the learning situation as similar as possible to the transfer situation.	If you're using a practice test for teaching students test-taking strategies, make sure that the practice test is similar to the test that will be given in class so that students make the connection and can apply the strategies easily.
Practice: Similar	Design activities that require students to get extensive practice on similar problems or tasks.	If you are teaching students to use mental images while reading, require that they describe their images from several sections in the same chapter or book and from several other similar types of readings.
Practice: Varied	Provide students with extensive practice on different types of problems or tasks.	Have students practice asking self-questions when reading literature, social studies, solving problems in science and math, and when writing essays.
Negative Transfer	Be alert to the possibility of negative transfer and help your students to be aware of it. Prior learning can interfere with learning new material when some information overlaps.	The vowel "i" in English also occurs in Spanish, but the pronunciation is different. In Spanish it is pronounced like "ee" whereas in English it tends to be pronounced as "eh" or "eye." Because of negative transfer interfering with learning the new language, the native Spanish speaker may have a tendency to mispronounce the English letter and the native English speaker may have a tendency to mispronounce the Spanish letter.

Concept	Guideline	Example
Prerequisite Knowledge	Make sure that your students have the prerequisite knowledge and skills before asking them to complete a complex task.	They must know what "spell check" is and how to use it in order to spell check a paper before turning it in.
Model	Give students a model of what needs to be learned.	To study literature, teach them a story grammar model in which they identify the key features of a novel, play, or short story. Demonstrate for them how to look for the main characters, setting, plot, crisis, and denouement. Such models aid understanding and memory.
Generalizations	Transfer is facilitated when students are asked to give many different illustrations of a generalization.	If you tell students that a sentence usually should not end with a preposition, give them several different examples of sentences that should be changed because they do end incorrectly with a preposition.
Strategic Knowledge	When students know when, where, why, and how to use their knowledge and skills, it is easier for them to transfer what they have learned. Understanding the appropriate context for using knowledge and skills helps them recognize when situations are appropriate for them to use what they already know.	If you want students to summarize something they read, explain that after reading something, summarizing helps them comprehend and remember what they read. The procedure involves selecting the most important points and concisely stating them in their own words.
Overlearning	Encourage students to "overlearn" important concepts and skills, that is, to learn them to the point that they are internalized as a part of their minds. Then the knowledge and skills are more likely to be used automatically when needed.	The multiplication tables are commonly taught this way because of the recognition that these mathematics facts need to be retrieved fluidly when solving a variety of problems.

(continued)

TABLE 2.4   *Continued*

Concept	Guideline	Example
Induce Familiarity	Help students learn to convert the unfamiliar to the familiar. Teach them to look for some part of the new material that has a relationship to something with which they are already familiar. It can be a similarity based on structure, function, shape, sound, size, color, or any other attribute that is meaningful. Connecting new and seemingly unfamiliar information with prior knowledge can make the new material more meaningful to students and help them apply their prior knowledge to new situations.	Learning chords on the piano can be related to simple mathematics.

transfer as the final stage of instructional approach. In 6PQ, the "process" stage requires the student to transfer what was learned during the session. For example, a student learning to compute the mean for a math class can use this skill to figure out how much money she/he spends each week on average or how many pages to read each night in order to finish a chapter in a week. A student learning to brainstorm ideas to include in an essay can use brainstorming to come up with possible ideas for a birthday present to buy for a friend. A student who learns to make mental pictures while reading a novel can transfer the use of mental imagery to remembering rules and formulas for chemistry. Many teaching methods have transfer or application built in as the final stage of the model. One example is the Learning Cycle Model in the chapter on science.

⚔ Assigning Homework

How often do you assign homework? Why do you assign homework? What kinds of assignments do you make? When and how do you communicate your expectations about completion of homework assignments? What factors do you take into consideration when making homework assignments?

Homework is a relatively controversial topic. Increasingly, there are criticisms of the quality and quantity of homework assignments and questions about whether it affects academic achievement. There is great variability in the frequency with which teachers assign homework, some never assigning it at all and others assigning it every day, including over weekends. Some schools have homework policies. Does yours? Do you coordinate your assignments with other teachers so your students aren't overwhelmed?

Research on homework shows that the benefits vary with grade. Elementary students do not benefit from it very much in terms of their academic achievement. Middle school students do benefit from it, and high school students benefit from it the most: twice as much as middle school students. For middle school students, the optimal amount of homework is 1–2 hours per night. For high school students, in general, the more homework the better, and the subject doesn't seem to matter.

What is the proper amount of time students should spend doing homework each night? Although there are variations in recommended amounts of time, the National Education Association and the National Parent-Teachers Association generally support the "10 minute rule," whereby 10 minutes is assigned for each grade level, so a 9th grade student would get 90 minutes of homework per night. The rule can be increased to 15 minutes if reading is included.

There are at least four different functions of homework:

1. practice, which is intended to reinforce what was learned in class;
2. preparation, so that students will benefit more from a forthcoming lesson;
3. creativity, whereby students engage in a project requiring them to synthesize what they have learned; and
4. transfer, where students apply what they learned in class to a new situation.

Which of these homework assignment functions do you use most often? Should you use others more? How do these functions relate to your instructional goals? The first two functions tend to be the most common. The last, while least common, potentially is the most important. What kinds of homework assignments do you or could you make that require students to extend their knowledge or skills to tasks or contexts different from the ones in class?

Other benefits of homework assignments, which can be especially beneficial to college-bound high school students, are that they can help develop effective study, time management, and independent learning skills. In addition, research shows that homework improves students' memory, comprehension, inquisitiveness, critical thinking, self-discipline, learning during leisure time, and attitude toward school. Homework assignments should be designed specifically to benefit student learning, not just made as a matter of policy.

To what extent are your students aware of your purposes and of the potential benefits of completing their homework assignments? An online resource for teachers to make homework assignments more effective is available at http://www.ed.gov/pubs/HelpingStudents/. It is a 40-page booklet organized around 18 tips from teachers.

Though it is not uncommon for students to complain about homework, parents also occasionally complain about it because it conflicts with family plans, extracurricular activities, or students' responsibilities at home. How do you handle such complaints? How can you help parents see homework as an opportunity instead of a threat? An online guide for parents about the importance of homework is available at http://www.eric.ed.gov/archives/homewrk.html.

If your students need help with their homework, from whom do they get it? How much help do they get? There is great variability across parents, from no help at all to doing the whole assignment for their children. Even uneducated parents can help their children with homework.

Unlike in the past, when students were primarily dependent on their parents or older siblings for homework help, now there are telephone hotlines and places online where they can get assistance. One of these, Homework Spot (http://www.homeworkspot.com), includes resources for students, teachers, and parents at the elementary, middle, and high school levels in virtually all subjects, such as social studies, science, mathematics, reading, writing, foreign languages, and fine arts.

How do your students feel about their homework assignments? To what extent do they see them as challenging or as busy work? To what extent does homework help students connect schoolwork with their own needs and interests? Are students frustrated because their family doesn't have a computer or Internet access, thereby impeding their ability to complete assignments? To what extent do students feel overwhelmed by how much time they must devote to their homework assignments?

To what extent do your students complete their homework assignments? What strategies do you use to encourage them to do so? Some strategies emphasize tangible rewards such as pizza parties or final grade points, whereas other strategies, such as contracts or checklists, emphasize student responsibility.

What do you do with students' homework assignments? Do you always collect them? Do you grade them? If so, how? Does the homework grade impact their report card grade? To what extent and how do you give students feedback on their homework?

Four research-based guidelines for homework have been identified, as follows:

1. Homework should serve a legitimate purpose, such as practicing a skill, exploring a topic on their own, and elaborating on a topic discussed in class.
2. You should make homework assignments that students are likely to complete. This means that they're not too long or difficult, but are challenging and interesting.
3. Try to promote parental involvement with homework, but not as disciplinarians or teachers.
4. Make sure homework isn't so excessive that it interferes with other activities at home or is inappropriate for student age.

To what extent are your homework assignments consistent with these guidelines?

⚔ Technology

To assist your planning of exciting, effective lessons, there are numerous online resources, such as Homework Spot, mentioned earlier. Resources include activities such as science fair projects, virtual fieldtrips to Machu Picchu, the Art Institute of Chicago, the Louvre Museum, the White House, Buckingham Palace, and interactive games on the Amazon Rainforest. InTime (http://www.intime.uni.edu) provides a comprehensive database of lesson plans and videos of their implementation, based on a comprehensive, sound, technology-rich pedagogical model for all grades and subjects.

Lesson planning ideas, including the Madeline Hunter model, and how to formulate behavioral objectives, are available at http://www.adprima.com/lesson.htm. To help you think reflectively about lessons you are planning, look at this site's material on common mistakes teachers make in writing lesson plans and how to avoid them. This site also includes information on print resources for planning lessons and several links to other excellent lesson planning sites on the Internet.

Differentiated instruction resources available online include CAST: Universal Design for Learning, at http://www.cast.org/publications/ncac/ncac_diffinstruc.html, and Differentiated Instruction, based on the essential question, "How do I effectively and efficiently reach all students in a heterogeneous environment"? at http://www.frsd.k12.nj.us/rfmslibrarylab/di/differentiated_instruction.htm.

A chapter online provides rationales for instructional methods promoting active learning, which can help you reflect on action and consider which methods are most suitable for your particular needs, and when, why, and how to apply them. This site, www.charlesdennishale.com/books/chapter_2_planning_for_active_learning.pdf, also provides ideas for evaluating lessons and guidelines on using a variety of technologies in teaching.

Information on planning and evaluating lessons using technology is available from http://www.escambia.k12.fl.us/instres/e2t2/ir_pande_ele.htm. The VISIT project has a rubric for evaluating lessons using technology at www.emich.edu/visit/VISITrubric.doc.

Summary

To teach reflectively and critically, it is important to manage instruction and use techniques strategically. Management includes planning, monitoring, and evaluating your teaching. Teacher self-questions can help you do this. Even the most effective instructional technique does not work in all situations and variety is necessary to prevent boredom. It helps to have a repertoire of teaching strategies and comprehensive knowledge about each of them to allow you to differentiate instruction and to be flexible in the classroom, shifting approaches as the situation requires. This strategic information includes knowing what the technique is, when and why to use it, and how to use it. This knowledge enables you to select the best technique for the particular context and consider alternative strategies if it appears that change is needed. Homework assignments should fulfill specific functions that are consistent with your instructional goals.

Resources

Carolan, J.; and A. Guinn. "Differentiation: Lessons from Master Teachers." *Educational Leadership*, February 2007, pp. 44–47.

Chaika, G. "Help! Homework Is Wrecking My Home Life." *Education World*, 2005. Retrieved July 10, 2006 from http://www.educationworld.com/a_admin/admin/admin182.shtml.

Clark, R.C.; and R. E. Mayer. E-*Learning and the Science of Instruction*. San Francisco: John Wiley & Sons, 2003.

Cooper, H. *The Battle Over Homework: Common Ground for Administrators, Teachers and Parents*. 2nd ed. Thousand Oaks, CA: Corwin Press, 2001.

Cooper, H. "Homework for All—in Moderation." *Educational Leadership* 58, no. 7 (2001), pp. 34–38.

Crawford, Glenda Beamon. *Differentiation for the Adolescent Learner*. Thousand Oaks, CA: Corwin Press, 2008.

Crie, M. "The Great Homework Debate: Making the Most of Home Study." *Teaching Today*. 2001. Education Up Close. Retrieved July 31, 2007 from http://www.glencoe.com/sec/teachingtoday/educationupclose.phtml/45.

Eddy, Y. "Developing Homework Policies." *ERIC Digest*. 1984. Retrieved July 31, 2007 from http://ericae.net/edo/ED256473.HTM.

Glazer, N.; and S. Williams. "Averting the Homework Crisis." *Educational Leadership* 58, no. 7 (2001), pp. 43–45.

Hall, T. *Differentiated Instruction*. Wakefield, MA: National Center on Accessing the General Curriculum, 2002. Retrieved July 23, 2007 from http://www.cast.org/publications/ncac/ncac_diffinstruc.html.

Hartman, H. J. "Teaching Metacognitively. In *Metacognition in Learning and Instruction: Theory, Research & Practice*, ed. H. J. Hartman. Dordrecht: Springer, 2001.

Hartman, H. J.; and R. J. Sternberg. "A Broad BACEIS for Improving Thinking." *Instructional Science* 21, no. 5 (1993), pp. 401–25.

Homework Spot. Retrieved September 20, 2007 from http://www.homeworkspot.com.

Kizlik, B. *Lesson Planning, Lesson Plan Formats and Lesson Plan Ideas*, 2006. Retrieved September 23, 2006 from http://www.adprima.com/lesson.htm.

Marzano, R. J.; and D. J. Pickering. "The Case For and Against Homework." *Educational Leadership*, March 2007, pp. 74–79.

McKeachie, W. *Teaching Tips*. 10th ed. Boston: Houghton Mifflin, 1999.

Milbourne, L. A.; and D. L. Haury. "Helping Students with Homework in Science and Math." *ERIC Digest*. 1999. Retrieved July 31, 2007 from http://www.ericdigests.org/2000-1/homework.html.

National Research Council. *How People Learn: Brain, Mind, Experience and School*. Expanded ed. Washington, D.C: National Academy Press, 2000.

Planning and Evaluating Lessons (n.d.). Escambia County School District. Retrieved September 23, 2006 from http://www.escambia.k12.fl.us/instres/e2t2/ir_pande_ele.htm.

Planning for Active Learning (n.d.). Retrieved September 23, 2006 from www.charlesdennishale.com/books/chapter_2_planning_for_active_learning.pdf.

Rosenshine, B.; and C. Meister. "The Use of Scaffolds for Teaching Higher-Level Cognitive Strategies." *Educational Leadership* 49, no. 7 (1992), pp. 26–33.

Salomon, G.; and D. Perkins. "Are Cognitive Skills Context-Bound?" *Educational Researcher* 18, 1 (1989), pp. 16–25.

Tomlinson, D. A. *The Differentiated Classroom: Responding to the Needs of All Learners.* Alexandria, VA: Association for Supervision and Curriculum Development, 1999.

Vail, K. "Homework Problems: How Much Is Too Much?" *American School Board Journal* 188, no. 4 (2001), pp. 24–29.

Vygotsky, L. *Mind in Society: The Development of Higher Psychological Processes.* Cambridge: Harvard University Press, 1978.

Reflective Classroom Communication

Whether you are instructing classes of students or teaching them one-on-one, teaching is a social interaction. Communication is one of the most basic aspects of the teacher–student relationship. Refined listening, speaking, and feedback skills are vital to effectively "get through" to students. This chapter addresses preconceptions, effective communication, listening, speaking, feedback, nonverbal communication, cultural issues in communication, communication breakdown and repair, and following directions.

Due to the social nature of teaching, effective communication is crucial. As a teacher, it's your responsibility to ensure that you really understand your students and your students really understand you. Sometimes the best teacher is the best listener, not the best speaker! Sometimes communicating is difficult due to different native language backgrounds of teachers and students. In some classes, four or five different native language backgrounds can be found in a single small group of students. What native languages are common around your school and classroom? To what extent will the students you teach have a different native language background from you?

Communication can also be hindered by students not having enough prior content knowledge to communicate effectively about what they are learning. Lack of vocabulary can lead to lack of understanding. For example, if a student needs help with sines and cosines or with mitosis and meiosis, but doesn't know these terms, it might be hard for the student to explain what problems he or she is having. What examples can you think of?

Communication skills of speaking and listening often are taken for granted because we do them all the time. But in teaching, it's essential that they are not just done, but are done carefully and effectively. Speaking and listening effectively are more complicated than we often realize, because speakers and listeners not only need to be careful and effective in *what* they say and hear, but also need to carefully attend to *how* they communicate, and what they do NOT say and what they do NOT hear. In addition, both speakers and listeners should attend to nonverbal as well as verbal information.

✎ Preconceptions About Communication

What are your views about communication? How valid are they? One expert in communications identifies five common myths about communication, which are addressed in Table 3.1 by explaining the reality.

TABLE 3.1 Myths about Communication	
Myth	**Reality**
Words contain meaning.	Without prior knowledge or experience to connect with words, they're meaningless. Meaning must be constructed by the person seeing or hearing the words.
Communication and information are synonymous.	Communication is the process of transmitting content or information and receiving feedback on the transmission. Without feedback, there is no real communication.
Communication doesn't require much effort.	Effective communication requires investing time, effort, attention, and thinking beyond yourself to considering the points of view of the people receiving the communication.
Communication is a product.	Communication is a process, not a commodity. Thinking about it as a product is a great obstacle to effective communication because the fact that something has been produced is often mistaken as evidence that it has been processed by the recipient. Just because you teach something doesn't mean that students learn it!
Good speakers are good communicators.	To be a good communicator, you need to be a good listener because listening promotes understanding and builds positive relationships.

Adapted from Robertson, E. *The Five Myths of Managers.* Strategic Communication Management, 2005.

Did you subscribe to any of these myths before reading Table 3.1? What might be the implications of harboring such myths about communication?

⋈ Effective Communication

Communication will be most effective if it occurs in a way that is consistent with how the student learns best. For example, some students learn best by listening, others learn best by seeing pictures or diagrams, while still others learn best by reading and writing about what they need to know.

One multiple intelligence theory suggests that all people have at least nine different types of independent intelligences, and have strengths in specific ones. The nine intelligences are verbal-linguistic, logical-mathematical, visual-spatial, musical-rythmic, bodily-kinesthetic, naturalistic, interpersonal, intrapersonal, and existential. Try to determine the strengths of each student and communicate information accordingly, to the extent possible. If a student's strength is linguistic intelligence, emphasize words (oral and written); if a student's strength is spatial, use pictures or diagrams; if the strength is bodily-kinesthetic, use physical movement to act out (dramatize) or role play the concept.

Some people are good at communicating with others (interpersonal) but not good at communicating with themselves (intrapersonal), whereas others have the opposite communication strengths and weaknesses. What are yours?

TABLE 3.2 My Communication Self-Assessment	
My Strengths as a Communicator	**My Weaknesses as a Communicator**

Because speaking and listening are so much a part of our everyday life experience, we all are likely to have experienced both effective and ineffective speaking and listening. Think about your own specific past experiences regarding the following:

1. When you heard a very effective speaker, what were the features that made the person's speech so effective?
2. When you have been effective at speaking, what was it that made your speech so effective?
3. When you have been a good listener, what was it that made your listening good?
4. When someone else has been a good listener for you, what made that person's listening so good?
5. When you have been effective in giving someone feedback on their performance, what is it that made your feedback effective?
6. When someone has given you effective feedback on your performance, what was it that made their feedback effective?
7. If you have a pretty good idea what the speaker is going to say when talking to you, is it good to finish the sentence for the speaker? Why or why not?

Use the seven questions above to stimulate your thinking and assess your strengths and weaknesses as a communicator in Table 3.2. Include your own ideas about the characteristics of effective communication.

⚔ Listening Skills

Listening is developmentally our first communication skill, and therefore it is often taken for granted. Good listening is sometimes hard work. What do you think some differences might be for a student who has a passive, superficial listener as a teacher, as compared to a student who is taught by an active, analytical listener?

Effective and Ineffective Listening Strategies

How good are you at listening? Almost everyone can benefit from being a better listener. Evaluate your own listening strategies by using or adapting the checklist in Table 3.3 to assess your typical listening behavior.

TABLE 3.3 Listening Self-Evaluation Checklist		
Rate your own listening by considering how typical each behavior is of you.		
Listening Behavior	**Typical**	**Not Typical**
Make literal interpretations rather than listening for implications and/or symbolic interpretations.		
Focus on words and isolated sentences rather than on the big picture of relationships between ideas.		
Concentrate on what you're hearing and shut out distractions.		
Listen selectively for important information.		
Pull ideas together into a whole (synthesize) and draw conclusions.		
Objectively evaluate what you hear, being openminded and without bias.		
Withhold judgment until after completely hearing a message.		
Assess whether evidence supports statements.		
Consider what information might be omitted.		
Evaluate the source of the ideas presented.		
Passively take in information rather than actively think about it.		
Relate what you hear to your own prior knowledge and experience.		
Create your own examples of ideas you hear about.		
Recognize when you do not understand something.		
Seek clarifying information when you don't understand something that seems important.		

(*continued*)

TABLE 3.3 *Continued*		
Listening Behavior	**Typical**	**Not Typical**
Translate what you hear into your own words.		
Listen carefully only when you are interested in the topic.		
Try to create an interest in a topic that didn't previously interest you.		
Persist in listening even when material is hard to understand.		
Consciously attempt to remember important or useful information.		

Self-questioning about your listening while in the act of listening is a good way to monitor or check up on listening so it can be improved. You might ask yourself questions such as those that follow, about how well you listen, and/or adapt ideas from the self-evaluation checklist.

Listening Self-Questions

1. How good of a listener am I?
2. In what situations do I do my best listening?
3. In what situations do I have trouble listening?
4. To what extent are my listening skills different at different times during the day?
5. To what extent do my listening skills differ in relationship to particular subjects?
6. How do my listening skills compare when listening to a person versus listening to music, a video, or a movie?
7. How do my in-school listening skills compare with my listening skills outside of school?
8. What strategies could I use to improve my listening skills?

Teach your students to self-assess their listening to their teachers, other students, family, and friends.

Factors That Interfere with Listening

Why is it sometimes hard to be a good listener, even if you have good intentions? Many times our minds wander and we just can't concentrate. What are some factors that affect your ability to be a good listener? Several external and internal factors that interfere with listening have been identified, as summarized in the graphic organizers in Figures 3.1 and 3.2.

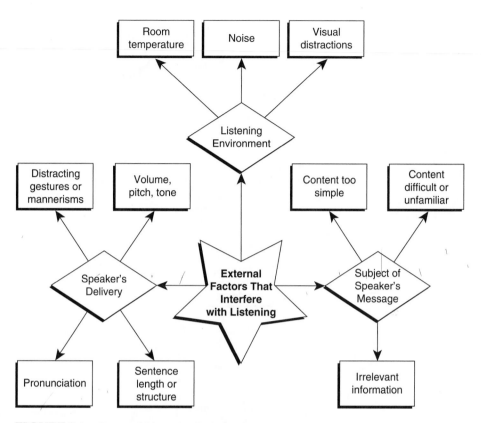

FIGURE 3.1 *External Listening Interferences*

Reflecting on your responses to the Listening Self-Evaluation Checklist in Table 3.3 and considering external and internal listening interferences in your classroom, how might you and your students become better listeners?

What Can Be Done to Improve Listening?

You and your students can use self-assessment results to plan application of strategies for more effective listening. Consider videotaping actual lessons in progress to more carefully examine listening behaviors and for students to reflect on and critically evaluate their own listening and other thinking/learning skills.

Two effective listening strategies are "reflecting the feeling" and "paraphrasing" (see Table 3.4). When communicating, it's often important to take into account your students' emotional states. Sometimes a student is so upset that personal concerns must be addressed before you can continue teaching. Once troubling emotions have been addressed, the student's mind is free to engage in learning. The same principle applies to a whole class that might be upset about something.

FIGURE 3.2   *Internal Listening Interferences*

Both "Reflecting the Feeling" and "Paraphrasing" involve verifying comprehension by restating and testing your interpretation of what someone communicated to determine whether your interpretation is right or wrong.

O.C.E.A.N. Model

This model has been used to summarize some important aspects of listening. The O.C.E.A.N. model approach is designed to help reduce internal and external interferences in the listening process. Although developed at Chemeketa Community College, it can be applied at all grade levels. Table 3.5 on page 44 explains and illustrates this approach to improving listening.

How might you use the information in the table and your own ideas to improve listening in your teaching in general and to address specific listening interferences in your classroom?

TABLE 3.4 Strategic Knowledge about Two Listening Strategies

Type of Knowledge	Reflecting the Feeling	Paraphrasing
What is it?	The listener verbally reflects the speaker's emotions.	The listener restates what the speaker said in his or her own words, focusing on the ideas, not the emotions.
Why use it?	It conveys understanding and empathy to the speaker and promotes awareness of his or her emotional reactions and how they might impact learning. Often, by acknowledging a student's feelings through reflecting them back, a teacher can refocus on the academic content targeted for the lesson or postpone instruction until the student is more receptive to learning.	It shows that you paid attention and understood what was said. It helps you stay actively involved, which encourages students to continue working. It enables you to check up on your comprehension and clarify or verify what was said. It enables you to reinforce students and build on their developing knowledge and understanding.
How to use it?	Acknowledge the student's feelings by verifying your impression of what the student is feeling and encouraging the student to talk about it. "So you're worried that when taking a test you're going to get so anxious that you'll forget everything you know, is that right?" Or, "You look worried, what's wrong?"	Translate what the student says into your own words to verify comprehension. You and/or students can paraphrase what was covered during a class as a mid-lesson review or end-of-lesson summary. Student: "I think what I wrote in the third paragraph sounds like the opposite of what I wrote in the second paragraph." Teacher: "So you think there's an inconsistency in what you wrote at different points in your essay?"

Speaking Skills

What kinds of things do you talk about with students? What kinds of things do students say in class? There are several aspects of your speech of which you should be aware and try to fine tune when talking with your students. Teachers are often aware of the importance of the content or *what* they say, but are often

TABLE 3.5   O.C.E.A.N. Model of Improving Listening

Component of Model	What It Represents	Example
O	Open channels of communication can be expressed both verbally and nonverbally.	Smile and say enthusiastically, "Good morning class!"
C	Caring attitude. Show students you are interested in their performance and progress.	"How did you do on last night's homework?"
E	Empathy. Try to realize and understand how students might react differently from you and each other. Express your understanding of how your students feel in particular situations.	After privately being delighted your student received a "B" when you feared he might get a "C," you can frown and say, "I'm sorry you're disappointed you didn't get an A," because you realize that he expected to do better.
A	Ask for suggestions on how to reduce interferences	"What do you think we could do so it's a little more quiet?"
N	Nonjudgmental attitude. Being openminded helps listening, whereas making premature evaluations interferes with listening.	Before concluding a student is headed in the wrong direction on a research paper, withhold your judgment until you have heard the entire plan. The student may be headed in the right direction and just needs time to explain it fully.

unaware of the importance of aspects relating to the style or *how* they communicate. Content issues include selecting relevant versus irrelevant information, the quantity and degree of completeness and specificity of information to be conveyed, and how the material is organized. Style issues include choice of vocabulary words, speed of speech, tone of voice, clarity of pronunciation, volume of speech, eye contact, enthusiasm, and nonverbal communication.

Listen more than you speak. Teaching should not be equated with telling or lecturing to students about the material to be learned. Effective speaking in a classroom context often is characterized by the teacher acting as a coach who guides student learning—not just a lecturer who fills students' heads with required information. To be effective, adapt your speech to the needs of the particular individuals and situations. See Cultural Issues in Nonverbal Communication for suggestions regarding effective interaction with students from culturally different backgrounds.

Teaching can be improved by audio taping (or videotaping) some classes so you can hear how you come across. When listening to such tapes, ask yourself questions such as "To what extent did I allow the students to speak without me interrupting? Did I allow enough "wait time" for students to think silently about their answers before I asked for an answer or followed up with another question?"

Communication can affect the teacher–student relationship. Students cannot develop trust and confidence if you do not listen actively and carefully. Students cannot understand what teachers are trying to teach them if you don't speak clearly, using an appropriate tone and an appropriate pace.

One social aspect of teaching is considering who does the most speaking and who does the most listening. It may be tempting for you as the teacher to do a significant amount of speaking because students often expect to obtain information and skills from the teacher by watching and listening. Teachers often expect to provide this knowledge from speaking. However, the best pattern is actually the opposite! Keep in mind that the ultimate goal of teaching is for the student to be able to function effectively without the teacher. By encouraging students to do most of the speaking, they work more with the content toward the targeted instructional objectives.

Students learn from your feedback on their performance about how versus how not to approach and think about the material. By listening to how a student works with the material, you can guide the student to work with it more effectively. With you as the listener and students as speakers, they are forced to think through ideas and gain independence and confidence with the material to be learned. Students can feel overpowered by your expertise when you do too much talking. Choose your words carefully. Speak clearly, simply, and respectfully. Do not "talk down" to students.

✹ Feedback

Classroom discussions are useful for deepening students' learning and for helping you assess students' understanding of and progress in learning important knowledge and skills. Other important dimensions of classroom communication are students' comfort in asking questions and your responses to their questions. To what extent does your classroom environment communicate that questioning is appropriate and even desirable?

Like discussions, students' questions can help you assess their comprehension of and progress in learning important knowledge and skills and help you evaluate their understanding of how they are supposed to perform classroom activities. Classrooms that discourage discussions and questioning tend to inhibit learning.

Another feedback technique is eliciting a summary from students of what you have covered midway through and/or at the end of a learning unit. You can either ask an individual student to orally summarize or ask everyone in class to write a summary. You could provide such a summary, but getting students to summarize is better for helping them to reflect on what they are learning. A third approach is to elicit a summary from students, and then provide your own summary so that students can evaluate theirs with reference to a specific standard. This method may be best because it requires both students and teachers to be reflective thinkers.

Your comments can help students "own" their progress and motivate them to continue working. Prioritize and focus on your goals; don't criticize irrelevancies. If your goal is to improve a student's ability to organize ideas in an essay, then do not focus your attention on every spelling and punctuation error. Be specific in your feedback so students have a clear idea about what you see as the improvements they have made and areas still in need of improvement.

As the old saying goes, "Catch them being good." Praising students for making genuine progress on academic or behavioral issues can help students recognize their accomplishments and encourage them to continue trying. Indiscriminant praise or praise for minimal progress can devalue your feedback and undermine students' efforts to improve.

The form and timing of feedback are important considerations. The following recommendations are based on Bruner's classic book, *Toward a Theory of Instruction:*

- Present feedback in a way that is useful to your students.
- Time feedback carefully for maximum impact—give it to students when they can use it to correct their mistakes or otherwise improve their performance.
- Ensure that students are in an appropriate frame of mind for receiving feedback—don't deliver it when they're in a state of "high drive" or anxiety.
- Translate feedback into the learner's mode or way of thinking about material or solving a problem to maximize its potential use.
- Avoid overloading students with criticism. We all have limited capacities for taking in information, especially criticism, so be selective and focus on the most important points rather than making a comprehensive account of all flaws at once.
- Structure feedback in a way that will encourage independent learning, so that students do not become dependent on your feedback. For example, instead of telling students the correct answer, pose a question that will lead students to think in the correct direction and find the answer on their own.

Additional information on feedback is included in Chapter 2, Managing Teaching Reflectively. What are your strengths and weaknesses in implementing these principles?

✄ Nonverbal Communication

Nonverbal communication or "body language" can be described as the idea that it's not what one says, but what one shows through subtle, often unconscious, physical messages that captures the essence of nonverbal communication.

Body movements—facial expressions, arms, legs, posture, and even styles of hair and dress—send out cues to others that reflect the communicator's emotional reactions in social situations.

Research has shown that nonverbal communication is often affected by gender and by the status of the people engaged in communication. Typically, higher-status individuals, like teachers, reveal more assertiveness in their nonverbal communication than do lower-status individuals, like students, who reveal more passivity and subjugation. A similar pattern occurs depending on gender—males typically reflecting assertiveness and females typically reflecting passivity and subjugation. However, these patterns are generalizations and do not take into account cultural and individual factors that affect nonverbal communication.

Strategies for successfully using nonverbal communication in the classroom include maintaining eye contact with your students, having an open facial expression and relaxed body language, using gestures to accompany spoken language, and moving around the classroom to keep students interested and alert.

To what extent are your nonverbal behaviors consistent with these characteristics?

Cultural Issues in Nonverbal Communication

Research suggests that there is striking consistency in many messages conveyed nonverbally by people from different cultural backgrounds. Examples are in Table 3.6.

Try to pick up on nonverbal messages communicated by students. Make sure you're aware of and control the nonverbal signals you send to your students. A writing teacher observed, "Although I have learned to bite my tongue and control my enthusiasm for my own ideas, I can never control my feelings completely. In fact, my attitudes come across loud and clear: I flinch involuntarily at ideas I dislike; I nod my head wildly when the student feeds me a line I like."

Do you know how and what you communicate nonverbally? How sensitive are you to nonverbal communication of others? What types of nonverbal

---

TABLE 3.6 Cross-Cultural Nonverbal Communication of Emotions

Emotion Represented	Sadness	Genuine Warmth	Anger	Disgust	Fear	Surprise	Determination
How emotion is expressed nonverbally	Corners of lips are down. Eyebrows raised.	Smile. Lips turned up. Outer corners of eyes crinkled.	Jaw pushed forward. Lips pressed together.	Wrinkled nose.	Upper eyelids raised.	Eyes wide open. Eyebrows raised.	Lips pressed together.

cues do you tend to pick up? How do you use this information? How might teacher smiles and chuckles be used effectively while working with students? How might they interfere with teaching? What do you generally think when you see someone yawn? How do you think your students might feel about you yawning?

Research also shows that people are not always aware of the signals they send out nonverbally. Sometimes people intend to send one message but actually convey a different one. For example, holding two fingers up in a V shape in the U.S.A. is a peace signal, but in Britain, that same gesture, with the palm facing you, is the equivalent of giving someone the finger!

⚔ Cultural Differences in Communication

In many teaching situations the teacher and students bring with them a set of communication habits, values, and perspectives that are influenced by their cultural backgrounds. Students born and raised with values from the "mainstream," white, middle class culture in the U.S.A. are often used to asking questions and often take somewhat of an active role in learning. Many students from other cultural backgrounds are raised with a different set of traditions. Students from some cultural backgrounds are more used to a passive role in learning and are not comfortable asking questions of their instructors.

Avoid assuming that your students have the same communication habits, values, and perspectives that you do. Similarly avoid assuming that all students from any particular cultural/ethnic background will have the same values, habits, and perspectives. Try to view and understand each student as a unique individual. Sometimes limited English-speaking ability and heavy accents can interfere with teaching and learning. Teachers working with English as a Second Language students need to be especially sensitive to cultural issues in communication, as do teachers whose own native language is other than English. A Web site with valuable information differentiating Asian from American cultural values and behaviors is http://www.csupomona.edu/~tassi/gestures.htm.

Teachers need to speak and listen very carefully when working with students from culturally different backgrounds. In addition to the influence of cultural background on verbal interactions, it can also affect nonverbal communication. Even the physical proximity of a student and teacher working together, and physical gestures, like a pat on the back, can be affected by cultural background. Some cultures are used to working in close physical proximity and to using touch in communication. In some cases, people from other cultures are more comfortable with greater physical space between them and are uncomfortable with touching.

Again, do not make assumptions, but try to tune into your own communication patterns as well as the reactions of each individual you teach. Try to use "politically correct" language with students so that you don't offend those from different backgrounds. How might an African-American student feel if referred to as "colored"? Examples of cultural differences in communication are included in Table 3.7, from http://www.maec.org/cross/table4.html.

TABLE 3.7   Examples of Verbal and Nonverbal Communication Contrasts Among Some African Americans and Some Anglo Americans

Some African Americans	Some Anglo Americans
Hats and sunglasses may be considered by men as adornments, much like jewelry, and may be worn indoors.	Hats and sunglasses are considered utilitarian by men and as outerwear to be removed indoors.
Touching another's hair is generally considered offensive.	Touching another's hair is a sign of affection.
Asking personal questions of a person met for the first time may be seen as improper and intrusive.	Inquiring about jobs, family, and so forth of someone one has met for the first time is seen as friendly.
Use of direct questions is sometimes considered harassment, e.g., asking when something will be finished, is like rushing that person to finish.	Use of direct questions for personal information is permissible.
"Breaking in" during conversation by participants is usually tolerated. Competition for the floor is granted to the person who is most assertive.	Rules on taking turns in conversation dictate that one person has the floor at a time until all of his or her points are made.
Conversations are regarded as private between the recognized participants; "butting in" may be seen as eaves-dropping and not tolerated.	Adding points of information or insights to a conversation in which one is not engaged is sometimes seen as helpful.
The term "you people" is typically seen as pejorative and racist.	The term "you people" is tolerated.
Listeners are expected to avert eyes to indicate respect and attention.	Listeners are expected to look at a speaker directly to indicate respect and attention.
Speakers are expected to look listeners directly in the eye.	Speakers are expected to avert eyes, especially in informal speaking situations.
Confederate flags and Black lawn ornaments are considered offensive and racist.	Symbols of the Old South, such as Confederate flags and Black lawn ornaments, are considered acceptable by many.
Purposely including a minority person in group activities is seen as tokenism.	Including a minority person in group activities is seen as democratic.
Adoption of dance patterns or music of another cultural group is suspect or considered offensive.	Adoption of dance patterns or music of another cultural group is seen as a free and desirable exchange.
Talking "Black" by outsiders without authorization is an insult.	Borrowing of language forms from another group is permissible and encouraged.
Showing emotions during conflict is perceived as honesty and as the first step toward the resolution of a problem.	Showing emotions during conflict is perceived as the beginning of a "fight" and an interference to conflict resolution.

Cultural differences in communication can directly impact on understanding content in teaching. For example, when a teacher listened to her culturally different student reading a Langston Hughes poem aloud, she noticed that the student's rhythms and intonations were completely different than her own. Subtle differences can obscure important aspects of meaning. As a result of cultural differences, teachers and students sometimes encounter a communication gap between teaching styles and students' natural learning styles. Some teachers observing these differences misinterpret them as deficiencies. Make sure you don't make that mistake!

Try to record a class on video or audio tape to analyze your own communication patterns (verbal and nonverbal) as well as those of your students. Obviously, videotapes are better for examining nonverbal communication. What are your strengths and weaknesses? Does anything surprise you about how you communicate? How is your communication consistent and inconsistent with your students? How could you improve your communication to be more in tune with your students?

⚔ Communication Breakdown and Repair

In the following example, a high school teacher asks a student about an after-school lecture on drug and alcohol abuse that was given in the school auditorium. The teacher had been absent from school that day and didn't attend the lecture, but wanted to know what she missed.

Teacher: Did you go to the lecture on drug abuse after school yesterday?

Student: Yes, I went to part of it.

Teacher: Why were you there for only part of it?

Student: The speaker was very annoying so I left early.

Teacher: I'm disappointed in you. There was important information being presented and you shouldn't have let your personal biases against the speaker interfere with your learning things you really need to know.

Student, sounding annoyed: What are you talking about?

Teacher: You're not going to like every speaker in every lecture you hear and should learn to be more tolerant for your own good. Did he talk down to you? Did he have a heavy accent?

Student: The man who gave the lecture wasn't the problem. It was the electric speaker on the wall of the auditorium that had a broken wire so the sound was crackling and I couldn't make sense of what was being said! All the seats in the front were taken so I left. Last night I called a friend who was sitting in the front to find out what I missed.

What happened in the scenario described above? What were the causes of the communication breakdown? Has this type of communication experience ever happened to you? How can you and your students become aware when comprehension has broken down? What are the dangers of miscommunication? Miscommunication can be a major stumbling block in learning. In order to communicate effectively, a person must be aware of her/his own strengths and weaknesses in speaking and listening.

Recognizing Communication Problems

The biggest danger in miscommunication is not knowing it has occurred. People are not always aware when misunderstanding occurs. They often believe they have effectively communicated the message they want to send when in fact the message did not come through as intended. People sometimes hear what they expected to hear despite what was actually said.

Lack of understanding can occur as a result of incomplete information; ambiguous, vague, or confusing words and concepts; inconsistent, conflicting information; and erroneous information. Teachers and students should learn to monitor or check up on the communications they send and receive to catch communication problems when they occur. It's easier to clarify understanding if a problem has been detected! Awareness of the breakdown of understanding is the first step, and it paves the way for the second step, repair of understanding through clarification.

What were the causes of the communication breakdown in the preceding example? What can teachers do to help themselves and their students become aware when comprehension has broken down? There are at least three strategies for recognizing problems of meaning.

1. *Independent Recognition.* Check up on your own understanding and be alert to the possibilities of misunderstanding. Without the benefit of feedback from an outside source, by using one's own knowledge and reasoning when examining the information in its context, awareness of a comprehension breakdown can emerge. In the sample dialogue above, the teacher could have activated prior knowledge of lectures in the auditorium, pictured the electric speakers on the wall, and realized that the word "speaker" was ambiguous in the context. Then she could have asked the student a clarifying question.

2. *Disconfirmation.* Analyze information from other sources and look for feedback that specifically invalidates or validates one's interpretation, to stimulate recognition of misunderstanding. In the example above, when the teacher communicated the interpretation that the student left because of annoyance with the *lecturer,* that interpretation was *invalidated,* thereby showing that misunderstanding had occurred.

3. *Relational Recognition.* Look at information as a network of relationships instead as separate pieces. Use knowledge from related units of information to elaborate on and clarify understanding. For example, if the teacher knew the student was in the back of a lecture hall and needed amplified sound to hear the lecturer, the teacher might have realized that "speaker" could have meant something other than the lecturer. This awareness involves understanding information in its particular context.

Clarifying

Clarification can occur by figuring something out for yourself using your own **internal** resources, or by seeking information from outside **external** resources. If you're alone or in a situation where you can't communicate with anyone or access supplemental information, you're dependent on your ability to clarify internally.

Strategies for figuring out what something means on your own, internally clarifying, include examining the context of the communication for relevant clues. You can self-test the implications of possible interpretations using potential statements such as "If she means... then..., but if she means... then...." You can also activate prior knowledge that may be useful in general or in the specific situation, and selectively combine this information to apply to the specific situation.

For example, in the scenario above, if the teacher recalled her own experience in the large lecture hall she might have remembered that occasionally she had similar problems understanding the lecturer. She might have been less hasty in jumping to the conclusion that the student let personal biases interfere with learning. She might have asked a clarifying question, such as "What speaker are you referring to? Do you mean the presenter or are you talking about the electric device on the wall?"

Internally clarifying is important for independent thinking and learning. Research suggests that high-achieving students prefer to try to internally clarify their confusion before going to an outside source, whereas low-achieving students immediately seek clarification from an outside source, by asking either open-ended or closed questions. There are different types of external clarification strategies. While asking someone a question is an example of using an external source of information to clarify understanding, so is using a dictionary.

Research suggests that when asking someone a clarifying question, it's generally best to ask **open-ended** questions that require **elaboration** and maximize the amount of information elicited instead of **closed questions** that require **yes/no** answers and minimize the amount of information elicited.

Following is an example of external clarification by a closed question.

> **Teacher:** Did you mean that you had a problem with the conclusion of your essay because you forgot to include a conclusion in your essay?
> **Student:** No.

Compare this example of a closed question with the following external clarification by asking an open-ended question.

> **Teacher:** What did you mean about having had a problem with the conclusion of your essay?
> **Student:** I mean I forgot what I was supposed to include in the conclusion. I wrote a conclusion but didn't put the right stuff in it. I wrote the conclusion based on what I remembered the assignment to be, but didn't check out the directions and example on the handout, so I left out a lot of the points I was supposed to include.

What kinds of clarification strategies do your students generally use? You might ask them questions like the following to find out and to discuss when and how to clarify information, including differences between internal and external clarification.

1.   Shakira was confused about what she was reading in her social studies book for homework about the civil rights movement in the 1960s. She didn't understand whether people were marching because they didn't want to have to sit in the back of a bus any more, or because they were tired of being treated unfairly in a lot of different ways. If you were Shakira, what would you be most likely to do?

     a. Decide that it doesn't matter why they were marching, it's just important to know they were marching for their civil rights. (no clarification)

     b. Try to figure out the reason they were marching by rereading the chapter and looking for clues. (internal clarification)

     c. Ask your mother to read the chapter and ask her why the people were marching based on what was said in the book. (external clarification by open-ended)

     d. Show your mother the part of the chapter that confused you and ask, "Were the people marching because they didn't want to have to sit in the back of a bus any more?" (external clarification by closed questions)

2.   Tony's teacher returned a math quiz with a comment written at the bottom of the page saying "wrong formula." Tony wasn't sure which problems this comment referred to because several of them had points taken off. If you were Tony, what would you be most likely to do?

     a. Assume it refers to all problems where you lost credit. (no clarification)

     b. Ask the teacher, "Which formulas were wrong?" (external clarification, open-ended question)

     c. Ask the teacher, "It's just the last two problems, near your comment that had wrong formulas, right?" (external clarification, closed question)

     d. Carefully look at which problems had points taken off and see if you made careless mistakes that might account for losing credit or whether it's probably a case where the formula was wrong. (internal clarification)

Discuss with your students the advantages and disadvantages of different approaches to clarifying understanding, and how the specific situation can affect the type of clarification strategy that's best in the particular context.

⚔ Following Directions

How well do you and your students follow directions? One of the most common communication problems in academic situations is the failure to follow directions. Many times, if you examine a student's wrong answer, you will find that it is the "right" answer to the "wrong" question. Students tend to misinterpret communications to say what they expected or hoped they would be asked rather than focusing on what is actually asked. This communication problem happens on many tasks: objective tests, essay tests, in-class questions and learning activities, research projects, and homework assignments.

Try out the following activity with your students by giving them a handout with the 10 steps below. It's designed to test skills in following directions. Have them take out a piece of paper for this activity.

1.   Read all the directions before doing anything else.
2.   Write your name in the upper left-hand corner of the paper.
3.   Fold the paper in half, length-wise.
4.   Write your name on the outside of the folded paper.
5.   Print the letters of the alphabet beneath your name.
6.   Add these numbers and write the sum underneath the alphabet: 3, 35, 9, 95, 308.
7.   Open up the paper and write your teacher's name in the upper right-hand corner.
8.   Write today's date under your teacher's name.
9.   Put the paper on the floor.
10. Do not do anything asked for in numbers two through nine. Do not say anything to anyone. Just raise both hands high and smile.

✂ Attention Exercises for Students

To help your students become aware of their strengths and weaknesses paying attention during class, put students in pairs and have them monitor each other's attention by having them observe and record these nine non-attentive behaviors (see Table 3.8) during a lesson.

TABLE 3.8   Attention Checklist

Non-Attentive Behavior	Present (Record time)	Absent
yawning		
doodling		
fidgeting		
reacting to distractions		
eye movements away from the lesson		
turning head away from the lesson		
talking to another student		
reading or writing something unrelated to the lesson		
sleeping or nodding off		

Have the observers tally the number of incidences of each of the behaviors. Before giving students the results of the observations, have them evaluate themselves on the same behaviors, providing their own tally of the number of instances during the same time. Then have students compare their self-ratings with the objective observations by other students. Have the students switch roles so that everyone is observed and everyone is an observer. After everyone has been observed and done a self-assessment, discuss issues such as the following:

1. What topics can you concentrate on for a long time? Why?
2. What topics and activities do you have trouble concentrating on for a long time?
3. What are the differences between topics and activities you can concentrate on relatively well and those you have difficulty concentrating on?
4. What kinds of situations or events interfere with your concentration?
5. What do you tend to do when you stop concentrating? Why?
6. How might you improve your concentration?

✖ Technology

The "Fact Monster" Homework Center Web site has resources in many subjects, including geography, history, mathematics, science, and language arts. It also has links to material for improving students' speaking and listening skills. Included is a useful list of words that are commonly mispronounced and suggestions for how to give an oral report. It also includes material on reading, writing, and study skills.

USA Today has an online Web site, "Idea: Success Stories," with a variety of K–12 teacher resources. One of them is called "Today's Debate" and is geared toward using newspaper editorials to have students debate as a way of improving their communication skills.

Another resource, sponsored by Microsoft "Home Magazine," recommends that teachers and parents communicate with each other about what happens in the classroom via e-mail. A research report from Harvard, available online, suggests that contrary to some beliefs, parent involvement is important for students' achievement in high school and beyond. Online resources for teachers to communicate effectively with parents can be accessed at http://teacher.scholastic.com/professional/parentconf/.

Strategies for assessing students' speaking and listening skills are available in an online summary of research available from the Educational Resources Information Clearinghouse on Reading and Communication Skills.

To help students become more reflective about their communication skills, there are technology-based self-evaluation strategies that can be used or adapted for specific students. You can model for your students how to self-evaluate by videotaping your own speaking and listening skills and critiquing yourself. An online listening self-evaluation rubric is available at http://www.ell.nie.edu.sg/innerPages/programmes/Special/Rubrics/Documents/Listening%20self%20evaluation.Chaney.doc.

Summary

Teaching is a social interaction that depends on effective communication. Become aware of your own strengths and weaknesses in speaking, listening, and giving feedback as well as what you communicate nonverbally, especially when working with culturally diverse students. Learn and teach your students about obstacles to effective communication, strategies for identifying communication break-downs, and techniques to improve all aspects of communication. Various online resources are available for improving and assessing students' speaking and listening skills and for helping teachers and parents communicate with each other.

Resources

Bruner, J. *Toward a Theory of Instruction.* New York: W.W. Norton & Co., 1966.

ComResources Online (n.d.). Retrieved August 16, 2006 from http://www.natcom.org/ctronline/nonverb.htm.

Culture, Communication and Language (n.d.) Retrieved August 18, 2006 from http://www.maec.org/cross/4.html.

Doucet, J. Classroom Communication. (n.d.) Parents talk to Teachers with Email. Retrieved July 31, 2007 from http://www.microsoft.com/canada/home/familyandfun/2.1.18_classroomcommunication.aspx.

Exploring Nonverbal Communication (n.d.) Retrieved August 16, 2006 from http://nonverbal.ucsc.edu/.

Fact Monster. Homework Center (n.d.). Retrieved October 22, 2006 from http://www.factmonster.com/homework/speaklisten.html.

Fast, J. *Body Language.* New York: Pocket Book, 1974.

Gardner, H. *Multiple Intelligences: New Horizons.* New York: Basic Books, 2006.

Gestures: Body Language and Nonverbal Communication. Teachers' Asian Studies Summer Institute Web Page. California State Polytechnic University. Retrieved October 10, 2006 from http://www.csupomona.edu/~tassi/gestures.htm.

Lebaron, M. Cross-Cultural Communication. 2003. Retrieved August 16, 2006 from http://www.beyondintractability.org/essay/cross-cultural_communication/.

Mead, N. A.; and D. L. Rubin. Assessing Listening and Speaking Skills: ERIC Digest. ED263626. 1985. Retrieved October 10, 2006 from http://www.ericdigests.org/pre-923/speaking.htm.

Nonverbal Behavior Nonverbal Communication Links (n.d.). Retrieved August 20, 2006 from http://www.usal.es/~nonverbal/introduction.htm.

Patrikakou, E. N. "Adolescents: Are Parents Relevant for High School Students' Achievement and Postsecondary Attainment?" *Research Digest.* 2004. Retrieved October 10, 2006 from http://www.gse.harvard.edu/hfrp/projects/fine/resources/digest/adolescence.html.

Professional Development Center: Instructor Development Resource: Module 3 Classroom Communication and Learning Theories (n.d.). Retrieved August 20, 2006 from http://planet.tvi.edu/idc/modules/IDR3ClassroomCommunicationsWeb.htm.

Robertson, E. The Five Myths of Managers, Strategic Communication Management. 2005. Retrieved July 11, 2007 from www.gov.im/lib/docs/dhss/communicationstrategy2006finalve.doc.

Williams, G. L. "Self-Evaluation in Speaking and Listening." *English Journal* 61, no. 1 (1972), pp. 68–70.

Emotional Aspects of Thinking and Learning

To be successful, it's important for you to address more than students' knowledge and skills when helping them think and learn. An often overlooked or neglected element is the students' emotions. Students need to be emotionally prepared to think and learn and to use what they have learned. A key part of your job is to help develop in students those emotions that aid learning. To think and learn effectively students need to be motivated, to have positive attitudes, and to know how to control their emotional states of mind. How would you rate your students on these characteristics?

Why is it that sometimes even students who you know are intelligent don't do very well? At least 20 emotional stumbling blocks to intelligent performance have been identified in multiple intelligence research. One is a lack of perseverance, or giving up too soon. Another is perseveration, or refusing to stop even when it is obvious that nothing constructive is occurring. A third emotional obstacle is being motivated by external factors, which tends to have a short-term impact, rather than being motivated by internal factors, which tends to have a longer-term impact. Multiple intelligence theories hold that we all have some degree of self-knowledge or "intrapersonal intelligence," which includes self-awareness of our feelings and how they are expressed. Therefore, as a teacher you have an opportunity and responsibility to your students.

⚔ Motivation

To examine the importance of personal motivation in thinking and learning, consider the following. Mentally picture a student who is motivated to learn. What are the characteristics of that student? How does that student learn in class compared to one who is unmotivated? What motivates you to learn? What decreases your motivation? How would you define the concept of motivation in your own words? Reflecting on factors influencing your own motivation can give you insights into your emotions that affect thinking and learning. Motivation is defined as a set of conditions that initiate, direct, and sustain behavior. For example, Janine's family purchased a piano, which gave her the desire to start piano lessons (initiate behavior). She especially liked to play jazz and focused on that (direct behavior). Janine's love for the piano grew and she continued taking piano lessons (sustain behavior). This example is of intrinsic or internal motivation, which has characteristics shown in Figure 4.1

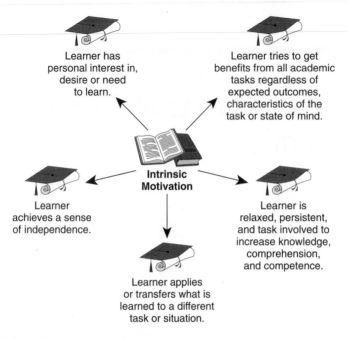

FIGURE 4.1   *Characteristics of Intrinsic Motivation*

In contrast, extrinsic or external motivation is characterized by a student emphasizing a desire for rewards such as grades, praise, and/or privileges. Often teachers try to motivate students by giving them easy tasks with a high probability of success. The reward is a good grade and perhaps praise. When working with very weak or insecure students, this may be a good approach to begin, but it should be temporary.

Motivation research has found that students really need challenging tasks where they have a moderate probability of success, defined as about 50 percent chance of success. Tasks should be slightly more difficult than students' current level of ability. However, even when tasks are structured to engage learners, students must have the organizational skills and motivation to do the work. Sometimes they begin working on a challenging task, but don't persist until it is complete. Making student work public can help motivate students to continue, even when the task becomes difficult or frustrating. Encouraging students to work together can also help motivate them to persist with challenging tasks.

Encourage your students to take intellectual risks. Help them understand that making mistakes and failing are important and beneficial parts of the learning process. Expert learners are not error free. They learn from their errors by thinking reflectively, analyzing why they made them and planning how to improve their future performance.

Help students examine and discuss their persistence on difficult/boring tasks and consider whether they have expended appropriate time and energy. Help them identify and evaluate the approaches they use and, as appropriate, offer alternatives. Discuss the scope of motivation. Emphasize that it is a continuous process, because it initiates, directs, and sustains behavior. Question your students. Find out "what makes them tick," and use this information to enhance their motivation when needed.

Although certain common factors generally impact many students, such as grades and the desire to earn a decent living, not everyone is motivated by the same influences. Consider what motivational factors influence each of your students individually. How could you help a student broaden the sources of motivation? How would you evaluate these various motivational factors? Which should you emphasize developing in your students? Why? How would you go about it?

Your students should experience their lessons as engaging, enjoyable, and meaningful. In this chapter we explore strategies for promoting these feelings in your students. We will look at strategies that are best for working with multicultural students.

Reflective teaching includes thinking about your own learning experiences and gaining insights from them. When you were in school, what subjects and learning activities did you find most interesting? Think about why they interested you. How might you use such reflection to motivate students?

Research shows that intrinsic motivation, which comes from within the learner, is better than extrinsic motivation, which comes from outside the learner, for promoting and sustaining long-term, meaningful learning. Although intrinsic motivation is multidimensional, it most commonly is associated with building on learners' needs, interests, and experiences.

Intrinsic Motivational Framework for Culturally Responsive Teaching

A framework for culturally responsive teaching has been developed for use when teaching multicultural students. It is based on understanding the value of intrinsic motivation. This framework is broadly applicable regardless of gender, socioeconomic class, race, ethnicity, religion, region, family background, and the subject being taught. The rationale for this framework is that emotions are affected by culture and influence motivation, which in turn affects school performance and achievement. According to this framework, some sources of intrinsic motivation transcend culture. These include curiosity, making meaning from experience, being active, and initiating thought and behavior. If you effectively motivate students, then your teaching is culturally responsive.

The Intrinsic Motivational Framework for Culturally Responsive Teaching has four components.

1. Establishing Inclusion: so students and the teacher feel connected to each other and enjoy mutual respect;
2. Developing Attitude: by personal relevance and choices creating favorable dispositions;
3. Enhancing Meaning: making thoughtful learning experiences that challenge students and include their values and perspectives;
4. Engendering Competence: creating learning experiences in which students succeed and recognize their effectiveness in learning something they consider to be worthwhile.

These motivation principles should be incorporated into your teaching. Do you have activities and/or strategies for each of them? How might you supplement your lessons to further enhance the incorporation of these principles?

Social Insight

Culturally responsive teaching is related to the concept of "social insight," which is one of the characteristics shown to differentiate expert teachers from novices. Social insight involves tuning into students' culture and their behavior inside and outside of the classroom. By tuning into their culture, expert teachers can understand their students' thoughts and behaviors. The expert also has an awareness of verbal and nonverbal communication, values, culture and ethnic identification, as well as general features of the culture such as music and clothing styles, world view, behavioral style, and reasoning methods. When working with multicultural students, expert teachers construct multiple standards for events, their perceptions, and their interpretations.

Social insight is especially important when teaching adolescents. They are likely to have disdain and disrespect for teachers who don't "get it" and consequently act out in class, thereby lessening the effectiveness of instruction. To what extent are you tuned into your students? How do your students perceive your degree of social insight? What strategies do you use to find out about their beliefs, attitudes, and preferences? What could you do to increase your social insight?

A specific area requiring understanding is bullying. How good is your insight into bullying both in your classroom and involving your students outside the classroom? Bullying is a major issue during adolescence, and your awareness of it and ability to address it constructively can affect your students' behavior, attitudes, and academic achievement. Bullying can be physical, such as tripping, pushing, or even sexual abuse. Bullying can also be psychological, such as threatening, name calling, or picking on someone. It's not uncommon for students to resist going to school in order to avoid being bullied. Victims of bullying may suffer mental health problems, with depression, anxiety, and even suicide attempts. Because one of the main causes of bullying is a student being perceived as different, try to cultivate your students' acceptance of people who are different from them in race, culture, socioeconomic status, and physical characteristics, such as being fat or having pronounced skin blemishes. Having them reflect on bullying from the perspective of the person being bullied might enhance their empathy and encourage students to be more caring about peers.

Do you ever exercise power by bossing and bullying your students? Bullying creates feelings of intimidation and resentment, and undermines respect, so a short-term advantage is often followed by a long-term disadvantage.

Reflective teachers have social insight about their students' and their own emotions and interactions. Awareness and control of negative behavior patterns such as bullying can lead to improved social relationships and higher levels of academic achievement.

A few areas of motivation have been of particular concern to teachers. They include motivating students to use what they learn, motivating students to be responsible for their own educational outcomes, motivating them to come prepared to the classroom, and motivating students to take an active role in their own learning both in and outside of the classroom.

Motivation Principles

What influences motivation? Students are likely to give up on an activity if it does not meet their needs, if it does not make particular sense, if it is conducted at a level that is incomprehensible, or if it is presented in a humiliating or insulting way. Tension between your teaching style and a student's learning style can also decrease motivation. What can you do to increase student motivation? (See Table 4.1.) You can help the student recognize the personal value of the activity, develop a strong sense of confidence that she or he will be able to master the material, and anticipate success in the learning experiences rather than failure.

What can you do to enhance the motivational impact of a presentation? Present instruction clearly in a simple-to-understand, easy-to-follow manner, avoid arousing negative emotions in students and attempt to arouse positive emotions. Empathize with students' reactions and be aware of how the material appears to the student. To do this you must have a realistic understanding of each student's needs and point of view and then adapt instruction to the student's level of experience and skill. Continuously consider where the student is coming from and inspire enthusiasm by communicating genuine interest in the subject.

What can you do to provide rewards that will increase student motivation? Provide (immediate) feedback on work so that long-term retention is enhanced and use realistic, appropriate praise for work well done or for continued efforts to master material. Don't overdo praise and make students dependent on it. Praise students selectively—only when you feel they really need outside support or when they accomplish something truly admirable.

TABLE 4.1 Strategies for Enhancing Student Motivation		
Motivational Principles	**Reasons and Strategies**	**Examples**
Help students overcome feelings of helplessness.	Success alone does not work. It's necessary but not sufficient. Students need to be able to interpret success as resulting from the strategies they used. The Links to Success model, described later in this chapter, is one successful approach to eliminating students' feelings of helplessness. Help students focus on strategies rather than outcomes in order for them to attribute successful outcomes to their own actions.	That was a good diagram for setting up and solving problem number 3.

(continued)

TABLE 4.1 *Continued*

Motivational Principles	Reasons and Strategies	Examples
Praise has a positive effect on students only if the teacher praises an aspect of performance that is relevant to the task.	If praise is used indiscriminately, it can undermine students' beliefs in their ability. Do *not* praise something like handwriting unless clear handwriting is the specific task.	It was good to see you proofreading your paper before turning it in. Your corrections will make it a better paper!

Help students develop positive self-perceptions.	Use the self-perception continuum (Figure 4.2), which ranges from general to specific, to identify which self-perception you will have a student focus on at a specific time.
	
	    Self-esteem is a feeling of general self-worth.
	
	    General academic self-concept is how a student feels about him- or herself as a learner.
	
	    Subject-specific self-concept is a feeling about learning potential in a particular content area.
	
	    Self-efficacy is a task-specific feeling about potential success.
		Self-esteem: I'm a good member of my community. General academic self-concept: I'm a good student. Subject-specific self-concept: I'm good in English, but not in math. Self-efficacy: I'm good at solving equations in algebra, but not at doing proofs in geometry.

Although extrinsic rewards can be effective, they are generally overused and can have a hidden cost.	Encouraging students to become controlled by factors external to themselves, such as rewards or praise, can undermine intrinsic motivation and lead to dependency on outside forces. Phase out extrinsic rewards and emphasize internal benefits.	If you get a good grade on this test, you will be excused from taking the next two quizzes.
Research on intrinsic motivation shows benefits of giving students choices and feelings of personal control over learning.	Choices plus a sense of control increase interest and involvement in learning.	What topic would you like to address in your essay? When do you want to begin writing it, in class today or tonight for homework?
Telling students that they did not work hard enough may actually decrease their feelings of self-efficacy.	Let students know that effort is important, but the amount of effort is sometimes not as important as the type of effort students make. If they spend more time (equated with making greater efforts) using the same ineffective learning strategies, their increased efforts will not be very fruitful, and they will be even more frustrated. Sometimes students can work less hard by using more effective learning strategies. Working smarter improves the payoff from effort.	Don't be upset that you didn't get an "A" on that test. What's most important is that you started to use the relaxation and test-taking strategies we went over and you did much better than on the last test. Don't work harder or longer, work smarter.

general_____specific

Self-esteem   general academic   subject-specific   self-efficacy
                self-concept   self-concept

FIGURE 4.2   *Self-Perception Continuum*

Research tells us that students need to feel that they have some control over their environment and that they can influence or shape it to increase their ability to learn from instruction. Students need to understand that their successes and failures are due to their own efforts, which they can control. When they perceive that they have some control, their performance improves. Learning to attribute academic performance to effort and use of particular strategies, rather than native ability or external influences, can improve academic achievement.

Motivating Students to Be Responsible and Come Prepared

Students are most likely to come prepared for class if they expect the lesson to be interesting, relevant to their personal needs, something they can succeed at, and if they believe that the outcomes will meet their expectations.

Student effort and persistence are affected by:

1. Believing they develop their competence on specific tasks with your assistance;
2. Knowing what is expected of them in the short and long term and knowing their own strengths and weaknesses;
3. Having personal standards against which to measure their performance;
4. The ability to judge whether their performance has met their standards; and
5. Being able to self-direct and self-correct ("constructive failure"), through analyzing their errors and their own states of mind (intellectual and emotional aspects).

You can follow five basic steps to help students to do their best.

1. Identify a specific goal.
2. Specify personal benefits of achieving this goal.
3. Review the current status in achieving the goal.
4. Specify strategies for reaching the goal.
5. Identify specific criteria for reaching the goal.

Motivating Students to Use What They Learn

To what extent do your students use their effective, reflective thinking and learning strategies when they need to? Recent research on learning emphasizes the importance of attending to higher-level thinking and emotional aspects of learning in addition to the traditional focus on content and basic skills. Learning is best when it is active, meaningful, retained over time, and transferred to a variety of contexts. One often neglected but vitally important aspect of learning is that often students have the requisite knowledge and skills for performing complex tasks but do not use them. The skills remain **inert.** Sometimes this is because students are not motivated or confident enough to apply them. And, sometimes students simply do not recognize when situations call for use of particular knowledge and skills they already have. (See Transfer section in Chapter 2.)

Some individuals fail to use the strategies and knowledge they already have because of

1. minimal motivation,
2. minimal transfer,
3. attributing their successes and failures to external factors beyond their control,
4. classroom practices that do not support strategy use.

Teachers often do not present strategies in enough different contexts for students to generalize their use effectively. Impulsive students not only need to learn to eliminate distractions, focus their attention, and slow down when applying what they have learned, but also need specific instruction on how to plan, monitor, and evaluate their performance. Teachers can model thinking aloud to systematically externalize obvious and hidden thoughts.

To help motivate students to use what they have learned, you can specifically guide their thinking about what they have learned with reference to memory, context, procedures, and value.

- *Memory:* Students must remember what they have learned. They should consciously plan to use specific strategies to help them remember important information. Which memory strategies are most effective? Memory is easiest when learning is meaningful and students can connect their knowledge. Graphic organizers are excellent tools for helping students understand and visualize relationships between ideas so that they can be remembered when needed. Writing summaries is also a good memory strategy.
- *Context:* Students must know **when and why** to use what they have learned. All the knowledge and skills in the world won't help students if they don't know when is the right time to use them. What cues can they use to determine if it's an appropriate situation to use particular knowledge/skills?
- *Procedures:* Students must know **how** to use/do what they have been taught. Teachers should emphasize approaches for both storing information in memory and retrieving it from memory. How can they figure out or remember the steps, strategies, and sequences needed?
- *Value:* Students must recognize personal meaning and benefits of what they have learned. For example, have students create a graphic organizer (and perhaps write an essay) on how better English will help them get a job or how math will help them with a career as a scientist.

Motivational Progress Chart

A progress chart may be useful for motivating students to come prepared for, and to be active in, learning. The chart can focus on an individual student or on a group. The progress chart can state the specific objective, why it is targeted as an objective, when and how the objective will be met, and the ongoing status of each component. You can use symbols such as those in Table 4.2 to record progress on specific plans.

In addition to assessing their objective status in achieving targeted learning objectives, students can benefit by learning to make more subjective, qualitative judgments about their own progress. For example, rather than viewing the writing of the research paper as unfinished for a long six weeks, the table reveals significant achievements each week, such as completing an outline or beginning a draft.

Sometimes it may be more motivating to a student to subdivide higher-level objectives, such as writing a research paper, into a series of lower-level objectives, such as preparing an outline, writing a first draft, getting feedback, and so forth. You can chart progress on these lower-level objectives to help the student see progress over shorter periods of time. Students often need steady feelings of making progress to motivate them to continue working.

TABLE 4.2 Sample Progress Chart				
Specific Learning Objective	**Why**	**How**	**Date**	**Status:** − not done / partly done + completed
Write research paper.	Required and counts for 30% of grade. Will need to do in college.	Choose an interesting topic. Develop a schedule.	2/16	+
		Search library and online for journals, books.	2/23	+
		Make an outline.	3/14	+
		Do a section at a time.	3/21	/
		Get feedback on drafts and revise.	4/12	/
		Proofread final copy before submitting.	4/26	−

Students can be taught a variety of strategies, such as those in the list below, to assess their progress or performance. See more on self-assessment in Chapter 7.

1. Reflect on whether and how the task was performed successfully.
2. Observe someone else performing the task successfully.
3. Hear someone comment on the student performing a task successfully.
4. Compare one's performance with someone else's.
5. Obtain a good grade for task performance.
6. Feel a sense of accomplishment for performing a task.
7. Obtain feedback on task performance.
8. See a connection between specific efforts and their outcomes.
9. Use a personal standard to assess one's own performance.
10. Identify one's own physiological or psychological state—attention, fatigue, stress, confidence.

⚔ Attitudes That Influence Reflective and Critical Thinking

Emotional factors that affect teaching and learning are numerous and varied. They include motivation, attitudes, and values. An attitude is a feeling for or against something, resulting in a relatively enduring tendency to react favorably or unfavorably to an idea, person, or situation. Attitudes toward school, self, the world, academic tasks, and testing all can have a direct impact on how students think, learn, and perform in school. Each is different from, but related to, the others. Following are some attitudes that impact students' thinking and academic performance. Make sure you have a clear understanding of their differences, in terms of both what they are and how they are developed.

Predispositions

Students enter classes with personal and cultural attitudes toward authority figures, their role as students, the importance of learning, and the value and usefulness of knowledge and skills. All of these are factors that affect students' willingness to participate in a class, to persevere with academic tasks, and to take intellectual risks.

Predispositions affect students' perceptions of the relationship between schooling and future needs/goals as well as their willingness to pursue further education. A student entering a classroom with a predisposition to learn from and use what the teacher presents is likely to have a very different learning experience from a student who views school as a rite of passage or merely a social meeting place. Often students are predisposed to be anxious about learning and taking tests in particular subjects because of the perceived difficulty of the subject matter. Anxiety can occur because of parental pressure and expectations regarding their children's school achievement, the students' own self-perception, and gender stereotypes.

Suggestions for improvement include

- Discuss short- and long-term benefits intended for each topic/task;
- Cultivate student self-control over learning and performance (e.g., time management);
- Encourage students to challenge and question authority;
- Systematically relate schoolwork to everyday life and future goals;
- Model, encourage and reward persistence, intellectual risk taking, toleration for ambiguity, intrinsic motivation, and delayed gratification.

Curiosity

Students differ in their sense of wonder and desire to know about the world. Curiosity involves an interest in and alertness to problems, events, ideas, and individuals. It is best accompanied by a questioning attitude and a sense of inquisitiveness, through which students can satisfy their thirst for knowing the what, the why, and the how. Research shows that students with a high degree of curiosity are more likely to be interested in, appreciate, and benefit from the education process than students with little curiosity.

Students like to be challenged. Research indicates they find tasks that involve a moderate probability of success, defined as 50 percent, most satisfying. This moderate probability of success is also associated with intrinsic motivation. Don't attempt "error-free" environments. Students can learn a great deal from their mistakes, especially if you provide feedback that is prompt, specific, and informational. Theory and research indicate three conditions needed for risk taking to have successful outcomes, as follows:

1. Students must be given choices of materials and activities that have different levels of difficulty and varied degrees of probable success.
2. Rewards for success must increase with the difficulty of the task.
3. There must be an environment that accepts errors and assists in correcting them. (See "error analysis" in the chapter on assessments.)

Suggestions for enhancing students' curiosity include

- Create a warm, accepting environment where students feel free to take intellectual risks.
- Have discussions in which students play with their own ideas, build on the ideas of others, examine dilemmas, and confront conflicting ideas or information.
- Model and encourage an interested, skeptical, and inquiring attitude.
- Teach students questioning and self-questioning strategies.
- Make students' "brains itch" by posing provocative problems/questions students don't expect or aren't used to, using novelty, surprise, or questions with no clear, immediate, single answer (e.g. "What would happen if no one ever died?") and by not giving them the answers to selected problems/questions to encourage student discovery.

- Encourage creative problem solving instead of one "right" answer.
- Make interdisciplinary and cross-cultural connections.
- Assign learning tasks that require doing, not just remembering.

Reflective Style

Students show general tendencies to be reflective or impulsive across time and tasks. The reflective style is associated with longer thinking time, cautiousness over performance, and fewer errors. The impulsive style is characterized by shorter thinking time, carelessness in performance, and more errors. Adopting a reflective style can help ensure "precise processing," which some view as the key to higher-order thinking. Dewey characterized reflective thought as intentionally turning ideas over in one's mind and giving them active, serious, and systematic consideration. He viewed reflective thinking as an aim of education because it transforms blind, routine, and impulsive action into intelligent action, which enables inventing, problem solving, and creating enriched meaning.

Suggestions for developing reflectiveness include

- Model reflective thinking, patience, thoroughness, and carefulness.
- Ask questions that require reflection (e.g., Why and how do you think the wheel was invented?).
- Model and require "wait time" of at least a few seconds to think before raising a hand to answer selected questions.
- Model and encourage thinking aloud.
- Let students know that counting on their fingers and moving their mouths when they read are acceptable strategies. Both are signs of carefulness.

Attributions

Attributions refer to the reasons people give for their successes and failures. Attributions can be divided into two dimensions: stable–unstable and internal–external. Stable–unstable refers to how consistent the attributions are over time. Stable refers to the person using the same types of reasons to explain success or failure over and over again. Unstable refers to giving one kind of reason on one occasion and another type of reason another time. For example, Phil says equations are always difficult for him to solve (stable), but that some division problems are easy and some are difficult (unstable).

Internal–external refers to where the person assigns responsibility for her/his successes and failures—inside the self or outside the self. For example, Teres says she didn't do well on her history test because she didn't study enough (internal). Susan says she didn't do well on her psychology test because her family interfered with her study time (external). Alan says he got a good grade on his first math test because he was lucky and he did poorly on his second math test because he was jinxed (external).

Students' explanations of their successes and failures have important consequences for future performance on academic tasks. Research shows there are four common ways students explain their successes and failures:

Effort — "I could do it if I really tried."
Ability — "I'm just not a good writer."
Luck — "I guessed right."
Task difficulty — "The test was too hard."

Attributions are related to

1. expectations about one's likelihood of success;
2. judgments about one's ability;
3. emotional reactions of pride, hopelessness, and helplessness;
4. willingness to work hard and self-regulate one's efforts.

Feelings of helplessness are created over a period of time by belief that failure is due to lack of ability. Students who see a relationship between their own effort and their own success are more likely to use learning strategies such as organizing, planning, goal-setting, self-checking, and self-instruction.

The Links to Success model was designed to help "at-risk" students develop attributions that will motivate them to succeed. However, this approach can benefit a wide range of students. The four Links to Success are

1. Proximal goals. These are short-term rather than long-term, specific rather than general, and challenging (but reachable) rather than easy. (For example, This week I'll manage my time so that I have three extra hours to study.) Teach students to anticipate and overcome obstacles, monitor their own progress while goals are being pursued, and evaluate whether they achieved their goals at the end of the specified time. "I'll know whether I accomplished this goal by writing down how much time I study and comparing that to how much time I studied last week. Possible obstacles to my achieving this goal are . . . I will overcome these obstacles by . . ." When they don't achieve their goals, teach students to determine why they didn't and what they could do differently next time.

2. Learning strategies. Teach students to apply effective strategies, such as summarizing and clarifying, that emphasize meaningful learning and can be used across subjects and situations. They replace ineffective approaches, such as repeating, which tends to emphasize rote memorization.

3. Success experiences. Structure moderate difficulty tasks for students, but ensure they are likely to succeed. Students' evaluating their success in achieving the proximal goals, emphasizing **learning** ("How much progress did I make?") rather than **performance** ("What grade did I get?"), is the goal.

4. Attributions for success. Encourage students to explain their successes in terms of their personal efforts, strategies, and abilities. The teacher's role here is to give students feedback on why they succeeded or failed and to help students give the appropriate explanation. Was an answer incorrect, or incomplete? Was there a careless mistake? Make sure students understand why an answer is incorrect. Ask questions such as, "What did you do when you tried to answer that question/solve that problem?"

Openmindedness

The extent to which students' mental attitudes are open or closed affects how they process information. Being openminded is often associated with being free of bias or prejudice, both of which inhibit consideration of new ideas. Openmindedness is often considered one of the key attitudes underlying critical thinking. It allows one to more objectively determine whether information should be accepted or rejected.

Research shows that students who are openminded are more likely to see connections between differing beliefs whereas students who are close-minded tend to treat beliefs as isolated from each other. Consequently, openminded students might be more likely than close-minded students to see relationships between concepts across subject areas as well as connections between knowledge and skills learned in school and non-school applications, thereby promoting transfer.

Suggestions for enhancing openmindedness include

- Help students view the world relativistically (in terms of degrees and alternatives) rather than absolutely (all or none and one right answer or way).
- Model and encourage students to withhold judgment until sufficient evidence and reasons exist.
- Model and encourage respecting the right of others to have beliefs and values different from one's own.
- Have students argue from positions different from their own, and show students how to use opposing viewpoints as tools for critically evaluating lines of reasoning.
- Help students avoid overgeneralizing the implications of ideas and events.
- Accept students' valid answers and methods even if they are not the ones you or the book had in mind.
- Identify relationships between ideas instead of treating them in isolation.
- Cultivate the habit of differentiating between fact and opinion.

Have your students reflect on and critically evaluate themselves on these attitudes and develop individual plans for self-improvement in one particular area. A journal is a good strategy for them to record their plans, their implementation, and to monitor their progress. It's also a good way for you to evaluate their approaches and provide them with feedback for improvement by periodically collecting their journals and making comments.

✄ Subject-Specific Emotions

In addition to the emotional factors affecting academic performance in general, there are also emotional responses to individual subjects.

Consider these questions: How do students' emotions affect their performance in specific subjects? For example, which subjects tend to evoke the most anxiety in students? In which subjects do students experience the most test anxiety? What factors affect subject-specific anxiety? To what extent does test anxiety vary with the subject area? How do students' emotions influence their performance in your subject area(s)?

For native speakers of English in the United States of America, subject-specific anxiety is most common in mathematics and next most common in science. However, there is some evidence that test anxiety is highest in physical science. For many non-native speakers of English in the U.S., English often evokes the most anxiety. Consequently, reflective teaching includes considering how academic activities (tests) and cultural factors (native language) might affect your students' anxiety in particular subjects.

Extensive research shows subject-specific differences in students' academic self-concepts. Some students feel confident about their ability to do well on verbal tasks but are pessimistic about their ability to do well in mathematics. For other students it's the exact opposite.

What kind of frame of reference do your students use when thinking about their subject-specific learning abilities? Research tells us that students who make self-comparisons have more positive attitudes than those who make comparisons with other students. Help your students focus on their own progress in learning in a specific subject instead of focusing on how they compare with their peers.

Some emotional responses to specific subjects are desirable. For example, when teaching literature from an aesthetic perspective, students' emotional responses to text are valuable because they facilitate their engagement in reading and their connections with the characters and events. Often teachers deliberately choose literature that will stimulate and provoke their students in an effort to create emotional responses to text. Emotions also influence reading of information-oriented writing.

Self-Regulation of Emotions

This section shows how you can help students have greater control over their attitudes and motivations. Positive self-talk is important for learning in general and in all subjects. Reflective learners are aware and in control of the messages they give to themselves. They "tune in" to what they are silently thinking and feeling and use silent self-talk to modify these thoughts and feelings in a more desirable direction, eliminating negative self-talk, either neutralizing it or converting it to positive self-talk. Coping self-statements and self-reinforcers can help students manage their emotional states in academic situations. The key to controlling an undesirable mental state is first becoming aware of its existence. Each of these strategies requires reflective thinking.

Coping self-statements are self-talk techniques that can help the learner set the stage for a positive learning experience and help motivate a student to do his/her best. Self-reinforcers can reward a student for doing her/his best. Three subject-specific examples are given in Table 4.3.

TABLE 4.3   Self-Talk Techniques for Developing Attitudes that Foster Thinking

Subject	Coping Self-Statements	Self-Reinforcers
Reading	Reading will help me do better in all my subjects.	Now that I'm using better reading strategies, I understand more in both my history and science books.
Writing	I need to write well so that I can become a journalist.	I'm glad I revised my essay after catching those mistakes. Now I'm on my way to being a professional writer!
Math	If I work hard preparing for all the math quizzes, I'll do much better on the end-of-unit test.	My extra studying paid off. I did the best I've ever done on the end-of-unit test.

⚔ Technology

Bullying is a major problem in the schools, especially for students in grades six through ten. Several videotapes are available on this problem and include strategies for addressing the problem of bullies as well as interviews with students who have been bullied and others who are reformed bullies. TeachSafeSchools has extensive resources on the topic at http://www.teachsafeschools.org/bully_menu6-2.html. Bullying and violence prevention are both addressed by Safe Youth, http://www.safeyouth.org/scripts/media/index.asp.

Videos addressing the issue of violence in schools and with adolescents in particular offer suggestions for helping students become nonviolent. Such videos explore the causes of violence in teenagers and recommend strategies for teachers and parents to use to counter violence.

The Internet has a variety of resources for helping you promote the development of positive emotions in your students. As part of their formal Learning Standards, the State of Illinois identifies three standards for social/emotional learning for grades K–12:

1. Self-Regulation. Develop self-awareness and self-management skills to achieve school and life success.
2. Social Interactions. Use social awareness and interpersonal skills to establish and maintain positive relationships.
3. Standards. Demonstrate decision-making skills and responsible behaviors in personal, school, and community contexts. Available at their Web site are five levels of benchmarks for each of these standards, describing what students should know and be able to do at different grade levels.

A wonderful online article at Kidsource on strategies for nurturing the emotional-social development of gifted children has suggestions you can adapt or use for many other children as well. In addition to identifying gifted students' strengths, it shows corresponding problems that might arise due to those strengths. For example, the strength of intrinsic motivation might be accompanied by resistance to taking direction and being strong-willed.

The Advocates for Youth Web site has over 30 lesson plans on a variety of issues relevant to emotional development in adolescents. Examples include Gender Roles and Relationships, Body Image, and Addressing Discrimination.

Summary

Reflective teaching recognizes that the emotional side of learning is just as important as the intellectual side. Emotions for improving thinking and learning include both motivation and attitudes. Though some facilitate thinking and learning, others inhibit them. Some are general and apply across subjects, others are subject-specific. In addition to developing positive emotions in students, reflective teachers help students become reflective learners who are aware of their emotions and control them to improve thinking and learning. Videotape and Internet resources can help you address the emotional and social needs of your students.

Resources

Advocates for Youth (n.d.). Retrieved October 10, 2006 from http://www .advocatesforyouth.org/lessonplans/index.htm.

Alderman, M. K. "Motivation for At-Risk Students." *Educational Leadership* 48, no. 1 (1990), pp. 27–30.

Ames, C. "Motivation: What Teachers Need to Know." *Teachers College Record* 91 (1990), pp. 409–21.

Blum, R. W. "A Case for School Connectedness." *Educational Leadership*, April 2005, pp. 16–20.

Bruner, J. *Toward a Theory of Instruction.* Cambridge, MA: Belknap, a division of Harvard University Press, 1966.

Clifford, M. M. "Students Need Challenge, Not Easy Success." *Educational Leadership*, September 1990, pp. 22–26.

Darling-Hammond, L.; and O. Ifill-Lynch. "If They'd Only Do Their Work!" *Educational Leadership*, February 2006, pp. 8–13.

Dewey, J. *How We Think.* Chicago: Henry Regnery Company, Gateway Edition, 1933.

Eison, J.; and C. Bonwell. Active Learning: Creating Excitement in the Classroom. ASHE-ERIC. 1991. ED 340272.

Everson, H. E.; S. Tobias; H. Hartman; and A. Gourgey. "Test Anxiety in the Curriculum: The Subject Matters." *Anxiety, Stress and Coping* 6 (1993), pp. 1–8.

Felder, R. M.; and B. A. Solomon. Learning Styles and Strategies. Retrieved July 22, 2007 from http://www.ncsu.edu/felder-public/ILSdir/styles.htm/.

Gardner, H. *Frames of Mind: The Theory of Multiple Intelligences.* New York: Basic Books, 1985.

Gordon, R. L. "How Novice Teachers Can Succeed with Adolescents." *Educational Leadership*, April 1997, pp. 56–58.

Hall, E. T. *The Silent Language.* Garden City, NY: Anchor Press, 1981.

Kagan, J.; and N. Kogan. "Individuality and Cognitive Performance." In *Carmichael's Manual of Child Psychology. Volume I,* ed. P. Mussen. New York: Wiley, 1970, pp. 1273–1365.

Karolides, N. "Teaching Literature as a Reflective Practitioner: Script and Spontaneity." *The Wisconsin English Journal* 32, no. 2 (Fall 2001), pp. 16–19. Retrieved July 22, 2006 from http://www.uwrf.edu/wej/.

Kohn, A. *Punished by Rewards: The Trouble with Gold Stars, Incentive Plans, A's, Praise, and Other Bribes.* Boston: Houghton Mifflin, 1999.

Marsh, H. "Verbal and Math Self Concepts: An Internal/External Frame or Reference Model." *American Educational Research Journal* 23, no. 1 (1986), pp. 129–49.

Raising Nonviolent Children in Violent Times (n.d.). A Meridian Production. SR Publications. Media on Child Development. Retrieved October 10, 2006 from http://www.srpublications.com/child-development/categories/emotional_development.htm.

Shaw, J. "Bullies." SR Publications. Media on Child Development. 2002. Retrieved October 10, 2006 from http://www.srpublications.com/child-development/categories/emotional_development.htm.

Social/Emotional Learning. Illinois Standards. Retrieved October 22, 2006 from http://www.isbe.state.il.us/ils/social_emotional/standards.htm.

Sternberg, R. J. *Intelligence Applied: Understanding and Increasing Your Intellectual Skills.* Orlando: Harcourt Brace Jovanovich, 1986.

Webb, J. T. "Nurturing Social-Emotional Development of Gifted Children." 1994. ERIC EC Digest #E527. Retrieved October 22, 2006 from http://www.kidsource.com/kidsource/content2/social_development_gifted.html.

Wigfield, A.; and J. S. Eccles. "Test Anxiety in Elementary and Secondary School Students." *Educational Psychologist* 24, no. 2 (1989), pp. 159–83.

Williams, B.; and M. Woods. "Building on Urban Learners' Experiences." *Educational Leadership*, April 1997, pp. 29–32.

Wlodkowski, R. J.; and M. B. Ginsberg. "A Framework for Culturally Responsive Teaching." *Educational Leadership*, September 1995, pp. 17–21.

Reflective Classroom Management

This chapter focuses on thinking about the structure of the classroom environment. The purpose is to help you to construct effective strategies for classroom management, to recognize problems or challenges that may occur, including cultural issues, and to develop strategies for managing them. Appropriate questions to ask yourself are: How do you view yourself as a classroom manager? How smoothly does your classroom run? What kinds of problems tend to arise? How do you handle them? What are your strengths and weaknesses as a classroom manager? How might your students rate your classroom management skills? Although there are no quick fixes or magic solutions, generally it's better to be proactive than reactive in managing the classroom.

⚔ Constructive Classroom Environment

One preconception about classroom management is that effective managers use different strategies or react differently from ineffective managers when confronting classroom problems or conflicts. Research, however, shows that the key difference is that effective classroom managers prevent problems from arising or spinning out of control by using **proactive** strategies. As a reflective teacher, it is important for you to evaluate your knowledge about your students' personal, cultural, and social characteristics and consider how they might impact classroom behavior. This knowledge can help you create and maintain a well-functioning learning environment.

Proactive classroom management includes engaging learners, minimizing disruptions, and fostering constructive student interrelationships. No single instructional method is likely to accomplish this routinely. What methods have you found to be most successful? Part of teaching reflectively is experimenting with various approaches and evaluating their effectiveness in your classroom. Use feedback from your experience to help you apply even more effective methods in the future.

To create a positive classroom environment make sure your expectations, directions, requirements, time limits, and evaluation methods are clear so students feel secure engaging in academic activities. Establish boundaries and provide structure. Provide an environment using multiple modalities—for example, both oral and written—to accommodate students with different learning styles or preferences.

If you expect specific classroom behaviors and attitudes, model them for your students. Explicitly express that these are the ones that you want to see reflected by them. Then monitor their performance and give them specific feedback. Suggestions for providing feedback are discussed in Chapter 3, Communication.

A research-based approach to classroom management derived from looking at and combining the results of numerous studies identifies four critical factors:

1. Classroom Rules and Procedures: their design and implementation;
2. Disciplinary Interventions: teacher as the "first line of defense";
3. Teacher–Student Relationships: how the quality affects student behavior;
4. Mental Set: teacher awareness of and control over the classroom environment.

Although all four of these factors require you to think about possible problems that might arise in the classroom and how you might prevent or solve these problems, "mental set" is the essence of reflective, critical thinking.

Research shows there are fewer behavior problems if students are actively involved in the lessons. There are fewer management problems when you use instructional time effectively. By offering students choices over either activities or how to accomplish the goals you set for them, students are likely to have more ownership over their work and complete their assignments more enthusiastically and with fewer disruptions.

To be proactive, teachers must anticipate potential management problems. Research on effective classroom managers shows use of several approaches including "withitness," overlapping, smoothness and momentum, and avoidance of the Ripple Effect.

Withitness, a term coined by Kounin in his research on effective classroom managers, refers to a heightened and pervasive tuning into what is going on in the classroom, even when students may think you're not paying attention. Good withitness can gain you a reputation of having eyes in the back of your head. You achieve withitness by monitoring student behavior and communicating an ongoing awareness of what is going on in the classroom. This practice enables you to keep tabs on students' behavior and intervene immediately to prevent problems from snowballing.

To what extent do you have withitness in your classroom? Do you ever ignore misbehavior hoping that it will end without you having to intervene? Although ignoring misbehavior used to be recommended as a way to extinguish undesirable behavior through non-reinforcement, recent research has demonstrated that it's usually more effective to deal with problems as they arise.

Do your students tend to act up when there are lulls in activity? A second management technique called **overlapping** requires doing more than one thing at a time, such as giving directions while passing back graded papers. Expert teachers use this strategy to maximize efficiency, keep students engaged, and eliminate slow downs or down time that can contribute to boredom and disruptions.

Do you have down times in your classes? Do your students tend to act up when there is a lull in activity? To what extent do you use overlapping? How might you use it more? Demonstrate *smoothness and momentum* moving in and out of activities. Avoid slow downs and delays between activities. How might you achieve smoothness and momentum from one activity to the next?

Effective classroom managers also are aware of the **Ripple Effect**—the contagious spreading of attitudes or behaviors through social learning processes of observation and imitation of other students. For example, if one student acts up and gets away with it, others might soon follow. If you show hostility while disciplining a student in front of the whole class, the rest of the students are likely to feel your hostility as well, though that wasn't your intention.

Expert classroom managers prevent problems rather than react to them. They carefully plan lessons to maximize smoothness, momentum, and engagement. And they vigilantly monitor classroom behavior, verbal and nonverbal, so they are aware of and can control problems before they intensify and get out of control. Gaining this level of classroom management is often the greatest source of apprehension for novice teachers.

What techniques do you use to ensure your classroom runs smoothly? Do you keep students actively engaged in learning with little down time and few disruptions? What types of behavior and management problems tend to occur most often in your classes?

⚔ Social Insight and Intelligence

Another dimension of successful classroom management involves social insight and culturally responsive teaching, which are both related to the concept of social intelligence. They are also discussed in Chapter 4 on Emotions. One multiple intelligence theory has a category called social intelligence (or interpersonal intelligence), which involves being able to identify and respond to the motivations, moods, desires, and temperaments of other people. All people have this type of intelligence, but to different degrees. For some people social intelligence is a strength, for others it's a weakness.

How would you rate your own social intelligence? To what extent does it depend on the situation you are in? How would you evaluate your ability to identify your students' motivations, moods, and desires? How would you rate your ability to respond to those feelings in your students? To increase the chances of having a successful relationship with students, convey the feeling that you are genuinely interested in their successes and are not just passing time or collecting a paycheck. If you are frequently absent or late, students will feel that teaching and your students are not very important to you.

Research has made clear that social insight is especially important when teaching adolescents. Social insight in regard to adolescents is a type of expertise representing a second type of "withitness." It involves awareness of adolescent culture and understanding how this impacts on classroom behavior. Social insight also includes respecting the feelings of others by not treating them as inferiors through patronizing or condescending speech, behaviors, or attitudes. It also includes being tuned into the characteristics of your students' interests, cultural value, and practices. A student might act out in class, not because of a slow down or boring activity, but because he wants to impress someone else in the class. A student might not participate in class because she is embarrassed by her accent or limitations in speaking English. She might be intellectually engaged, but socially insecure. Novice teachers usually have to work at developing this type of social insight, especially if their students come from cultural backgrounds different from their own.

Another multiple intelligence theory has a category called "practical intelligence," a type of social intelligence that focuses on how people effectively interact with and negotiate their environments. This type of social intelligence is often referred to as "street smarts." It requires **tacit knowledge**—knowledge of things that are important to know and know how to do, but that aren't explicitly taught and must be figured out by oneself. There are three strategies people use to intelligently interact with their environment. Part of intelligence is knowing which of these strategies to use in any particular situation.

Consider the problem of having trouble making progress during a class and communicating effectively because of a noisy environment. Loud noises from a construction crane or tractor might intrude into the classroom. One strategy is *adapting* to the environment, or changing your behavior to adjust to the demands of a situation. For example, you may adapt by speaking louder and asking students to strain to listen.

Although sometimes considered the hallmark of intelligence, adapting is not always the best approach. Sometimes *selecting* a new environment is a better way of meeting one's needs and interests. For example, you may choose to move the students to a room in the library, which is on the other side of the school, for quiet.

Another way of responding to the environment is *shaping* it, that is changing the environment so that it better meets one's needs. For example, you may close a window to shut out the sounds of the crane or tractor. When dealing with problems that arise in the classroom, it is wise to consider and evaluate strategies based on these three general types of approaches within the context of the specific situation.

Social intelligence includes building good student–teacher relationships and adopting proactive approaches. Again, the goal is to prevent problems to begin with instead of having to react to them later on. It's very important for you to be aware of and in control of your own emotions and social interactions. However, sometimes even if you as the teacher do all the "right things," conflicts or problems can arise in the relationship. Teaching can be a delicate relationship because often it blends both professional and personal involvements.

Remember that there is a natural imbalance built into the teaching situation; you are the stronger, more expert person, the student is the weaker, less expert person. Be sensitive to each student's feelings and protect the student's self-esteem. Insulting and humiliating students—even for the noble purpose of trying to motivate them to change—is unacceptable. Although you and the other students might find sarcasm humorous, a student targeted by a sarcastic remark is likely to feel ashamed, defensive, and bitter. Such attitudes are not likely to promote positive behavior change.

Expect all your students to succeed. When you expect your students to learn, they generally achieve at higher levels than when you don't expect them to learn. Teacher expectations tend to be self-fulfilling prophesies. In addition, students who feel you don't expect them to learn are more likely to feel academically inadequate and to seek attention from you and/or their peers by engaging in disruptive behaviors.

It's also important to be patient because not everyone learns at the same pace. Rushing students can inhibit their thinking and make them feel inadequate. It also gives the wrong message about the value of silent time for reflective thinking instead of impulsive answering. Nonverbal signs of impatience can communicate as loudly as words!

❧ External Control

One goal of classroom management is to move from external controls with strict rules and punishments, where students behave when the teacher is present out of fear of being punished, to internal controls, where students behave because they value appropriate behavior because they know it is the right thing to do. External control provides short-term behavior changes and empowers the teacher at the expense of students' autonomy and self-control. In the long run promoting student responsibility and self-control will lead to longer lasting, more positive behavior change.

Punishment at its best teaches students what NOT to do; it doesn't teach what a student is supposed to do. Operating under external controls, students focus their energies on getting away with misbehavior rather than doing the right thing. They do not have the incentive to internalize control and responsibility. To emphasize responsibility instead of obedience, inform students of standards of acceptable behavior, make sure students understand the rules, guidelines, and consequences of violating them, respect the students' dignity, and handle discipline problems privately. Draw up a social contract with a student who misbehaves to develop guidelines for future behavior. You can renegotiate the social contract as needed.

When problems arise, use your hunches and trust your instincts. Be prepared to deal with unexpected problems. Address specific discipline problems discretely and confidentially. Maintain a soft voice and cool head throughout a conflict or disruption. Apply a practical problem-solving approach that uses common sense, motivate students to take responsibility for their own behavior, and encourage students to care for each other. This approach is holistic, embeds cooperation, responsibility, caring, and respect.

Don't rely on rewards. Avoid turning students into "reward junkies." Build a caring and interactive classroom community. Respect your students' pride and dignity. If students' emotional needs are not being met, or if what they're learning doesn't make sense to them and they feel helpless, they are likely to try to get attention, power, revenge, or whatever else they need to feel satisfied. They may even resort to violence against themselves or others. Everyone wants to feel empowered and respected, to have choices, meaningful experiences, and a sense of belonging.

⚔ School Connectedness

How connected did you feel to your school as an adolescent? Why? How did your school connectedness or lack of it make you feel? Why? How did it affect your behavior in class? Out of class? Consider why it had these effects on your behavior.

School connectedness is especially important for adolescents. As a reflective teacher you can use insights from your own experiences to help you understand how your students might feel about their connections to your class in particular and the school in general. Although this self-analysis is valuable, it's not sufficient. Observe and inquire to find out about your students' feelings regarding school and classroom connectedness. Try to discover how you might enhance their feelings of connectedness and how they might benefit.

How connected do you feel to your students? Why? Novice teachers sometimes feel too connected to their students, especially when there's not much of an age difference. Feeling too connected to your students can be just as problematic as not feeling connected enough! What might be some problems from feeling too connected to your students? What might be some consequences of not feeling connected enough?

Research shows us that school connectedness has two major benefits. It increases students' chances of academic success through more motivation, better attendance, increased engagement in learning, and higher levels of achievement. It decreases the likelihood of students engaging in destructive behaviors including bullying, vandalism, substance abuse, pregnancy, violence, and suicide. Which of these benefits are particularly appropriate to target for your students? For example, if your students have problems with substance abuse, are there resources and strategies already in place in your school? Is prevention and treatment of substance abuse already part of the curriculum? How do your students learn to cope with the numerous and diverse pressures that confront adolescents almost universally? In addition to what they learn in school, what messages do students get from their homes and larger communities (including houses of worship) about risky activities such as sex, smoking, and drinking? To what extent are you aware of the norms, expectations, and values in your students' homes, cultures, and communities? How might you learn more about them?

According to research there are three characteristics of schools that promote feelings of connectedness while also fostering achievement:

1. positive and respectful adult–student relationships,
2. high academic standards accompanied by strong support from teachers, and
3. an emotionally and physically safe environment.

How would you rate your classroom in particular and your school in general regarding these three characteristics? Which one would you consider the greatest strength? Why? Which do you feel could use the most improvement? Why? Have there been professional development activities targeted at achieving these objectives?

Extracurricular activities sponsored by schools often help promote feelings of connectedness while enhancing the skills and broadening the experience of the students. But in some urban centers, such as New York City, many middle and high schools have cut these activities due to budgetary constraints. Does your school sponsor such activities as sports, band, 4H, chess, debate team, and theater? If such activities are sponsored by your school, to what extent do your students participate in them? Many urban schools do not have facilities for activities like football or soccer. If your school does not sponsor such activities, what other organizations in the community do or could help to fill this void? Did you participate in such activities as a student? How did this participation, or lack of it, affect you?

Research indicates there are three main threats to school connectedness: social isolation, poor classroom management, and lack of safety. Do your students have to worry about being bullied, physically threatened, or stolen from while in school or on the way to and from school? Do they have to worry about being teased or picked on by dominant social cliques? Do all of your students have at least one friend in your classroom? Do they have friends elsewhere in the school? If you don't know the answers to these questions, make it a point to find out!

⚔ Cultural Dynamics

A continuing theme in this book is the importance of thinking reflectively about and responding to individual differences in your students. Do you tend to think in terms of cultural stereotypes? Most schools and our society as a whole are increasingly multicultural. Ethnic diversity creates rich opportunities for personal and social development. It also brings challenges for teachers working with students from different cultural backgrounds with different values and customs.

Consider this example. Suppose you were teaching Sarana, who never looked directly at you when communicating and who never asked any questions. How would you interpret this behavior pattern? What might appear as a problem of shyness or lack of interest might actually be respectful behavior. Some cultural backgrounds teach that it is disrespectful for a student to have eye contact with a teacher and that it is disrespectful for a student to ask questions of a teacher, even if the student does not understand something important. Students from some cultures are accustomed to passively listening, watching, and writing during class and are very uncomfortable when asked to speak, even to answer a relatively simple question.

How should you handle such situations? Should you adapt to the student's needs and disregard eye contact and questioning? Should teachers and students be matched on the basis of cultural background so there is less conflict in values and expectations? Should you shape your students' behavior and attitudes so that they are consistent with your expectations?

A key aspect of reflective teaching is deciding on the best way to respond to different situations that arise in the teaching environment—deciding when to adapt, when to select, and when to shape. There is no one right way to react in all such situations. It is unrealistic for you to try to adapt to all of the different cultural backgrounds that might be represented in your classroom. Students must learn "code switching," that behaviors and attitudes appropriate at home and in their community might be different from behaviors and attitudes that are appropriate in school and in society at large, and they must learn to make the adjustment.

Teaching students from a variety of cultural backgrounds made one teacher aware of issues related to minority students' assimilation in education and coping with the problems of the dominant culture, which imposes its values and standards. He discovered that multicultural students have to learn the culture as well as the curriculum. Many students must learn the language as well. An important insight was recognizing the impoverished perspectives and cultural blinders imposed by single-culture backgrounds and expectations. Single-culture students frequently see their own culture as dominant and their assumptions and biases are reflected in their personal and social relationships as well as in societal institutions. This tends to create rigidity and tunnel vision, which lead to significant disadvantages when contrasted with students who have multicultural backgrounds. They have a broader, richer, and more relativistic perspective that aids in their appreciation of alternative viewpoints and the ability to deal with new situations.

To what extent do you make assumptions about your students because of their race, ethnicity, family background, gender, socioeconomic status, or where they live? It's common to make implicit or explicit assumptions based on such factors, so reflective teachers try to become aware of them and make sure they don't influence their attitudes toward and expectations of their students. For example, sometimes teachers assume that because students live in a farm community or an urban ghetto, they are not likely to go to college or seek careers as doctors, lawyers, business executives, or college professors.

To counteract the potential limits such expectations might have on students' school achievement, reflective teachers try to treat each student as an individual with motivation, capabilities, resilience, and cultural strengths. A recent framework for urban learners contrasts this view with the old view of them as unmotivated, lacking abilities, at risk, and culturally deprived. The *Urban Learners' Framework* emphasizes attention to students' experiences, including home, community, and school, which influence their development of beliefs, values, language, knowledge, and behavior. These include in-school experiences such as the curriculum, norms, rules, and school culture; and out-of-school experiences such as responsibilities, use of leisure time, and regular activities at home and in the community. Do you systematically think about how each of your students' in- and out-of-school experiences might affect their academic achievement?

Teachers' effectiveness with urban learners largely depends on their ability to connect schoolwork with students' strengths and experiences. The goal is to help students become independent learners with awareness and control over their own destiny and to aid them in becoming good citizens. An instructional model developed from this perspective on urban learners is a four-step process of reflection. It emphasizes taking the time to carefully think about how the curriculum can be most effectively taught. The steps of reflection are

1. Make learning meaningful by reviewing subject matter. Ask yourself questions such as "What subject matter really matters to them ?" "What do students already know about this subject?" "How might this subject be used in their communities?"

2. Connect curricular content to students' interests and experiences. Ask yourself questions such as "How will students relate to what they are supposed to learn?" "What in- and out-of-school experiences might affect students' learning and performance in the classroom?" "How can I find out more about students' lives outside of school?"

3. Begin lessons with activities building on students' strengths to make them feel part of the curriculum. Ask "How can I build on students' in- or out-of-school experiences to help them connect with this part of the curriculum?" "What do my students do well outside of school?" "What interests my students when they're not in school?"

4. Reflect on what happens in class to gain new insights and consider changes that might improve the lessons. Ask questions such as "How consistent was this lesson with the view of students as motivated, capable, resilient, and with cultural strengths?" "How can I modify the lesson to better connect with students' in- and out-of-school experiences?" "To what extent did the lesson help develop students' abilities to be independent learners?" "How could I modify the lesson to focus more on students' roles in the greater society?"

In some cases gender issues might arise. Males from some cultures might be uncomfortable being taught some subjects by a female, which may create "academic culture shock" and affect learning. Think about how a situation like this might be handled. What are some ways that teachers can build positive relationships with students from backgrounds different from their own? What are some ways teachers can build positive relationships with students of the opposite sex or a different sexual orientation?

⚔ Social Skills

Figure 5.1 summarizes some social skills that are important ingredients in a successful teacher–student relationship. Which do you feel are your strengths? Which are your weaknesses? Think about your own examples for each social skill listed. For example, you might show supportiveness and caring by saying, "I'll let you use your study period to finish your homework because of the family emergency you had to attend to last night."

⚔ Classroom Rules and Procedures

Involve students in formulating classroom rules, procedures, and consequences. This promotes ownership and makes it more likely that students will understand and follow them. This will also ensure that they feel the rules, procedures,

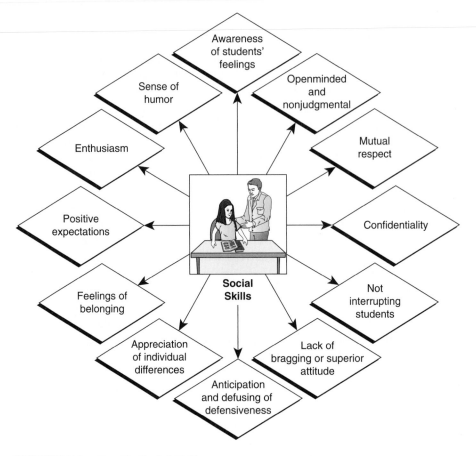

FIGURE 5.1   *Specific Social Skills*

and consequences are fair. Make sure that the classroom rules are realistic, consistent with your own values, and don't violate any of the rules in your school. Be consistent in how you apply them so that students don't feel singled out or treated differently. If you post them in the room, there's no excuse for students to say that they forgot the rule.

"Classroom Procedures" refers to methods of getting things done. If the methods are written down and standardized, class can function smoothly. Time can be saved, and students will experience the class as having continuity and being predictable. By being routinized, students feel secure because they know what is expected. Classroom procedures can be developed for activities such as collecting and returning homework, taking tests, requesting a hall pass, distributing handouts, moving chairs to form groups, exiting the classroom for an assembly, and virtually any other regular classroom tasks.

When establishing a procedure, clearly describe the expected behavior and explain the reason or rationale. Solicit and use students' input whenever it's feasible. Give a step-by-step demonstration and monitor students' comprehension and memory of the methods and sequence. Give students the opportunity to practice the procedure and give them feedback. As with class-room rules, procedures can be posted on a classroom wall so that everyone is aware of your expectations. Consistency is very important, whether working with an individual student or several students. If a rule or procedure is neces-sary, enforce it. If it isn't working, discuss and change it.

Consequences should be decided on as soon as rules and procedures have been formulated, and should be made explicit. As with rules and procedures, student input into the consequences of violating rules and procedures will pro-mote ownership and acceptance. It's too late to decide on consequences after the rule has been broken or procedure not followed. Respond to the situation as soon as possible, so that it doesn't spin out of control. Disruptive behaviors can spiral if not addressed immediately.

⚔ Negative Teacher Behaviors

When dealing with rules violations, it's important to maintain your own self-control. Avoid acting if you're feeling hostile or upset because you might have a negative tone of voice or body language. Calmly and privately convey your reaction to students' misbehavior. You could go to a corner of the classroom, out in the hall, or wait until after class. Privacy and confidentiality are important for preserving the teacher–student relationship.

Avoid strategies and communications that put students on the defensive. Use a non-threatening approach, such as an "I Message" (discussed later in this chapter). This focuses on your feelings of disappointment or concern, and en-courages students to reflect on their behavior without making them feel defen-sive or humiliating them. As a result, students are more likely to change their behavior rather than shut down.

Don't wait until after a misbehavior has occurred to develop penalties for student misconduct. One recommendation is to establish a graded list of penal-ties that will fit many occasions, which can be developed with input from stu-dents to ensure their ownership over the fairness of the consequences. Post these on the wall or otherwise make them available to students so that everyone knows the consequences of misbehavior. Reflecting on potential penalties can prevent students from engaging in negative behaviors. If you don't have a graded list of penalties, consider alternative approaches to handling the situa-tion, which might include detention; withdrawing privileges; using a problem-solving approach such as the No Lose Method or Peer Mediation (discussed later in this chapter); requiring a written reflection on the problem in the form of an apology, essay, journal entry, or social contract; or involving an outside re-source, such as a school counselor, the principal, or parents. Save contacting parents as a last resort, and call them about a problem only if you have already called them about something positive regarding their child so that they don't feel defensive when you call.

After the consequence has been decided on, reestablish a positive relation-ship with the student(s) so that there isn't a long-term negative effect on the teacher–student relationship. Then monitor the student's behavior to give specific feedback, positive or negative. It's best to "catch them being good," praising and encouraging students when they do well. Monitoring can be done by informal observations or more formally through use of a behavior checklist.

Following is a list of twelve teacher behaviors that can undermine teacher–student relationships and lead to a classroom environment that impedes thinking and learning. Do you engage in any of these behaviors? If so, how often? Under what circumstances?

Burke's "Dirty Dozen" of Teacher Behaviors That Can Erode the Classroom Climate*

1. Sarcasm   Students' feelings can be hurt by sarcastic put-downs thinly disguised as "humor."

2. Negative Tone of Voice   Students can "read between the lines" and sense a sarcastic, negative, or condescending tone of voice.

3. Negative Body Language   Clenched fists, a set jaw, a quizzical look, or standing over a student in a threatening manner can speak more loudly than any words.

4. Inconsistency   Nothing escapes the students' attention. They will be the first to realize the teacher is not enforcing the rules consistently.

5. Favoritism   "Brown-nosing" is an art and any student in any class can point out the "teacher's pet" who gets special treatment. There are no secrets in a class!

6. Put-Downs   Sometimes teachers are not aware they are embarrassing a student with subtle put-downs. If you expect students to encourage others rather than put them down, model positive behavior.

7. Outbursts   Teacher are sometimes provoked by students and they "lose it." These teacher outbursts set a bad example for the students, create a negative climate, and could lead to more serious problems.

8. Public Reprimands   No one wants to be corrected or humiliated in front of his or her peers. One way to make an enemy out of a student is to make him or her lose face in front of other students.

9. Unfairness   Taking away promised privileges or rewards; scheduling a surprise test; "nit-picking" while grading homework or tests; or assigning punitive homework could be construed by students as being unfair.

10. Apathy   Students want teachers to listen to them, show them they are important, and empathize with them. If teachers convey the attitude that teaching is just a job and students are just aggravations who must be dealt with, students will respond accordingly.

11. Inflexibility   Some students may need extra help or special treatment in order to succeed. A teacher should be flexible enough to "bend the rules" or adjust the standards to meet students' individual needs.

12. Lack of Humor   Teachers who cannot laugh at themselves usually have problems motivating students to learn, and usually have boring classes.

*Burke, K. *What to Do with the Kid Who . . . Developing Cooperation, Self Discipline and Responsibility in the Classroom.* Palatine, IL: Skylight Publishing Co., 1992.

Teaching, like all professions, has its ups and downs. You can help prevent problems from occurring and solve problems that arise by anticipating them and having a repertoire of strategies to address them. It seems natural to hold students responsible for problems that arise, but it helps for you as a teacher to reflect on your own behavior and attitudes to see if they are inadvertently contributing to problems. Often social problems are two-sided. The problems and solutions described below can help make you aware of some of the types of problems that may occur and let you know you are not alone in experiencing them. They can also stimulate your thinking about possible troubleshooting approaches.

⚔ Troubleshooting Potential Problems and Solutions

What are types and examples of problems and solutions from your own knowledge or experience? Which problems do you consider the most common, most important, or most difficult to deal with? How might you handle each of the situations in Table 5.1?

Problems may be student-based or teacher-based or both. What other problems might occur?

Some students refuse to participate in class or they may react to teachers' questions with no response or very brief and superficial answers. This problem may be due to not being prepared, not paying attention, or boredom or frustration because the material is too easy or too difficult. Some students come from schools or cultures where passivity in a learning situation is the norm so they may need to really stretch to become more active learners.

Make it clear from the first day of class that you expect students to actively participate and contribute to their own learning, including asking you questions if they are unclear about a point, would like to know more about a topic, or have a different point of view. If students understand why their active participation is expected and the values of active learning and reflective, critical thinking are understood, they are more likely to accept them. To try to build relationships and mobilize students to be actively involved, teachers can empathize and say something like, "I used to have a hard time working in a group too" or "It took me a long time to feel comfortable asking questions in class, I remember it very well!"

Sometimes passivity is due to fear of embarrassment. Students are afraid to express their ideas because they don't want to be wrong or appear stupid. In this case it's important to help students understand that everyone makes mistakes. During class discussions, when there is no penalty for being wrong (as there is on a test, paper or project to be graded), mistakes can be great learning opportunities. Create a classroom environment that promotes intellectual risk taking. Help students recognize that your class is a "safe" environment for making errors.

Often passivity is due to shyness. Getting to know a shy student better often helps. Involving a student through building on an area of special knowledge or interest can help break the ice. When the student does contribute, smile or otherwise help the student feel good about participating in class.

TABLE 5.1 My Classroom Problems and Solutions		
Problem: A Student Who	**In Your Classroom?**	**Potential Solution Strategy**
Is unprepared for class		
Doesn't take education seriously		
Is too angry or upset to work		
Is ready to give up		
Is passive		
Resists thinking		
Is disruptive		
Dislikes the subject		
Seeks power struggle with you		
Sees you more as a friend than a teacher		
Flirts		
Uses illegal drugs or alcohol		
Consistently is late or absent		
Has conflicts with others		
Constantly seeks attention		
Doesn't do assigned work		
Doesn't pay attention		

Students often believe it's the teacher's responsibility to give students information and correct their mistakes instead of guiding them to do the work themselves. Teaching-as-telling is the traditional model of instruction, but recent research shows it to be much less effective than approaches in which the teacher is more of a coach than a transmitter of information. Many teachers remain more comfortable with the traditional method, often because this is how they were taught, and may feel it is their job to lecture and fix students' mistakes. This expectation is a result of preconceptions or misconceptions of what good teaching is all about and what the teacher's role should be.

During the first day of class, make it clear that your job is to help students become effective, independent learners who do not need to have a teacher around for them to be able to self-correct and learn. Help students develop the habit of taking responsibility for and control over their own thinking, learning, attitudes, and behavior. Use your leadership skills and personal strength to keep students from manipulating you into doing more than you should.

Students unused to taking responsibility may show little ability to handle frustration. Many times these students feel hopeless, act out in class, and disrupt other students' learning as well as their own. These students then get discouraged, feel immobilized, and freeze up or block. They make statements such as "It's beyond me," "I'll never get it," "I'm stuck," "I just don't know what to do," "I don't know what you want," "I studied for the test and still got a 'D.'" To address this problem, determine what the student does know and discuss that. This helps validate positive aspects of their knowledge. Use the students' prior knowledge as a foundation. Build from existing knowledge in simple steps, moving progressively toward more complex material.

Offer continual support and reinforce success consistently. Help students learn to organize their work, such as class notes and assigned papers. Give students strategies to help them feel greater control over their own destiny and see that their outcomes are due to their own correctable actions. When they feel academically empowered, they are less likely to be disruptive during class.

Occasionally students dislike specific teachers and/or subject areas. Rather than denying or defending against the negative feelings, it is usually more constructive to let the student express all the negative attitudes and criticisms. Using a neutral tone of voice, ask the student to tell you specifically what he or she does not like. Express genuine interest in finding out what is bothering the student and make it clear you want to do what you can to improve her/his attitude. Get a complete list of complaints, summarize them to make sure you have heard and understood them all, thank the student for this feedback, and invite future contributions of this nature. Then consider implementing one of the problem-solving approaches discussed in the next section.

Problem-Solving Approaches

Problem Ownership

Problem ownership refers to identifying who has primary responsibility for a problem. Ownership can be an important component of identifying and defining the problem, and is often necessary for identifying an appropriate solution. The purpose of determining problem ownership isn't to assign blame; it's to develop a better understanding of the problem, the people involved, and the context. There is often a tendency to blame someone else for a problem and not take personal responsibility, but the person who owns the problem is usually the one who feels the conflict or pain directly and knows the most about it.

An important first step is to get the student to recognize that a problem exists. Once there is **awareness** of a problem, it is possible to take steps to **control** the problem. Ask the student to explain the problem. Ask questions such as "Who experiences the problem most directly? Why?" Try to identify the "real problem" and what the participants in the conflict feel. Paraphrase and verify your interpretation to make sure you understand what the student is expressing. In student-owned problems, students experience upsets or problems that distract from learning. In teacher-owned problems, the teacher experiences problems with unacceptable student behavior and is distracted from instruction.

Accepting problem ownership helps participants in the conflict understand each other and communicate about the problem more effectively. It also helps guide the solution process as the problem owner takes responsibility for helping solve the problem. Problem ownership fosters a sense of self-reliance and improves classroom management through student self-control instead of extrinsic rewards or punishments. Once ownership has been established and accepted, use a win-win problem-solving model such as the No Lose Method.

No Lose Method

The No Lose Method attempts to create win-win outcomes to problems. Teachers should try to identify the "real problem" and use a problem-solving model and write down the steps for trying to solve the problem. The problem-solving process is considered win-win because it is intended to ensure that no one loses face. The No Lose Method has the following six steps:

1. Define the problem: Determine what each person wants and specify the behaviors involved. Active, analytical listening and reflecting the feeling, where the teacher periodically paraphrases what the students say, can help clarify the problem.

2. Generate many possible solutions: Brainstorm possible solutions. Remember that brainstorming means *generate but do not evaluate ideas.*

3. Evaluate solutions: Discuss the advantages and disadvantages of each potential solution.

4. Make a decision. Rank order the top three solutions and explain why the first one is the best. No solution can be selected unless everyone agrees to it. If none is acceptable, brainstorm again.

5. Plan to implement the solution: Specify what will be needed, assign responsibilities, and establish timelines.

6. Evaluate the solution's success: Judge how well the solution is working and whether changes are needed.

Peer Mediation

Peer mediation is a popular way to help students resolve conflicts. It's best for other students to be the peer mediators. Peer mediators do not impose solutions; rather, they help the "disputants" work out their **own** solution to the conflict. Mediators work alone or in pairs. In peer mediation programs, a cadre of students is trained to help their schoolmates resolve disputes.

Research suggests that peer-mediated agreements work 80 to 89 percent of the time and are more successful than principal-imposed solutions. The greater success is due to *disputants owning the solution* because they hammered it out themselves. Peer mediation is similar to the No Lose Method, but adds two important features. Disputants pledge to live up to the solution selected. In some cases the solution is put in writing, like a contract, and the disputants sign it. A basic principle of peer mediation is that if the disputants agree on a solution, everyone must respect it, even if they do not consider it the best possible solution. The mediator checks with the disputants to see if they are sticking to the agreement. You can use behavior checklists to record the frequency of targeted behaviors in the peer-mediated contract.

Peer mediation is appropriate for same, but not all, student conflicts. It is NOT intended for conflicts involving weapons, drugs, violence, illegal activity, or blatant injustice. These need to be handled by the administration.

The following are the *basic steps* in peer mediation:

1. The disputants and mediators come together, which can happen in many ways.
2. Disputants agree to participate in the process.
3. The mediator lays down the ground rules.
4. Each disputant tells her/his side of the story and expresses her/his feelings, speaking only to the mediator.
5. The mediator paraphrases, summarizes, and asks clarifying questions.
6. The mediator tries to help disputants see the conflict as a problem they must solve together instead of a competitive situation with a winner and a loser.
7. The disputants brainstorm ways to resolve the conflict.
8. The disputants agree on the best solution.
9. Disputants pledge to live up to the solution selected, sometimes putting the solution in writing and signing it.
10. The mediator checks with the disputants to see if they are sticking to the agreement.

To select peer mediators, school administration generally surveys students to identify whom they trust and would feel comfortable talking to. Administration selects some mediators so there is a balance of gender and ethnicity. Once selected, mediators need to be trained in a variety of skills. It is recommended that mediators receive 15–20 hours of advanced training with follow-up every two weeks. Skills include communicating, listening, paraphrasing, clarifying, summarizing and asking neutral questions, detecting underlying causes of conflicts such as differing perceptions or assumptions, how to diffuse anger and develop empathy between disputants, and self-control to keep the mediation confidential.

Additional Troubleshooting Strategies

I Messages

If you are disturbed with something one of your students is doing, send "I Messages" telling the student how you feel about it and how her/his behavior affects you. For example, "I get upset when I see you arguing with your group members because I'm afraid you're not going to have time to complete your assignment." Why send I Messages? Because they avoid negative evaluations of students, protect the teacher–student relationship, and are more likely to result in the student being receptive to dealing with the problem. I Messages are effective strategies when confrontation is called for. They allow you to express your feelings in an assertive, nonjudgmental, and straightforward way.

There are generally three parts to an I Message: describe the behavior that is causing the problem, the consequences of that behavior, and your feelings. For example, the statement "I get upset when you come late to class because it disrupts the lesson" includes all these components. I Messages are preferable to "You Messages" such as "You should be here on time for class" because they make students feel less defensive. Nobody really likes being told what to do. I Messages convey your feelings without giving someone orders.

Reflecting the feeling

Reflecting the feeling is a listening skill that conveys understanding and empathy to the speaker. Reflection of feeling involves "holding up a mirror" to the speaker so the speaker can become more aware of how his or her emotional reactions are affecting the learning process. Often, by acknowledging a student's feelings through reflecting them back, a teacher can refocus on the academic content targeted for the class. This strategy is discussed in more detail in Chapter 3, Reflective Classroom Communication.

Do you already use strategies like these? How might you adapt or use some of these approaches for your own classroom needs?

✄ Technology

Available free, online is a practical guide for reflective classroom management based on scholarly research on classroom management and discipline. It emphasizes the importance of teachers' reflective and critical thinking.

To help students become reflective about their own classroom behavior, there's a video/DVD/audio "Teaching Self-Discipline," available from National Professional Resources, which emphasizes students self-monitoring their behavior. This video focuses on students setting their own goals, applying themselves, directing their own behavior, making decisions about their own actions, and moderating their actions in accord with their peers.

"The Teacher's Guide" Web site has numerous classroom management resources, such as articles and links to other information on the Internet. Topics include discipline stages, discipline techniques, techniques that backfire, the honor system, managing inappropriate behavior, and working with shy or withdrawn students. The "Teachernet" site (http://www.teachnet.com/how=to/manage/index.html) also has links to classroom management topics, including cheating, tattletales, bathroom breaks, contracts, and sending "violators" to "court." However, the biggest resource of them all appears to be "The Really Big List of Classroom Management Resources" which has over 420 resource links, including one entitled "The Really Best List of Classroom Management Resources." However, the site warns that some of the links no longer work and others have been sold and may take you to unsavory places on the Internet!

A whole series of videos on classroom management is available from the Irving Independent School District in Irving, Texas. The series is briefly described at their Web site: http://www.irvingisd.net/one2one/classroom_management/cm_video_series.htm.

Summary

Effective classroom managers reflect on difficulties that might emerge in the classroom and plan instruction and proactive approaches that minimize problems. The emphasis is on student responsibility instead of obedience to your rules. When problems do occur, critically evaluate the situations and address them immediately using strategies that preserve the student's dignity as well as the teacher–student relationship and smooth functioning of the rest of the classroom. Internet and video/DVD resources can help teachers develop a repertoire of classroom management techniques and help promote reflective classroom management in themselves and their students.

Resources

Aronson, E.; N. Blaney; C. Stephen; J. Sikes; and M. Snapp, *The Jigsaw Classroom*. Beverly Hills, CA: Sage, 1978.

Blum, R. W. "The Case for School Connectedness," *Educational Leadership*, April 2005, pp. 16–20.

Burke, K. *What to Do with the Kid Who . . . Developing Cooperation, Self Discipline, and Responsibility in the Classroom*. Palatine IL: Skylight Publishing Co., 1992.

Classroom Management. The Teacher's Guide (n.d.). Teacher Created Resources. Retrieved July 31, 2007 from http://www.theteachersguide.com/ClassManagement.htm.

Classroom Management Video Series. Irving Independent School District (n.d.). Retrieved October 22, 2006 from http://www.irvingisd.net/one2one/classroom management.htm.

Cohen, R. *Students Resolving Conflict: Peer Mediation in Schools*. 2nd ed. Tucson, AZ: Good Year Books, 2005.

Cohen, R. (n.d.). The School Mediator's Field Guide. Prejudice, Sexual Harassment, Large Groups and Other Daily Challenges. School Mediation Associates. Retrieved July 31,2007 from http://www.schoolmediation.com/.

Curwin, R. L.; and A. N. Mendler. *Discipline with Dignity*. Alexandria, VA: Association for Supervision and Curriculum Development, 1988.

Evertson, C. M; and A. N. Harris. *COMP: Creating conditions for learning*. Nashville, TN: Vanderbilt University, 2003.

Gardner, H.; and T. Hatch. "Multiple Intelligences Go to School: Educational Implications of the Theory of Multiple Intelligences." *Educational Researcher* 18, no. 8 (1989), pp. 4–9.

Gordon, T. *Teacher Effectiveness Training*. New York: Peter H. Wyden, 1977.

Knapczyk, D. Teaching Self-Discipline. National Professional Resources 2004. Retrieved July 31 , 2007 from http://www.nprinc.com/classmgt/tsdi.htm.

Kounin, J. *Discipline and Group Management in Classrooms*. New York: Holt, Rinehart & Winston 1970.

Martin, W. The Really Big List of Classroom Management Resources, 2006. Retrieved July 31, 2007 from http://drwilliampmartin.tripod.com/classm.html.

Marzano, R. J.; J. S. Marzano; and D. J. Pickering. *Classroom Management That Works: Research-Based Strategies for Every Teacher.* Alexandria, VA: Association for Supervision and Curriculum Development, 2003.

McKeachie, W. *Teaching Tips.* 10th ed. Boston: Houghton-Mifflin, 1999.

Singh, A. (n.d.) Toward a Comprehensive Practical Guide for Reflective Classroom Management. Retrieved July 31, 2007 from http//www.mun.ca/educ/faculty/mwatch/win97/introsin.htm.

Sternberg, R. J. *The Triarchic Mind: A New Theory of Human Intelligence.* New York: Viking, 1988.

Williams, B.; and M. Woods. "Building on Urban Learners' Experiences. "*Educational Leadership,* April 1997, pp. 29–32.

Wlodkowski, R. J.; and M. B. Ginsberg. "A Framework for Culturally Responsive Teaching." *Educational Leadership,* September 1995, pp. 17–21.

Woolfolk, A. *Educational Psychology.* 7th ed. Needham Heights, MA: Allyn & Bacon, 1998.

Students' Reflective and Critical Thinking

To what extent do your students think about their own thinking and learning? How skilled are they at assessing their knowledge, thoughts, and actions? What are their strengths and weaknesses in reflective and critical thinking? What strategies enhance such thinking? Think about your own reflective and critical thinking skills and when, why, and how you use them in academic and everyday life activities. How did you acquire them?

Many experts have acquired their most valuable reflective and critical skills without a conscious awareness of their existence and without recognizing that some students lack these skills. In his classic book, *How We Think*, Dewey (1933) defined reflective thinking as "Active, persistent, and careful consideration of any belief or supposed form of knowledge in the light of the grounds that support it and the further conclusions to which it tends." Experts differ from novices in how they think and what strategies they use.

Reflective and critical thinking involve both reflection on action and reflection in action, as described by Schon in his classic works on reflective practice. Numerous strategies can help students become more reflective, critical thinkers and learners. Some of the important thinking skills discussed in this chapter include critical thinking, memory strategies, being a self-directed learner, low- and high-level cognitive skills, time management, and test-taking skills.

Students generally learn and appreciate these techniques best when they are applied to specific content in specific courses and academic tasks. The second half of this book addresses reflective and critical thinking in specific subjects. This chapter concentrates on general characteristics of critical and reflective thinking that transcend specific academic content. Chapter 7 on assessment has a rubric for evaluating critical thinking. It also discusses an error analysis procedure to help students critically evaluate their own past academic performance, master the material they missed or didn't apply effectively, and plan for future improvements.

✵ Critical Thinking

Critical thinking has both cognitive and emotional components. Cognitive components include analyzing and judging assumptions, evidence, and arguments. Emotional components include openmindedness, inquisitiveness, and truth seeking. Teaching for critical thinking involves helping students to reflect on, analyze, and evaluate their thinking before, during, and after learning. These types of thinking can help students to determine their progress and decide what to believe or do. Reflection in action helps students analyze and evaluate their behaviors and connect them with their feelings while they are working. The purpose is to increase understanding and use this enhanced understanding to inform actions so that they can be performed more effectively in an ongoing situation. Reflection on action helps students learn from their own past performance so they can think and learn more effectively, improving planning for how they will approach tasks in the future.

Novice critical thinkers tend to have preconceptions about the nature of knowledge and view it in terms of the quantity of information regardless of its quality. To them, assessment of their effectiveness comes from outside sources, especially authority figures, rather than from themselves. Help your students learn to think critically before they get to college so that they will be more successful in their college courses. Many beginning college students tend to think "dualistically," dichotomizing the world into two realms, such as good versus bad, right versus wrong, us versus them, or success versus failure. They believe there is one right answer to each problem and that authorities know these answers. They believe that these answers should be memorized by hard work. They also believe there is only one way to correctly approach a task or problem, and don't recognize that often there are several alternative, acceptable approaches. (For more details on the theory underlying these ideas, visit the Perry Network: http://www.perrynetwork.org/.)

By the time students leave college they are more likely to think critically, by thinking more in terms of "multiplicity" and "relativity." Multiplicity refers to recognizing there is a diversity of legitimate opinions and values where right answers aren't known yet. Everyone has a right to one's own opinion and no one can claim that an opinion is wrong. Relativity refers to knowledge being qualitative and dependent on the context in which it occurs. Analyses and comparisons are made possible by recognizing diverse opinions, values, and judgments, which are derived from evidence, logic, and coherent, reliable sources.

How can you help your students become better critical thinkers? Strategies include encouraging them to think aloud and make graphic representations of their work, such as papers they are writing or problems they are solving. These strategies are effective because they externalize the students' thinking processes, which makes it easier for students to evaluate their own thinking objectively. Once again, awareness facilitates control over thinking.

Self-questioning is another powerful technique that promotes critical thinking. By asking and answering questions such as "How can I state this in my own words?" or "Does this make sense?" students are directed toward reflecting on and critically evaluating what is understood, what is unclear, and what is and isn't known. In the process of answering such questions, students sometimes discover that their initial understanding was incomplete or incorrect. This discovery can reveal some important preconceptions that interfere with learning.

TABLE 6.1 Critical Thinking Checklist			
Critical Thinking Behavior	**Progress Rating**	**Critical Thinking Behavior**	**Progress Rating**
Understand the question/task		Differentiate fact from opinion	
Know how to approach the question/task		Differentiate main from supporting ideas	
Express ideas clearly		Judge ideas for quality	
Elaborate on ideas adequately		Judge quality of source	
Organize ideas logically		Make logical deductions	
Ensure answer is complete		Interpret information accurately	
Verify answer fits question		Make appropriate inferences	
Check answer for mistakes		Ensure evidence supports conclusion	
Remember important concepts		Consider multiple points of view	
Stay openminded		Reflect on action, before and after actions occur	
Be aware of biases		Reflect in action, while actions are occurring	
Recognize assumptions		Analyze quality of arguments	

Some people prefer checklists to self-questioning. Students and teachers can use checklists to assess their application of critical thinking skills. Help your students develop their own progress charts or checklists. A sample critical thinking checklist might include the behaviors in Table 6.1, and progress could be rated on a scale from 1 to 5 indicating none to extensive.

This is an analytical approach to evaluating critical thinking because it rates each behavior separately. A rubric for holistically evaluating critical thinking is in Chapter 7 on assessment.

✂ Remembering Reflectively

"Last week I taught my students how to factor polynomials. At the end of the week most students did it by themselves and did it perfectly. At the beginning of the next week we were almost back to ground zero."

What happened in such a short time? Have you experienced teaching something only to find that it has been forgotten by the next class? Just because students seem to follow along with a lesson in class doesn't guarantee they can remember, understand, and/or apply what was "learned." A frustrating circumstance for many students is the fact that they "study hard," but frequently cannot remember or apply the material. These students often try to overcome the problem by "studying harder," but because they continue to study in ineffective ways, the material is still not remembered or used effectively. As a result they may believe that they suffer a learning deficiency or simply don't have the ability to learn whatever they are studying. The solution is more often studying *smarter* than studying *harder*.

Try the learning activity that follows, which is designed to help you work with students who have trouble remembering.

Learning Activity: Study the list of words below for one minute only. Try to remember all the words on the list. The order is not important.

1. List: piano, chair, saxophone, table, guitar, drums, toothpaste, bed, lamp, desk.
2. Cover the list and write as many words from it as you can remember in any order.
3. Compare the list of words from step 1 with the list you wrote for step 2.

How did you try to remember those words? What method(s) did you use?

There are many different ways of remembering information. Some ways are generally better than others, but much depends on such factors as the individual, content, and purpose. The simplest memory strategy is repetition—stating the material over and over again—exactly the way it was presented. This strategy is called rote learning. Rote learning is characterized by memorizing isolated pieces of information and/or memorizing without understanding. Rote learning works quite well if you look up a phone number and repeat it over and over as you dial. It may work well for remembering a social security number or home address, but it is one of the least effective strategies for most academic work. Sadly, it is a commonly used approach for many students who think they have trouble with their memory. The problem is not their memory. The problem is their method of remembering.

When asked to define "effective learning," two categories emerged from teachers' responses: long-term retention and application, including transfer to new situations. Meaningful learning requires students to make connections between new information and information they already have. In meaningful learning, the learner tries to make sense of all the information even when it seems that there are many separate and distinct pieces of unconnected data. Students who use meaningful learning will normally try to organize or group information according to some common theme. The common theme joins the separate information into groups rather than many pieces. If separate pieces of information can be remembered as one group, the task of remembering is greatly simplified. For example, in the learning activity above, all the terms except one could be organized into two groups: musical instruments and furniture. Toothpaste stands out because it doesn't fit in either group. Information that stands out tends to be remembered more easily.

The particular organization of material sometimes depends on the individual. Frequently, organization that is helpful for one learner is of limited value for another. At the same time, some organization is almost always better than none at all. Due to our limited capacity to hold information in our short-term (working) memories, we need to find economical and powerful ways to organize and represent information. Effective organization and representation strategies can help learners best utilize their memory capacities. Common memory strategies that are forms of rehearsal include rereading material; using flash cards; reciting names, concepts, or definitions; and underlining/highlighting. Other common approaches involve mnemonic techniques of simple associations such as first letters, locations, and images.

Ask your students to reflect on and critically evaluate their memory strategies. The best memory techniques tend to be those that emphasize the learner's use of prior knowledge. Using prior knowledge enhances meaningfulness through active, personal construction of ideas and their relationships. Effective memory techniques are those that emphasize insight into concepts and relationships instead of memorization of them. The more concepts and their relationships are understood, the lighter is the burden on memory.

The goal is also important when it comes to memory. Many times students want to remember material only long enough to use it for a test. When remembering is done with this goal in mind, students usually treat the material to be learned very superficially. This goal is usually short-sighted. In many cases, students need long-term memory of the information because it is likely to be a building block for later learning. It's more efficient to learn it well initially and save time by avoiding having to relearn it in the future. For information to last in memory, students need to use it and think about it more deeply. Help them think about ways to store or record the material to be remembered and ways to retrieve or recall what they have stored as well. Writing summaries fosters comprehension and can aid both storage and retrieval.

You can demonstrate a variety of examples of effective memorization. For example, what happens when you have to go somewhere for the first time? Usually at the beginning you have to get directions and follow them carefully so you don't get lost. If you go there often, eventually you can get there automatically without even having to think about where you are going. You can go on "automatic pilot." You have had so much practice that memory of the location and how to get there is well-ingrained in your mind. It has become internalized, second nature, and is a part of you.

That is what is meant by automaticity or "overlearning." Automaticity is another principle for improving memory. There are some concepts or skills that are so basic that learners need to be able to use them automatically. For example, what would it be like to read a book if every time you read you had to try to remember what all the letters and words stood for? This principle explains why ESL students often must spend much more time reading their texts than students for whom English is their native language. Multiplication tables are an example of a math content that needs to be on "automatic pilot" because these math facts are so fundamental. Extensive and varied practice can help students learn information or skills to the point of automaticity. Automaticity aids performance, especially on complex problems or tasks, because the more knowledge and skills that are on "automatic pilot," the more mental energy can be devoted to other aspects of a problem or task. How could you help students get the practice they need so they can put important concepts and/or skills on "automatic pilot"?

One of the most important concepts is that effective memory often depends on **planning** to remember **early** in the studying process. It's often too hard to retrieve information when it's needed if a memory cue or technique wasn't part of the initial learning process. Teach students to think about and develop strategies for how they are going to store and recall information to be learned while they are studying it. For example, to remember some major chords in music, use the strategy of thinking about the first note in the chord as starting with the thumb, like C for a C chord, then adding every other finger and note, that is three and five, in this case E and G for the C chord.

Graphic organizers, such as Figure 6.1, can be excellent tools for integrating learning, enhancing understanding, and promoting long-term memory. Deciding what to include in graphic representations and how to organize them as

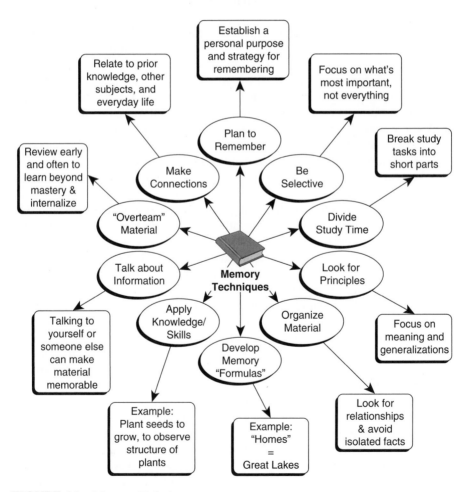

FIGURE 6.1   *Memory Techniques*

well as actually drawing them helps students store important information. Graphic organizers are effective tools for note taking, reviewing, self-testing, and remembering. While taking a test, mentally picturing the completed graphic organizers can help students to recall important ideas and the relationships between them. See Chapter 7 on assessment and Chapter 9 on reflective and critical reading for further discussions of graphic organizers.

Encourage students to experiment with a variety of memory strategies in all of their subjects. They shouldn't assume that the same memory technique is appropriate for all subjects or for all tasks within the same subject. The basic rule, however, is that whenever possible, emphasize memory with understanding rather than rote memorization. Memory techniques, such as summaries, that emphasize main ideas and meaningful relationships between units of information are generally superior to techniques that emphasize arbitrary relationships or fragmented information.

Understanding information has a direct relationship to memory. The more students understand about the information they are expected to know, the less of a burden there is on their memory. If students understand a concept, they can reconstruct it more easily and do not have to depend on rote memorization. Emphasize meaningfulness and connections when students are learning.

⚔ Experts Versus Novices

Be flexible about accepting how your students initially organize their knowledge. Research shows that the superior knowledge of experts is not only in the quantity of information, but also in the organization of that information. Consequently, you and your students may deal with exactly the same information in substantially different ways. Organization of information improves over time as the learner gains more experience and knowledge. For example, once individual pieces of music are learned, they may be grouped into categories such as classical, rock, or jazz. Further familiarization may bring grouping into subcategories such as bebop, boogie woogie, swing, ragtime, Dixieland, and improvisational jazz.

You are a subject area expert whereas your students are subject area novices. Communicate clearly the ways you think about the organization of the material in a subject. When you make connections within and between topics, those connections may be even more important than the individual topics because they reveal important relationships and show how a subject is organized.

The situation may be compared to two people looking at a hidden-3D picture. Experts see a deep underlying structure that creates a new and three-dimensional picture with the objectively same information. They know how to look at and organize the information. Novices just see the two-dimensional images immediately apparent on the surface; there is simpler organization and fewer connections. If you teach students how subject matter is organized by experts, then students can use this knowledge when taking notes, reviewing notes or a text, and preparing for a test. Three major differences between experts and novices are shown in Table 6.2.

TABLE 6.2 Differences Between Expert and Novice Thinkers	
Experts	**Novices**
Construct a richly cross-referenced, hierarchical knowledge base.	Construct a poorly cross-referenced incomplete, amorphous knowledge base.
Focus on deep structures.	Focus on surface features.
Strategize before solving a problem.	Jump into solving a problem without strategizing

⚔ Self-Directed, Reflective Learners

A major goal of teaching is to create students who no longer need your help to learn. This purpose can be described as creating a self-directed, self-regulating, or independent life-long learner, who has the following seven characteristics:

1. Self-motivates, self-confident. Self-motivation means the student is motivated to learn for learning's own sake. Self-confidence means the student feels that she or he can succeed. This includes feeling that one is the master of one's own educational destiny, knowing that individual efforts and strategies can affect academic performance and outcomes. (See the Self-Perception Continuum in Chapter 4 on emotions.)

2. Plans work; knows when, why, and how to use knowledge and skills. Self-directed learners plan their work on academic tasks, such as homework, papers, and studying for tests. Such planning includes knowing what material is to be learned and what knowledge and skills are needed for succeeding with particular material or tasks. Knowing when, why, and how to use what has been learned is vital for applying and transferring already learned knowledge. However, many teachers just teach "what" or factual information. What do you typically teach your students?

A. Knowing WHAT: Knowledge of facts, definitions, concepts, in a subject area. Declarative information is elicited by a "What" question. Each of the following questions seeks some declarative knowledge:
  - What is meant by a symbiotic relationship?
  - What is the meaning of the small 2 to the upper right of x in x^2?
  - What is clarifying?

B. Knowing WHEN and WHY: Knowledge regarding the situation in which and/or reasons why the student should apply some information or skill. Such contextual or conditional information is often sought by a "When" or "Why" question. This type of knowledge lets students identify conditions and situations in which it is appropriate to use specific information and skills. Each of the following questions seeks some contextual information:
  - Why is the economy of Poland more volatile than that of Finland?
  - Why is Herbert Hoover's presidency blamed for the Depression?
  - When do you clarify?
  - When do you use the quadratic equation?

C. Knowing HOW: Knowledge of how to apply information or skills students have learned. This includes methods, procedures, and techniques. A "How" question often activates procedural information. Each of the following questions seeks some procedural information:

- How is carbonic acid stored in tropical climates?
- How is the equation $x^2 + 5x + 6 = 0$ solved?
- How do you clarify?

Successful students think about these three types of knowledge differently. Successful teachers understand that factual and procedural knowledge are not enough. Students also need to know when and why to use their knowledge and skills. For example, even if Denny knew all the formulas that were going to be covered on the test (factual knowledge) and how to apply them (procedural knowledge), he could fail the test if he didn't know which formulas to use with which types of problems (contextual/conditional knowledge).

3. Monitors work in progress: comprehension, approach, and memory. Student self-checks comprehension, reflecting on whether and how well he or she really understands the material or a task, and if clarification is needed. While working, the student checks up on whether/how well an approach or strategy is working and decides whether to stay on course or change. The student assesses whether there is information already stored in memory that should be retrieved for a task, or if there is new and useful/important information that should be put into memory for future reference or use.

4. Controls self-messages and persists. Self-directed learners maintain awareness of and control self-messages to eliminate negative thoughts and feelings, which otherwise can undermine effective performance. Such learners persist even when faced with difficult, boring, or tedious tasks. (See Chapter 4 on emotional aspects of thinking and learning.)

5. Evaluates work, using internal and external feedback to improve performance. Self-directed learners evaluate schoolwork by looking not only at grades received, but also at your comments. Self-directed learners seek evaluations of their performance from external sources such as you, other teachers, peers, and themselves. In addition, they examine wrong answers and use them as learning opportunities by identifying error patterns and using error analyses to develop an action plan for transforming mistakes into future successes.

The worst situation occurs when someone is wrong, makes a mistake, or fails, but does not learn from the experience. In such cases, the failure is likely to be repeated! Self-correction is an essential part of self-directed learning, and it is an important component of both monitoring and evaluating performance. See Chapter 7 on assessment for details on error analysis.

6. Self-rewards. Self-directed learners don't need the approval of their teachers, peers, or parents. Their rewards come from within, such as the personal satisfaction of achieving their own goals, and can include treating themselves to something special for a job well done. See the chapter on emotions for a detailed discussion of motivation.

7. Transfers knowledge and skills. This includes application of knowledge and skills learned to other subjects, other situations in the same subject, and to everyday life. Being able to recognize similarities or make connections can help the learner know it's appropriate to use or adapt their existing skills or knowledge to new situations. (See Chapter 2, Managing Teaching, for details on teaching for transfer.)

Levels of Thinking Skills

Many students experience academic difficulty because they constantly focus on retaining subject matter content without first learning the intellectual skills needed to support that effort. In order for students to function intelligently, teaching needs to develop both low- and high-level cognitive skills as well as positive emotions (attitudes and motivation).

Lower-level cognitive "worker" skills perform the intellectual tasks decided on by higher-level "boss" (management) skills. Examples of lower-level skills include registering information (encoding), deciphering meaning (decoding), inferring, comparing, and combining. Higher-level cognitive skills include reflective and critical thinking skills needed for executive management processes such as planning, monitoring, and evaluating. Higher-level cognition involves "thinking about thinking," such as deciding how to approach a task. Research shows that higher-level cognitive skills involving reflection and critical thinking often need to be taught for the following reasons:

1. Teaching specific strategies, like the order in which to perform a particular task, will not give students the skills they need in the long run. Students must learn general principles such as planning, and how to apply them over a wide variety of tasks and domains.

2. Both the long-term benefits of training in lower-level cognitive skills and the ability to apply lower-level cognitive skills to new tasks appear to depend, at least in part, on training at the higher cognitive level as well as the lower cognitive level. Both levels are needed for effective cognitive performance.

3. Generally students have a history of blindly following instructions. They have not acquired the habit of questioning themselves to lead to effective performance on intellectual tasks.

4. Students with the greatest reflective skill deficiencies seem to have no idea what they're doing when performing a task.

5. Students often have problems of
    A. Determining the difficulty of a task.
    B. Monitoring their comprehension effectively (they don't recognize when they don't fully understand something, such as task directions, information in textbooks).
    C. Planning ahead (what they need to do, and how long each part should take).
    D. Monitoring the success of their performance or determining when they have studied enough to master the material to be learned.
    E. Using all the relevant information.

F. Using a systematic, step-by-step approach.

G. Jumping to conclusions.

H. Using inadequate or incorrect representations.

6. These reflective and critical thinking skills and knowledge, although important, often are not taught in school.

For more information on levels of thinking skills, see the categories of low-intermediate- and higher-level questions as well as Bloom's taxonomy in Chapter 8 on Teaching Strategies.

Strategies for Developing Self-Directed, Reflective Learners

In addition to teaching your subject matter, teach your students to systematically reflect on how they think, learn, remember, and perform academic tasks before, during, and after their work. Students can manage their own learning through reflection promoting self-awareness and self-control. This reflection should emphasize planning, monitoring, and evaluating.

- Plan. Before beginning, think about what is to be done, when to do each step, decide how it is to be done, consider alternative strategies, and determine why a particular way needs to be chosen. Examples: What steps should I take to write this term paper? What should I do first? What should I wait until later to do? Where can I find the information I need to answer this question? How am I supposed to conduct this experiment?
- Monitor. While working, check up on progress to determine how well you understand what you're doing, whether what you're doing is really leading you where you want to go, and whether you're forgetting anything important. Examples: Am I sure I understand what the teacher expects for this question? Is my answer heading in the right direction? Have I included all the major causes of the war in my answer? Am I leaving out anything important? What do I remember from my class notes that could help me solve this problem?
- Evaluate. After task performance, judge what you have done and how you did it. Determine what could have been done better and what you can do to improve performance next time. Develop a specific plan of action to improve performance. Examples: How well did I do on the test? How could I have done better? Did I make any careless mistakes? I'm going to remember to study my class notes while I'm reviewing the textbook to see where they overlap. That will help me have a better idea about what will be covered on the test. Next time I'll check more carefully before turning in my paper. The "I DREAM of A" models in Chapters 10 and 12 on mathematics and English, respectively, are subject-specific applications of these ideas. These models emphasize use of two reflection strategies: self-questioning and thinking aloud.

Another strategy for helping your students become self-directed learners is for you to be a role model and demonstrate examples of self-directed, reflective learning. Talk out loud to yourself, let students see and hear you plan, monitor, and evaluate your work and how you would approach tasks like theirs. It's a good idea to intentionally make mistakes so students can observe how you discover them and self-correct.

Questioning and self-questioning strategies are effective ways of promoting self-directed learners. Discuss and illustrate use of reflective and critical thinking in school and everyday life situations. Ask students questions such as "How would you plan, monitor, and evaluate a surprise party?" "How do you prepare for a test?" Model self-questioning for them. Have students generate and use self-questions. Habitual self-questioning may be the best way of improving reflective and critical thinking skills.

Research on self-questioning shows that questions created by the student are much more effective than questions given to the student by a teacher. It is preferable to have each student generate his/her own self-questions or to do this with a partner or in a small group. To stimulate and guide student thinking, provide sample questions for students to use as models. Self-questions such as "Have I left out anything important?" can help a student self-direct in identifying omission of important points or examples. Listen to students performing tasks while using their self-questions and give them feedback on their questions and answers. Encourage them to keep a readily accessible list of their own self-questions to use or adapt for the particular situation. It is important to regularly have students adapt their self-questions to the needs of the specific subject and specific situation, and use them to guide their performance before, during, and after a task. Self-questioning can have the following benefits:

- Improved awareness and control over thinking and thereby improved performance;
- Improved long-term retention of knowledge and skills;
- Improved ability to use knowledge and skills;
- Improved attitudes and motivation.

Practice is necessary but not sufficient. Make sure students understand when, why, and how to use strategies like self-questioning. Help them recognize contexts for their use and develop criteria for evaluating their effectiveness.

Finally, and most importantly, repeatedly emphasize, and demonstrate through your communications and actions, that students are responsible for and can control their own educational outcomes. Student performance should not be blamed on a teacher. Students earn grades, you don't "give" grades to them.

Help your students become effective thinkers and learners by working with them to develop important skills that underlie their intellectual achievement. Another of these, time management, can maximize their engagement with academic work outside of class.

✄ Time Management

How do you budget your time when preparing and implementing a lesson? Do you consider yourself a good time manager? Why or why not? What are your strengths and weaknesses as a time manager? One of students' most common complaints is that they do not have enough time for all the reading, studying, and other academic works they are assigned. Even excellent students tend to have trouble managing their time.

Too often students cram at the last minute on material they should have been learning over an extended period of time. Many students have competing social, extracurricular, and/or family responsibilities to balance with their academic work. Sometimes priorities get confused because short-term needs conflict with long-term goals. Research suggests the following four major factors may affect students' time management:

1. Setting goals and priorities—Ending conflicts between short-term and long-term goals;
2. Mechanics, including planning and scheduling;
3. Perceived control of time;
4. A general preference for organizing one's workspace and approach to projects.

Of these four factors, perceived control is the best predictor of grade point average. Controlling how time is spent is also related to measures of stress and self-evaluations of performance. Students who perceive themselves as having control over time also reported greater satisfaction with their job and life roles.

Time Management Tips

Determine whether your students are adequately managing their time and help them develop and implement good time management strategies. Have them reflect on whether they spend time in a way that is consistent with their priorities. The following recommendations can help your students improve their time management skills.

1. Set short-term goals and establish priorities. Sometimes students need a teacher's help clarifying their short- and long-term goals. An example of a short-term goal is to read a history chapter a particular week. An example of a long-term goal is to get into a good college. An example of a low-priority activity may be waiting in line to see a new movie. An example of a high-priority activity is preparing for an important test. Do students have conflicting priorities? If so, how do they handle them?

2. Keep a 24-hour time log of daily activities for at least a week. Logs should be kept from waking up to going to bed so students can figure out exactly how they are using their time. This provides a baseline for future time management plans. It will also help determine whether there is down time that could be used more effectively, such as waiting in line at the grocery store, riding the bus or subway, or doing laundry.

3. Use the log to compare how they spend their time with their stated goals and priorities. How much time is spent on low-priority versus high-priority goals? Is too much time being spent on low-priority goals? Is enough being spent on high-priority goals?

TABLE 6.3 Time Management Guidelines	
Time Management Scheduling Guidelines	**Explanations**
Things usually take more time than we think.	Research says to accurately predict how long a task is likely to take, estimate the time, then multiply by 3!
Fit the individual.	Most people are more alert and work more efficiently during one part of the day or night than another. Schedule activities accordingly.
Be specific.	What activities will be done? How much time is allotted for each?
Economize time.	Organize the schedule to create the most available time possible. Use down times.
Be flexible.	Modify schedules as needed. Expect the unexpected, such as emergencies and unanticipated demands.
Schedule fun and relaxation.	A happy, healthy person is generally a more efficient worker.

4. Develop a time management plan (schedule) that is more consistent with their own goals and priorities. Help students identify the strengths and weaknesses of their current schedule. Try to identify poor organizational habits, such as repeated trips from their study area to the kitchen, when better planning could lead to fewer trips and more available time. Determine whether interruptions or procrastination are factors in how time is being managed, and if so, identify strategies that can overcome these problems. Pay particular attention to time allocated for high-priority tasks, like keeping up with schoolwork so students can achieve their long-term career goals. The guidelines in Table 6.3 can aid scheduling.

5. Regularly monitor how time is spent in relationship to priorities. This should be an ongoing process. Check up on whether/how the time management plan is being followed and how it is working. By evaluating time logs, you and your students can examine whether and how the schedule is working. Students can benefit from finding more constructive ways to use "dead" or "down time." Even when traveling to and from school or standing in line at a grocery store, students can mentally review important concepts. Consider how your students feel about their new schedules. If they don't like the schedules, they probably won't be motivated to follow them.

Follow up this suggested list of activities with appropriate activities or discussions. Encourage discussions among students about their creative ideas for making the most of their time. Brainstorming, reviewing, reflecting on, and criticizing schedules and other time management strategies can help students make changes as needed.

Table 6.4 is an example of a time management plan for a high school student.

TABLE 6.4 **Sample Time Management Plan for Non-School Hours**			
Day of Week	**Time of Day**	**Activity***	**Results and Changes**
Monday	3–5:30	music lesson	
Tuesday and Thursday	3–5:30	sports/hobbies	
Wednesday and Friday	3–5:30	flexible, depending on goals and priorities**	
Monday–Friday	6:00–7:00	dinner/family, chores	
Saturday	9 AM–noon	schoolwork (homework, projects, studying for tests)	
	12:30–4	sports/hobbies	
	5:00–7:00	dinner/family, chores	
Friday and Saturday	7:00–midnight	friends/date	
Sunday	9 AM–noon	spiritual/family chores	
	noon–6 PM	flexible	
Sunday–Thursday	7:00–9:00 PM	schoolwork	
Sunday–Thursday	9:00–10:30 PM	phone, TV, and computer	
Sunday–Thursday	10:30 PM–6:30 AM	sleep	
Friday and Saturday	midnight–9:00 AM	sleep	

*Economy Strategies:

1. Bring homework for when traveling and for down time during activities.

2. Budget time based on needs, goals, and priorities.

3. Make sure to get enough sleep to be alert when needed.

**Goals and Priorities:

1. Get into a good college.

2. Develop a good social life and hobbies.

3. Continue to have a good family life.

4. Stay healthy.

⚔ Test-Taking Skills

How do your students prepare for tests? How do they think while they are taking tests? Learning how to improve skills in preparing for and taking tests is another very common student need. Students often engage in these important academic activities without reflecting on or critically evaluating their approaches and considering alternatives.

Test-preparation and test-taking strategies should be adapted to the particular type of test. Strategies for multiple-choice tests are different than strategies for essay tests. Some students have not had much experience with essay exams, whereas other students, especially those who were schooled abroad, have not had much experience with multiple-choice tests. Even students who are experienced with both types of tests often have never received explicit instruction in test-preparation and test-taking strategies.

What are some strategies you used when preparing for and taking multiple-choice and essay tests? Which strategies worked best for you and why?

There are several factors to take into consideration in test taking: the psychological state of the learner, her/his physiological condition, content knowledge, and basic testwiseness skills. The psychological state primarily involves the student's level of confidence and degree of relaxation/anxiety. To build self-confidence, the student needs

1. to have the knowledge and skills needed for the test content and questions;
2. a positive academic self-concept in the particular subject and positive self-efficacy for specific tasks or problems;
3. strategies for becoming aware of and controlling lack of self-confidence; and
4. relaxation techniques.

Another important psychological state in testing is avoiding impulsivity. Sometimes students get the wrong answer because they settle on something close to the right answer too quickly and stop thinking before they reach the correct answer. Being accurate and complete requires careful, deliberate thought, patience, and being reflective instead of impulsively jumping to the wrong conclusion. Recent research on adolescent brain development shows that their brains aren't completely mature in the areas responsible for impulse control until the early twenties. Consequently, adolescents often need guidance from adults to help them avoid acting impulsively.

The student's physiological state includes overall health, whether the student has had proper nutrition—not too much or too little to eat—and whether the student has had enough sleep. Lack of sleep is a common problem for students. If students cannot control their lack of sleep, they should be extra careful about attending to other aspects of being well-prepared for and strategic when taking a test. Recent research on brain development shows that nutritional deficiencies and sleep deprivation are common in adolescents.

The brain is the only organ in the body that doesn't store energy, so breakfast is especially important. Also, adolescent girls secrete chemicals that make them hungry. As a result, they often eat carbohydrates, which cause sleepiness.

Because their brains are bathed in melatonin in the morning, adolescents may be cranky and need adrenalin to get them going. Also, few adolescents regularly get the 9 hours and 15 minutes sleep research shows they need.

Test-Taking Tips

Give students practice tests so they can try out using some of the following suggested strategies. Guided practice with feedback can help students master various techniques so they can be used with ease during a test situation. Tips include

1. Know and understand test content and teacher expectations. Students should know all the material they are responsible for on a specific test. Have students predict or develop test questions and answer them or identify areas for further study. To what extent do your students know what you expect of them? For example, if it is an essay, is there a particular length it should be? How will it be graded? Will writing skills, such as spelling, grammar, and organization, be considered in the grading? Do some questions count more than others? Will the test present information exactly as it was presented in class or in their books, or will students be expected to transfer what they have learned to new situations? Discuss with your students why you think it is important for them to know the material, and how they can benefit from it.

2. Understand and follow directions. Encourage students to monitor their understanding of the directions and to ask questions if they are unclear about anything. Anxiety sometimes interferes with students' ability to calmly figure out what to do. Emphasize the importance of reading the directions carefully and making sure all the test items are answered as completely and accurately as possible within the allotted time.

3. Understand and answer the specific question asked. Identifying and defining the question or problem is perhaps the most important test-taking skill. If you examine students' errors on tests, you often will find students have given the "right answer to the wrong question." That is, students often misinterpret what the question is really all about and construct or select an answer to a related question rather than to the actual question. Sometimes it helps to break the question into parts.

Students can use other test items to find clues that might help them figure out the meanings of unclear terms or concepts and try to think back to the textbook and lectures where they encountered them. Recalling information related to the terms/concepts might help clarify their meaning. Students can try paraphrasing the question in their own words or diagramming it.

4. Use time wisely. Help students develop effective strategies and habits for managing their time when preparing for and taking tests. Students should learn to first review the entire test, and then to answer the questions they are sure of before moving on to the more difficult ones. Caution them against getting bogged down on difficult/time-consuming items, unless these items are heavily weighted in scoring. Encourage them to mark those items they skip so they can be identified easily when time permits returning attention to them. Administer practice tests under conditions like those in the real test, with similar questions, item formats, and time constraints.

5. Mark answers properly. For objective test items, students should make sure they have not marked more than one answer. Answer sheet responses must be correctly matched with the test question numbers. When skipping an item on an objective test with an answer sheet, the student must be very careful not to accidentally fill in the space intended to be blank with an answer to another item. This would throw off all subsequent items and could have a devastating effect on the student's score. Students need to determine when answers are to be based on course content or provided material, such as on reading comprehension tests, instead of when answers are to be based on their own prior knowledge and experience. Sometimes students' "right answers" are not what the teacher is looking for. Remind students to think critically and reflectively, and to avoid answering questions impulsively.

6. Guess intelligently. On multiple-choice, true-false, and matching tests, students should rely on guessing only after making a concerted effort to figure out the correct answer. Before guessing, they should use a process of elimination to eliminate options that are clearly wrong, such as outrageous, vague, or illogical choices. Teach students to use content on the test itself as clues about answers they cannot recall or doubt. Remind them to not leave multiple-choice answers blank when turning in a test, unless there is a penalty for guessing.

7. Plan essays. Research examining students' notes on test papers shows that students who plan their answers receive the highest grades. Graphic organizers, such as webs or concept maps, may be better for planning than outlines because outlines may be too linear for students to think flexibly about the main points, supporting details, and organization of the information to be included in the essay. Students need to know whether organization, grammar, spelling, and punctuation will count in grading and to budget time for editing essays for these factors as needed. They need to leave enough time to reread and revise an essay before turning it in.

8. Use memory strategies to recall important information. Constructing or recalling mental images of lecture scenes, notes, texts, and graphic organizers can aid memory of ideas and their connections. If students can't find the exact information when searching memory this way, they can look for related information. They should try to get a big picture of the overall context in which the material was learned. Self-questioning strategies can guide students through various searches. For example, "What did the diagram that she put on the blackboard have in it?" "Where is this in my notes?" Clues from other test items and answer choices can help students remember.

9. Self-pace. Help students learn to keep track of time during testing and to budget their time intelligently based on how the test will be graded. Students should tune into test starting and ending times, and monitor the amount of time remaining in relation to the amount and value of work to be done. Time budgeted should include time for answering the questions, checking answers, and making changes.

10. Check answers. Checking answers at the end of a test requires reflecting on and critically evaluating their accuracy and adequacy. Often students know the material, but make careless mistakes due to anxiety, feeling rushed, or a question/problem appearing to be too easy or too hard. If an answer has been changed, make sure the grader can clearly determine which is the answer intended. If a student decides to change an answer after reviewing her/his responses, the student should be very sure there is a good reason to change the answer (test content triggered student's memory of the correct answer). Many times students' first impressions are correct, and correct answers are changed to incorrect ones!

For math/science problem-solving tests, students should try to verify their answers, for example, by applying reverse operations, trying a different approach, and determining whether their answers make sense. For reading/language-based tests, encourage students to read the question and answer together as a unit to evaluate logic and coherence. Are their arguments developed sufficiently? Are they supported by valid and relevant reasons and evidence?

11. Know oneself. How reflective are your students about their test performance—considering both reflection on action and reflection in action? Students benefit from reflecting on and critically evaluating their own strengths and weaknesses in specific test content, in their attitudes, and in their test-taking practices before they take a test, while taking it, and afterward. Awareness of their strengths and weaknesses is the first step in control over them. Control strategies include performing error analysis (discussed in the chapter on assessment), monitoring self-talk to prevent negative self-fulfilling prophesies, and using relaxation techniques such as deep breathing, progressive relaxation, muscle tension/relaxation, imagery, and meditation.

Awareness of their attitudes during testing and maintaining a positive state of mind can prevent wasting valuable testing time and mental energy on negative self-talk, self-doubts, and worrying.

✍ Technology

A review of reflective and critical thinking from the Educational Resources Information Clearinghouse (ERIC) is available at http://www.ericdigests.org/2000-3/thought.htm. It recommends using questioning and problem generation as strategies for helping your students think critically and provides a comprehensive list of reflective thinking skills.

The Critical Thinking Community is online at http://www.criticalthinking.org. This community has a professional development area for K–12 teachers and resources including videotapes, DVDs, articles, and a series of curriculum materials called The Thinker's Guide. Video topics include teaching to standards, teaching writing, reasoning, creativity, problem solving, teaching content, and Socratic questioning. Topics of articles available free at this site include: A stage theory of critical thinking; Critical thinking: basic questions and answers; A critical mind is a questioning mind; and Critical thinking: Hispanic imperative.

Online tutorials on critical thinking include one on Argumentation and Critical Thinking, http://www.humboldt.edu/~act/HTML/, which is designed for college students but can benefit high school teachers and students as well. It includes tests and information on fallacies, validity, and formal logical structure. Another online tutorial, found at http://www.distance.uvic.ca/courses/critical/, focuses specifically on reading, writing, applying reasoning processes, and making reasoned judgments.

Another online resource on critical thinking is available at http://www.sbctc.ctc.edu/ewag/ewag0010/page9.html. It includes an article defining critical thinking and summarizing research from cognitive psychology, and provides links to information on instruction, reasoning, and assessment of critical thinking.

Summary

Although some students develop critical and reflective thinking skills independently, many need direct instruction to acquire and use them effectively. Experts differ from novices in how they think and learn, with experts being more reflective and critical. Self-questioning, checklists, and other approaches can be used to develop memory, critical thinking, test-taking, and time management skills and to help students become independent, self-directed learners. The Internet and videos/DVDs provide technological resources for developing reflective and critical thinking skills.

Resources

Dewey, J. *How We Think*. Chicago: Henry Regnery Company, 1993.

Dusenberry, P. (n.d.). *Teaching and Assessing Critical Thinking*. Retrieved July 31, 2007 from http://www.sbctc.ctc.edu/ewag/ewag0010/page9.html.

Ennis, R. *Critical Thinking: What Is It?* (1992). Philosophy of Education. Retrieved July 31, 2007 from http://www.ed.uiuc.edu/EPS/PES-yearbook/92 docs/Ennis.HTM.

Hartman, H. J. Developing Students' Metacognitive Knowledge and Skills. In *Metacognition in Learning and Instruction: Theory, Research & Practice*, ed. H. J. Hartman. Dordrecht: Springer, 2001.

Memory Improvement Tools (n.d.). Mind Tools. Retrieved July 31, 2007 from http://www.mindtools.con/memory.html.

Mestre, J. *Using Learning Spaces to Encourage Deeper Learning*. Educause Conference. 2004. Retrieved July 31, 2007 from www.educause.edu/ir/library/powerpoint/NLI0441.pps.

National Research Council. *How People Learn: Brain, Mind, Experience and School*. Expanded ed. Washington, DC: National Academy Press, 2000.

Perry, W. G. *Forms of Ethical and Intellectual Development in the College Years*. San Francisco: Jossey-Bass, 1999.

Price, L. "The Biology of Risk Taking." *Educational Leadership*. April 2005, pp. 22–26.

Samuel, S. Reflective Thought, Critical Thinking. ERIC Digest D143. 1999. ED436007. Retrieved July 31, 2007 from http://www.ericdigests.org/2000-3/thought.htm.

Schon, D. *Educating the Reflective Practitioner*. San Francisco: Jossey-Bass, 1987.

Sprenger, M. "Inside Amy's Brain." *Educational Leadership*. April 2005, pp. 27–29.

Student Resources: Critical Thinking Skills. 2003. Retrieved July 31, 2007 from http://www.distance.uvic.ca/courses/critical.

Test Taking Tips and Study Skills. 2006. Retrieved July 31, 2007 from www.testtakingtips.com/.

The Critical Thinking Community. 2007. Retrieved July 31, 2007 from http://www.criticalthinking.org.

Verlinden, J. (n.d.). *Argumentation and Critical Thinking Tutorial*. Humboldt State University. Retrieved July 31, 2007 from http://www.humboldt.edu/~act/HTML/.

Virtual Pamphlet Collection: Time Management. University of Chicago. Retrieved September 16, 2006 from http://counseling.uchicago.edu/resources/virtualpamphlets/time_management.shtml.

Wagner, R; and R. J. Sternberg. *Alternative Conceptions of Intelligence and Their Implications for Education*. Review of Educational Research, 1984, 54(4) 597–654.

Reflective Assessment Practices

Reflection is the essence of assessment because it requires careful, critical examination of your students' progress, which ultimately relates to your assumptions, instructional methods, materials, and activities and therefore mandates your own self-evaluation. The two overarching types of assessment are formative and summative. How do you use them to judge the effectiveness of your lessons and how students are progressing in achieving curricular objectives?

✕ Formative and Summative Assessments

Formative assessments are ongoing, informal measures on learning that elicit feedback on students' comprehension and progress and are used to refine instruction so that it better meets students' needs. Formative assessment may be characterized as reflection in action because it occurs while learning is progressing. It can be quantitative or qualitative. Examples include homework, quizzes, results of cooperative learning activities, and class discussions.

Summative assessments occur at the end of a learning unit, sequence, or period of time and are used to judge the effectiveness of the overall teaching–learning process. Summative assessment may be characterized as reflection on action as it occurs after instruction has occurred. Examples include final projects, teacher-made end-of-unit exams, report card grades, and standardized tests.

Many people have the preconception that assessment is only about summative evaluation, after learning, instead of seeing it as central to the learning process itself. It is a mistake to only look at assessment as reflection on action and ignore its importance as a tool for reflection in action so that the teaching–learning process can be enhanced while it is ongoing. To what extent and how do you use formative evaluation? To what extent do your summative evaluations give you a realistic picture of what students have learned deeply enough to remember long term and apply to new situations?

Another common preconception is that assessments must be quantitative, yielding a grade or score. However, qualitative assessments, such as the types of errors or confusions characterizing students' performance, can contain vitally important information for improving learning and instruction. Do you use both qualitative and quantitative assessments? How do you use the results of each?

A modern classic on assessment, *Knowing What Students Know,* has research-based recommendations from many and diverse experts who conducted a three-year study sponsored by the National Research Council. One of its principles is that assessment results should be used to improve teaching and learning, which requires thinking reflectively about assessment methods and outcomes.

⚔ Authentic Assessment

Recent research suggests that measurement strategies should be authentic in order to give meaningful evaluations of what has been learned. Authentic assessment is defined as evaluation methods that reflect real-world applications of the knowledge or skills that are being assessed. If you're assessing reflective thinking, then to be authentic the assessments should require everyday life applications of reflective thinking, such as deciding which methods are best for completing particular tasks.

Some teachers begin planning their lessons with authentic assessments as the desired outcome, and work backward from what they want students to do when assessed to designing lessons that prepare students for successful performance on authentic assessment tasks. This backward planning requires reflecting on the expected outcomes and choosing the most effective instructional materials and activities. TeacherVision cites the following as examples of authentic assessment tasks:

- do science experiments;
- conduct social-science research;
- write stories and reports;
- read and interpret literature;
- solve math problems that have real-world applications.

A four-step process for creating authentic assessments and a "toolbox" for authentic assessment are available online at http://jonathan.mueller.faculty .noctrl.edu/toolbox/. The Web site provides details on and guides teachers in implementing these four steps:

1. Identify the standards.
2. Select an authentic task.
3. Identify task criteria.
4. Create a rubric.

In addition to the many online resources for authentic assessment in general, there are Web sites for subject-specific online assessments, one of which focuses on mathematics: http://mathforum.org/sum94/project2.html.

⚔ Classroom Assessment Techniques

A modern classic, "Classroom Assessment Techniques," is an outstanding resource on assessment methods. It includes tools for both formative and summative assessments. Reflective thinking guided the authors' selection of assessment instruments based on criteria including whether the assessment would help them determine what students were learning in individual classrooms, whether there were implications for how teachers could change their behavior to improve student learning, whether the techniques were relatively easy to develop, and whether the results were easy to analyze and use.

One category of assessments focuses on subject matter learning and includes these five techniques: Focused Listing, Memory Matrix, Background Knowledge Probes, Directed Paraphrasing, and Documented Problem-Set Solutions. The Focused Listing procedure requires critical thinking as students list ideas that are central to an important topic. This technique helps the teacher assess the extent to which students recognize the most important points from a specific lesson or topic.

Many students have trouble differentiating important ideas from details, and this technique helps teachers determine whether students are seeing the forest or are caught up in the trees. Focused Listing can be implemented with individuals, pairs, or groups, and can be applied to a lecture students listen to, a videotape they watch, information from a site on the Internet, or something they read in their textbooks.

Memory Matrix is a two-dimensional table of rows and columns used to quickly assess what students remember about important content from a course and to judge their ability to organize that information into meaningful categories. Background Knowledge Probes are questions presented to students before material is covered to determine what they already know about the topic. They help teachers plan the most effective way to begin teaching the content to their students.

Directed Paraphrase requires students to explain what they learned to a particular audience using their own words. It helps teachers assess students' understanding and memory of important information. Documented Problem-Set Solutions require students to write down and explain steps they take in problem solving so they realize that solving problems effectively requires more than getting the correct answer, including reflection and understanding the problem solving process.

Another assessment category, which focuses on critical thinking, includes the Defining Features Matrix, Pro and Con Grid, Categorizing Grid, and Analytical Memos. In the Defining Features Matrix, students identify attributes of particular concepts. For example, should research for a report on environmental pollution be conducted using articles from the library or from the Web? What are the defining features of library material? What are the defining features of the Internet? Both are viable options for research, but by using this technique students (and teachers) are able to assess the advantages and disadvantages of each. Understanding the defining features of library versus web-based information helps students and teachers reflect on and critically evaluate the relative value of different information sources. For a concise summary of many of the Classroom Assessment Techniques, see http://www.utexas.edu/academic/diia/gsi/assessment/cats.pdf.

⚔ Characteristics of Effective Assessments

To be effective, assessment must include measurable goals, standards, and specific criteria against which to measure attainment, with honest, descriptive feedback that can be used to guide further teaching and learning. The eight steps below, on "Assessment as Feedback" from the New Horizons for Learning Web site, summarize key principles of good feedback previously identified by Thomas Gilbert in *Human Competence*. (See http://www.newhorizons.org/strategies/assess/wiggins.htm.)

1. Identify the expected accomplishments.
2. State the requirements of each accomplishment. If there is any doubt that people understand the reason why an accomplishment and its requirements are important, explain this.
3. Describe how performance will be measured and why.
4. Set exemplary standards, preferably in measurement terms.
5. Identify exemplary performers and any available resources that people can use to become exemplary performers.
6. Provide frequent and unequivocal feedback about how well each person is performing. This confirmation should be expressed as a comparison with an exemplary standard. Consequences of good and poor performance should also be made clear.
7. Supply as much backup information as needed to help people troubleshoot their own performance.
8. Relate various aspects of poor performance to specific remedial actions.

At this Web site, it is pointed out that students need both feedback and guidance from teachers. Feedback is defined as "information about what happened, the result or effect of our actions." In contrast, guidance is defined as giving future direction: what to do in light of what just happened. If you make a comment such as "Good work" on a student's paper, make sure that you explain specifically what in their work was good so students can use that information to guide their future performance. What strategies do you use to provide students with both feedback and guidance? What kinds of comments do you make? To what extent do you back up your comments with specific examples?

For assessment to be effective, there should be a continuous process of performance and assessment constituting a "feedback loop." Successful performance depends on having a "deliberate system of feedback loops" so that there are repeated opportunities to improve based on knowledge of results and strategies for revising and refining one's actions. To what extent do your assessment practices involve such feedback loops?

To be most effective for improving performance, students should receive feedback while they are engaged in the learning activities. The most useful feedback is given concurrent with performance (reflection in action), rather than after the performance has been completed (reflection on action). If the situation requires reflection on action, such as after students have taken a test, then to be most useful for students the feedback should be provided as soon as possible after they have taken the test. When do you provide your students with feedback on their performance?

All the feedback and guidance provided should be linked to instructional goals you previously explicitly and clearly communicated to the students. The feedback and guidance should also be related to strategies and skills that you recommended for achieving these goals. Otherwise, students are not likely to be able to take responsibility for adjusting their knowledge and study strategies/skills so they can improve their own performance based on your comments. To what extent do the feedback and guidance you provide directly connect with goals and strategies you have communicated to your students?

To what extent do you think about your assessment techniques and how well they measure what you have identified as important instructional goals? Research on assessing hands-on science suggests that there should be symmetry between curriculum and assessment, that assessment should be continuous, and that performance measures are needed to supplement traditional multiple-choice-type assessments in order to get a comprehensive picture of student achievement. Performance measures should emphasize science process skills, such as observing and inferring, not just getting the right answer.

Four performance assessments that can be used to assess science achievement are

1. lab notebooks recording students' procedures and conclusions;
2. computer simulations of hands-on investigations;
3. short answer paper-and-pencil problems in planning, analyzing, and/or interpreting experiments;
4. multiple-choice items developed from observations of students conducting hands-on investigations.

Effective performance assessment requires multiple iterations to revise performance based on students' experiences and feedback. Research suggests that shortcutting this process often leads to poor assessment and low-quality classroom instruction. Feedback is important for students in several ways: It helps them assess their mastery of course material, helps them assess their use of thinking and learning strategies, and helps them connect their efforts and strategies to their academic outcomes. The primary benefit of feedback is the identification of errors of knowledge and understanding and assistance with correcting those errors. Feedback generally improves subsequent performance on similar items. Research suggests that feedback can guide students in their use of learning strategies.

Research on how experts differ from novices in a subject can be useful for thinking about what to include in your assessments, as experts organize and use their information differently than novices. Most of the chapters in this book address the expert/novice distinction and therefore can provide subject-specific information to guide your assessments. As a teacher, your goal is to help your students, subject area novices, learn to think more like you, a subject area expert, in the content you're teaching. The modern classic, *How People Learn*, has a chapter devoted to this issue. Additionally, its chapter on Designing a Learning Environment discusses characteristics of an Assessment-Centered Learning

Environment, which can help you use assessments for both reflecting in action and reflecting on action.

⚔ Rubrics

Reflective thinking can be promoted by using rubrics for assessments. A rubric is a set of criteria or standards that are used to evaluate performance. By giving students a rubric on how you will evaluate their work, you can help them reflect on and critically evaluate whether and the extent to which they are meeting your objectives. But you can also teach students to create their own rubrics in cooperation with you. By giving them an opportunity to participate in establishing their own criteria, they may feel ownership, empowered, and motivated to meet the assessment standards. Student generation of assessment rubrics has been successfully achieved with middle school students.

A link to information on this effort is available at what is probably the most outstanding resource on assessment available free online, Kathy Schrock's page, "Teacher Helpers: Assessment and Rubric Information." It includes a wide variety of rubrics, from evaluating WebQuests to evaluating cooperative learning to subject-specific rubric links including evaluating physics labs! The site includes a tutorial for creating rubrics, articles on rubrics, and information on many other assessment techniques including portfolios, graphic organizers, report cards, alternative and performance-based assessments.

Rubrics can be analytical or holistic. Analytical rubrics examine one component of performance at a time. In contrast, holistic rubrics examine a group of performance components. Numerous and varied rubric resources are available at http://www.uwstout.edu/soe/profdev/rubrics.shtml.

The material in Table 7.1, from http://www.nden.k12.wi.us/tlcf/prob3.htm, is an excellent example of an analytical rubric for evaluating mathematical problem solving for use with story problems. It has a four-point scale that is applied to each of five components of solving a story problem.

Following is the Holistic Critical Thinking Rubric, an excellent and widely disseminated tool for evaluating critical thinking, which is available online at http://social.chass.ncsu.edu/slatta/hi216/learning/pnf.htm. This rubric can be used to evaluate critical thinking as applied to making a historical argument. Critical thinking by historians or anyone else requires constructing arguments based on solid evidence. In contrast, opinion, closed-mindedness, and irrationality reflect a lack of critical thinking. In such cases, one merely expresses preconceptions and biases not based on valid, supporting evidence. On the scale below, 4 represents the highest level of critical thinking whereas 1 represents the lowest level, by considering a set of characteristics rather than each characteristic individually, making it holistic rather than analytical.

4: Consistently does all or almost all of the following:

1. Accurately interprets evidence, statements, graphics, questions, etc.
2. Identifies the salient arguments (reasons and claims) pro and con.
3. Thoughtfully analyzes and evaluates major alternative points of view.

TABLE 7.1   Math Problem-Solving Rubric

Given a story problem, the student will use appropriate strategy to find the solution and use graphs and/or tables to illustrate and explain.

	Minimal(1)	Basic(2)	Proficient(3)	Advanced(4)
Understands the Problem	Student can't read problem—not sure what to do.	Student can read problem—can pull out numbers, not sure what to do.	Student can read problem, pulls out numbers, and operation may or may not be correct.	Student reads problem, pulls out numbers, and uses correct operation.
Computation	Pulls out numbers that may or may not be correct.	Pulls out numbers, operation and answer may or may not be correct.	Pulls out numbers, operation correct, answer may or may not be correct.	Pulls out numbers, operation and answer are correct.
Use of Tables/Graphs	Unsure of numbers involved, can't demonstrate how to use in table/graph.	Knows numbers involved, unsure of table/graph to use.	Knows numbers involved and table/graph to use, may or may not be completed correctly.	Knows numbers involved and puts them into table/graph correctly.
Explanation	Cannot explain why he/she did what they did.	Unclear, not concise, or incomplete.	Clear with some appropriate math language, not concise.	Clear, concise, and uses appropriate math language.
Satisfies All Requirements	Does not satisfy requirements of the problem.	Satisfies all requirements of problem, answer may or may not be correct.	Satisfies all requirements of the problem, answer partially correct.	Satisfies all requirements of the problem with correct answer.

SCORE TOTAL _____

Scoring Process **Advanced:** 19–20 **Proficient:** 15–18 No score of 2 in any area.	**Basic:** 10–14, no more than one area with a score of 1. **Minimal:** score <10

4 Draws warranted, judicious, non-fallacious conclusions.

5. Justifies key results and procedures, explains assumptions and reasons.

6. Fair-mindedly follows where evidence and reasons lead.

3: Does most or many of the following:

1. Accurately interprets evidence, statements, graphics, questions, etc.
2. Identifies relevant arguments (reasons and claims) pro and con.
3. Offers analyses and evaluations of obvious alternative points of view.
4. Draws warranted, non-fallacious conclusions.
5. Justifies some results or procedures, explains reasons.
6. Fair-mindedly follows where evidence and reasons lead.

2: Does most or many of the following:

1. Misinterprets evidence, statements, graphics, questions, etc.
2. Fails to identify strong, relevant counter-arguments.
3. Ignores or superficially evaluates obvious alternative points of view.
4. Draws unwarranted or fallacious conclusions.
5. Justifies few results or procedures, seldom explains reasons. Regardless of the evidence or reasons, maintains or defends views based on self-interest or preconceptions.

1: Consistently does all or almost all of the following:

1. Offers biased interpretations of evidence, statements, graphics, questions, information, or the points of view of others.
2. Fails to identify or hastily dismisses strong, relevant counter-arguments.
3. Ignores or superficially evaluates obvious alternative points of view.
4. Argues using fallacious or irrelevant reasons, and unwarranted claims.
5. Does not justify results or procedures, nor explain reasons.
6. Regardless of the evidence or reasons, maintains or defends views based on self-interest or preconceptions.
7. Exhibits closed-mindedness or hostility to reason.

What do you prefer, analytical or holistic rubrics? Although holistic rubrics are more efficient for grading, they are less able to provide specific details of strengths and weaknesses. You may want to use both analytical and holistic rubrics, depending on the particular situation.

⚔ Progress Evaluations

Checklists and Progress Charts

Checklists and progress charts are additional assessment strategies that teachers and students can use to reflect on and critically evaluate performance. Checklists generally indicate presence or absence of a skill. In contrast, progress charts show nuances of skill development A sample critical thinking progress chart students might use includes critical thinking skills, such as Table 7.2, which rates progress on a scale from 1 to 5, from no progress (1) to mastery (5).

TABLE 7.2 Critical Thinking Progress Chart	
Critical Thinking Skill	**Progress Rating (1–5, No progress to mastery)**
Understand the question.	
Know how to approach it.	
Differentiate main from minor points.	
Remember important concepts.	
Consider alternative approaches.	
Judge validity of the sources.	
Judge ideas for quality.	
Consider advantages and disadvantages.	
Select and use best ideas.	
Develop plan for approach.	
Use step-by-step systematic approach.	
Express ideas clearly.	
Provide evidence to support conclusion.	
Organize answer logically.	
Check for implementation of plan.	
Check for careless mistakes.	
Use feedback to improve performance.	
Fewer errors than last time.	
Different errors from last time.	

Portfolios

Reflective thinking of both teachers and students can be promoted and assessed by using journals and/or portfolios for either formative or summative assessments. Journals are like diaries or blogs because they're records of personal experiences and opinions. Portfolios are systematic records of work samples over a period of time, which document development. They are selective and representative rather than exhaustive collections of work. Both can be used as tools for self-assessment as well as for evaluation by others. Both are ways of identifying strengths and weaknesses and of documenting progress over time.

Teaching portfolios aid reflective practice by helping you conceptualize your teaching philosophy, and coordinate it with your instructional activities and techniques. They include not only lesson plans and reflective commentary on their implementation, but also samples of students' work for analysis and evaluation. A teaching portfolio can help you reflect on your teaching goals and philosophy and how teaching and learning in your classroom are consistent with them. They can guide you in making appropriate changes to your goals, philosophy, implementation, and assessment strategies.

Master Teachers certification by the National Board for Professional Teaching Standards (NBPTS) has established high and rigorous standards for what teachers should know and be able to do in order to improve student learning. The NBPTS has developed five propositions as the foundation for its certification of Master Teachers. They are

1. Teachers are committed to their students and their learning.
2. Teachers know the subjects they teach and how to teach these subjects to their students.
3. Teachers are responsible for managing and monitoring student learning.
4. Teachers systematically think about their practice and learn from experience.
5. Teachers are members of learning communities.

To what extent are you accomplished in each of these areas? You can use a teaching portfolio to reflect on your development in these important dimensions of mastery, whether or not you want to become nationally certified as a Master Teacher.

Portfolios are useful evaluation tools for both teachers and students. They can help you reflect on and critically evaluate how and the extent to which you and your students are meeting specific academic standards. Some schools use portfolio assessment as an alternative to evaluating student achievement based on traditional teacher-made and standardized tests.

Whereas portfolios used to be hard-copy records of work products, increasingly they are constructed electronically. Many schools now require students to develop and maintain electronic or digital portfolios to document their growth and progress in learning. An article in *Educational Leadership*, "Assessment to Promote Learning," examines high school students using digital portfolios to document their learning. The portfolios include not only text-based documents, but multimedia artifacts as well. Students are required to reflect on and evaluate their work, identify at the end of the year what they did best, state how they grew as learners, and plan academic goals for the next year.

⤤ Graphic Organizers

Graphic organizers, such as concept maps, are underutilized reflective tools for assessing teachers' thinking and students' learning. If you make a graphic organizer of material or a skill you want to teach, it can help give you a big picture of your goals and expectations and help you assess where you and your students might need extra time or effort for achieving your objectives. It can also help you identify and assess students' prior knowledge that you anticipate they will bring with them from previous classes and help you prepare to assess and address common preconceptions.

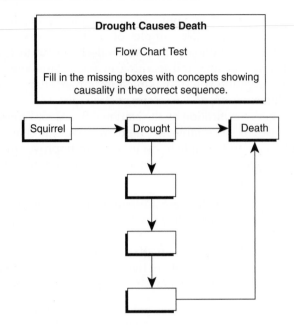

FIGURE 7.1   *Partially Completed Flow Chart Test*

Giving a partially completed flow chart, concept map, or Venn diagram for students to fill in the missing information can assess not only their content knowledge but also their understanding of how ideas relate to each other and to the big picture of the content you are covering. A partially completed flow chart can help you assess their understanding of a sequence of activities, stages, or processes. For example, if you want to evaluate students' understanding of how drought can cause the death of a squirrel, use the flow chart shown in Figure 7.1. In this chart, students are given the problem situation, a squirrel, drought, and death. Students must fill in the events induced by the drought that cause the squirrel's death, such as thirst, search for water, and no water available.

A partially completed concept map can help you assess student understanding of concepts and the precise relationships between them as identified by the linking words. To test students' understanding of the role of temperature in how ice becomes water vapor, give them a partially completed concept map such as that in Figure 7.2. Other information could be left out for different assessment goals. In this figure, most of the processes are identified and the students have to insert the correct temperatures and some of the processes at the appropriate stages of ice becoming water vapor.

A partially developed Venn diagram can help you assess students' understanding of part/whole relationships. For example, if you want to test how students would represent the concept that some animals live in the sea, give them a partially completed Venn diagram such as the one in Figure 7.3. In this figure the Venn diagram is already constructed for the students and they have to label the

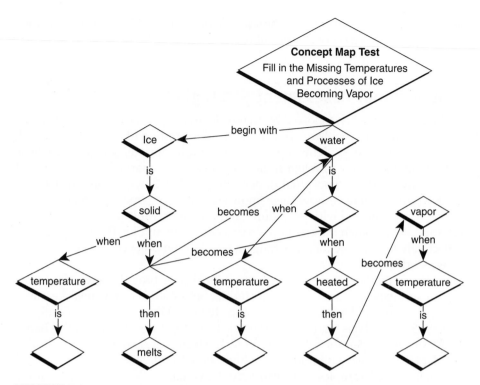

FIGURE 7.2   *Temperature and Process Test with Partially Completed Concept Map*

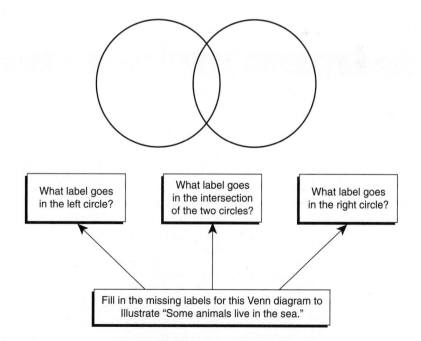

FIGURE 7.3   *Venn Diagram Test of Representation of "Some Animals Live in the Sea"*

left circle with "things that live in the sea," the right circle with "animals," and then label the center intersection "some animals live in the sea."

⚔ Additional Assessment Strategies

Problem posing, when followed by an interview, is a powerful assessment strategy for evaluating the development and understanding of concepts. Research suggests that good students are able to pose appropriate, solvable problems when responding to a problem situation or concept scenario, but they also had major flaws in their conceptual understanding. The flaws suggested that students were deficient in how their knowledge was organized in memory and how it was connected with procedures and problems. Most teachers could benefit from having such information about assessment and feedback and using it reflectively to improve their teaching and evaluation practices as well as to improve students' performance.

The handbook *Classroom Assessment Techniques* provides exercises focusing on students' self-assessments, including Self-Studies of Engaged Learning Time; Punctuated Lectures: Listen, Stop, Reflect, Write, and Give Feedback; Process Self-Analysis; and Self-Diagnostic Learning Logs. Although this handbook was developed for college teaching, the techniques are readily applicable or adaptable for use with middle and high school students.

Table 7.3, Examples of Constructivist Evaluation Tools, copied from the Internet, summarizes some recent approaches to assessment. See http://www.coe.tamu.edu/~kmurphy/classes/telecom98s/constructivist/table2.htm.

TABLE 7.3 Examples of Constructivist Evaluation Tools		
Example	**Source**	**Explanation**
Learning logs or self-studies of engaged learning time	Jonassen, 1996	Students track how long they spend on learning. Before they begin, they estimate how long they will spend learning. Then at regular 10–15 minute intervals, they log how long they actually spent learning.
Student rankings of course objectives	Jonassen, 1996	Students and teachers compare their rankings of course objectives. Teachers can use this information to facilitate learning for the student.
Think-aloud	Jonassen, 1996	As a student tries to solve a problem, s/he describes what s/he is thinking to others in a group. The group uses the information to define a procedure for solving the problem.

Example	Source	Explanation
Documented problem-set solutions	Jonassen, 1996	Similar to think-aloud, students describe what they do to solve problems—this time on paper.
Focused autobiographical sketches of students as learners	Jonassen, 1996	Before beginning a new topic, students write a 2–3 page essay on a previous learning experience on the same topic. The essay should include how successful the students were, how well they think they understood the material, and how they feel about the subject now.
Stump the teacher	Jonassen, 1996	Students think up questions that they think the teacher cannot answer. As the teacher attempts to solve the problems, he or she thinks out loud so students can follow the problem-solving process.
Cognitive interview	Jonassen, 1996	Students are asked to restate the context around a learning event. The interviewer may ask the student to restate again in a different order or to restate from a different perspective.
Essays	Jonassen, 1996	Students write an essay about a real-world problem from the perspective of a professional in the field. The audience of the essay should be one commonly associated with the problem.
Directed paraphrasing	Jonassen, 1996	Students read a selection and then restate it in their own words. This is similar to the executive summary attached to many business documents.
Analytical memos	Jonassen, 1996	Students develop an argument in a short essay. These memos can be used as a form of dialogue between the teacher, the students, and other students.
Classification/ decision matrix	Jonassen, 1996	Students list all items to be classified within a content domain. They list the features of the content domain. Then they match the examples to the features. This is similar to creating a database on paper.

(*continued*)

TABLE 7.3   *(Continued)*

Example	Source	Explanation
Diaries and journals	Jonassen, 1996	Students reflect on what they know and what they have learned. The teacher and student initiate a dialogue within the context of the journal.
Exhibits	Jonassen, 1996	Students put on a demonstration or live performance for the class or other audiences.
Experiments	Jonassen, 1996	Students perform hands-on laboratory work. This is not limited to science classes.
Concept maps	Jonassen, 1996	Students create a picture of how their knowledge is organized.
Oral debates	Jonassen, 1996	Students present and defend positions. They must be able to think on their feet.
Dramatic or musical performances	Jonassen, 1996	Students perform before a live audience.
Invented dialogue	Jonassen, 1996	Students create a conversation between historical characters to illustrate different sides of an issue.
Game creation	Rieber, 1996	Students create games within a content area. They must organize and synthesize their knowledge of the content domain in order to make the game work.
Virtual reality (VR) creation	Cronin, 1997	Students create virtual worlds to represent their knowledge.
Portfolios	McLellan, 1993	Portfolios can include recording learners' best compositions, game performances, multimedia projects, artwork, or problem solutions. Portfolios can be put on a CD, videotaped, and/or placed on local open access cable TV.

New trends in measurement, which are actual learning experiences, can help both teachers and students gain insights about their learning successes and difficulties and help them build on strengths and overcome weaknesses. These assessments require teachers and students to reflect on and critically evaluate their thinking and learning processes and outcomes.

Another good resource on a variety of assessments that can promote reflective and critical thinking is a special issue of *Educational Leadership* called "Assessment to Promote Learning." The lead article, "Seven Practices for Effective Learning," illustrates a rubric for evaluating students' graphic displays of data. It includes a three-point scale, with one showing little achievement and three showing a high level of achievement. Four categories are assessed: title of the graph, labels on the graph, accuracy of the data displayed, and neatness/readability of the graph. The scale and categories are represented in a chart. Below the chart is space for teachers to enter comments and identify goals/actions. This combination of quantitative and qualitative feedback can help students reflect on and critically evaluate their progress and plan for future improvements.

Another article in this issue addressed benchmark assessments. Are your students required to take state-sponsored benchmark tests? Do you administer your own benchmark tests in your classes? Benchmark assessments are formative evaluations, now required by many states, to monitor student progress in meeting standards before students have to take high-stake tests, summative evaluations that might be required for high school graduation.

Benchmarks can be useful tools for helping teachers and students reflect on and critically evaluate progress on meeting city, state, and/or national standards. The article on benchmarks emphasizes aligning the test with standards and curriculum, using the results for diagnostic purposes, and making the results user-friendly so it's clear how to help students achieve at higher levels.

⚔ Reflective Thinking on Tests

When your students get the wrong answer on an objective test, such as multiple choice, does that really mean that they don't know the material you were testing for? When students get the right answer, does that mean that they do know the material? You get glimpses into students' thinking on a multiple-choice (or true/false or matching) test by requiring them to explain their answers. Ask them to do "thought reports" explaining their answer choices. You're likely to discover that sometimes "Right is Wrong and Wrong is Right"! In some cases, students get the right answer for the wrong reason, whereas in other cases, they get the wrong answer, but their reasoning shows that they know the material you were testing them for, but somehow were confused by the question.

Research shows that asking students to explain their answers to test questions can be surprising and enlightening by revealing that sometimes students know more than you think just as sometimes they know less than you think! It's best to prepare students in advance for this type of test (multiple-choice items as described below), and give them guidelines about what constitutes good and bad thought reports.

Having such guidelines is especially beneficial if you **assign half credit to the answer** students select and **half credit for the explanation** of their answers. Knowing that they will be graded on their explanations tends to motivate students to study in a different way for this type of multiple-choice test. They study for deep understanding of the material instead of superficial recognition of the right answer. Analysis of students' wrong answers can help you reflect on why and how students misunderstood the material, critically evaluate your teaching strategies, and help you plan to teach more effectively in the future.

"Bad" explanations are characterized by preconceptions about the material, misunderstanding, misattribution, misapplication, confusion about related concepts, problems with vocabulary, confusing part/whole relationships, omission, illogical reasoning, and giving personal opinions instead of what was taught. Sometimes students get the right answer because they make a lucky guess, and sometimes their thinking is totally off track but they get the right answer anyway. By analyzing and evaluating their thinking, you can avoid perpetuating the false impression that they know the material just because they got the right answer.

"Good" explanations are characterized by using their knowledge to eliminate answer choices they know to be wrong, elaborating on the concept focused on in the question, logical reasoning, and giving their own example of the concept being asked about. Sometimes students use good information and good reasoning, but still get an answer that differs from what you expected. By analyzing their thinking, you can avoid penalizing them for what might actually be a creative answer to a question!

This approach to assessment looks beyond the product, or answer, to the process or thinking that resulted in selection of a particular answer. It helps students think about their own thinking—making them more reflective and more critical thinkers when preparing for and taking tests as well as when receiving their grade and your feedback on their performance.

Explaining answers to multiple-choice items can be done in all subjects and at all middle and high school grade levels. It is a good way to develop students' reflective thinking about their knowledge and how to apply what they know. Essay tests have a long history of fulfilling this function, but objective test items can also promote reflective thinking for both students and teachers.

⚹ Peer and Self-Assessment

Peer Assessment

An increasingly popular assessment method, especially well-suited for promoting reflective thinking, is for students to evaluate each other's work, commonly called peer assessment. The Pair Problem-Solving method described in Chapter 8 on Reflective Teaching Strategies is a peer assessment technique that has been used successfully with minority adolescents in mathematics and science. Peer Mediation is another form of peer assessment, used to address behavior problems. It is discussed in Chapter 5 on Classroom Management.

Criteria used and insights derived from peer assessment can be used not only to help each other, but for students to evaluate their own work. Peer assessment thus can have the double benefit of also promoting students' self-assessment. The external evaluation serves as a model for internal self-assessment.

Additional benefits of peer assessment include

- promoting deep learning;
- increasing feelings of ownership over the assessment process;
- improving motivation;
- encouraging students to take responsibility for assessing their own learning, developing their ability to be independent learners;
- viewing assessment as part of learning, so that mistakes are treated as opportunities for improvement rather than as failures;
- practicing the transferable skills needed for life-long learning, especially evaluation skills;
- improving critical thinking and self-judgments about academic work.

In English, students are often asked to give each other feedback on papers they have written, a process known as "Peer Editing." As a teacher, you provide students with specific criteria to use and communicate that students are responsible for giving each other feedback on specified dimensions of their writing according to the prescribed standards. Scoring rubrics are especially useful for this purpose as they help students be objective in evaluating each other's work. Peer editing helps students think critically about each other's as well as their own writing. It is best used as a stage in the writing process, in which students can use feedback they obtain from their peers to revise their papers before turning them in to be graded.

A Web site called "Read, Write, Think," sponsored by the International Reading Association and the National Council of Teachers of English, has a lesson plan on peer editing with hot links to online resources. This lesson plan, titled "Peer Edit with Perfection: Teaching Effective Peer Editing Strategies," identifies a three-stage process: compliments, suggestions, and corrections. This site also includes a tutorial on peer editing at http://www.readwritethink.org/lessons/lesson_view.asp?id=786.

Self-Questioning

One self-assessment strategy is *self-questioning,* whereby teachers and students pose questions about their learning and answer their own questions. Self-questioning increases awareness and control over one's own thinking. Teacher examples include "How well do students understand the diagram I put on the blackboard?" "What did students find most difficult to understand in the chapter they read for homework?" Corresponding student examples are "How well did I understand the diagram the teacher put on the blackboard?" "What did I find most difficult to understand in the chapter I read for homework?" Self-questions can be used for both formative and summative assessments.

By analyzing answers to self-questions, teachers and students can critically evaluate the learning strategies, skills, and processes they used as well as critically evaluate the products of their learning activities, such as portfolios, class presentations, solutions to problems, answers to test questions, and test grades.

One English teacher had her class generate self-questions for writing a report on Gods and Goddesses. As a homework assignment, students were asked to create questions for each step in the process of writing the report. In addition to students generating their own questions, they were asked to label the types of questions they constructed. Categories included goals, planning, organizing or outlining, checking your work, and evaluating. The teacher was able to evaluate students' understanding of their writing assignment by analyzing the questions they created. She compiled a list of questions from the class and gave each student a copy to put in their notebooks to guide their writing and self-assessments. Students enjoyed the assignment and said that having the list of questions would make the process of writing the report easier. Table 7.4 lists the student-generated questions. The chapter on Mathematics illustrates a similar lesson with high school students solving a related rates problem.

TABLE 7.4   Student-Generated Writing Self-Questions

Planning: Have I	Monitoring	Pre-Evaluating	Post-Evaluating
Asked myself something like "What should I do first, second, and third?"	Have I thought about my final goals while doing the task?	Have I proofread my paper carefully at least three different times?	Have I gone over work to see where the major mistakes were?
Established my goals before beginning the task?	Have I read the first part of the task to make sure that I am on the right track?	Is there any way that this can be improved before it is handed in?	Am I able to correct the mistakes for future work or should I seek help with the corrections?
Thought about the proper way to begin?	Have I thought about whether my work so far is correct?	Have I really done my best?	What can be improved for better work next time?
Organized my thoughts before beginning?	Do I feel confident with what I have accomplished so far?		
Established a logical order or written an outline for my task?	Am I sure that I have understood the directions and am following them?		

Error Analysis

What do your students do when they get a test back after looking at their grade? How many of your students never look at the test again? How many use the test as a resource for improving their mastery of material that was on the test? Error analysis is a specialized subset of self-questioning that can be especially useful in this era of high-stakes testing due to National Assessments of Educational Progress, the importance of SAT scores for college admission, states' assessments of content standards, and the federal No Child Left Behind law. Reflective teachers use error analysis to critically evaluate their instruction; reflective learners use error analysis to critically evaluate their learning.

The error analysis procedure outlined below is a technique for converting mistakes to mastery. It provides a structured opportunity for students to learn important course content they did not get correct on the first try. By analyzing their own errors, students can identify their own learning patterns and how to improve them.

Consequently, error analysis helps develop students' critical thinking about their own learning and test performance. It also helps students learn to connect their actions—for example, specific learning strategies—to their outcomes, such as grades on tests. The more students can connect their own outcomes to their own actions, the more likely they are to self-correct and become independent, self-directed learners who plan, monitor, and evaluate their work.

As a teacher you are encouraged to apply error analysis to two situations:

1. Teaching students to learn from their mistakes by figuring out what they got wrong, why, and how they will prevent future similar mistakes, thereby transforming failure into success.
2. Learning from your own mistakes in teaching by engaging in the same reflective thinking processes.

For both teachers and students, error analysis has three basic stages:

1. A. What did I do or get wrong? B. What is the right way or right answer?
2. Why did I make that specific mistake?
3. A. How can I use this information to make sure that I don't make the same mistake again? B. What specific strategy can I use to remember the correct information or approach?

Teacher Example

Science Test Situation: Over 75 percent of the class got the wrong answer to a question on what causes the change in seasons. Most said it was due to the distance of the earth from the sun.

1. What did I do wrong and what should I have done?

I didn't pay enough attention to the ideas students had about this topic before we covered it in class. I knew that they had some preconceptions about the importance of the distance of the earth from the sun, but I didn't make specific efforts to provide them with experiences that would help them see the limitations of their prior knowledge and understand why the correct reason is based on the tilt of the earth.

2. Why did I make this mistake?

I thought that my explanation and blackboard drawings were detailed and clear enough to overcome the invalid prior knowledge students brought to class.

3. A. How can I use this information to make sure that I don't make the same mistake again?

Next time, instead of just explaining the tilt of the earth to students, I'll have concrete objects representing the sun, moon, and earth for students to actually manipulate when I explain what does and doesn't happen. Instead of just listening to me, students will actively work with the concepts and discover the limitations of their prior knowledge.

B. What specific strategy can I use to remember the correct approach? I wrote in red on a large sticky note how many students missed the question on this test and gave the same wrong answer. Also, I described exactly what activities students will do to help them overcome this very common preconception, which several students have in every class I've ever taught. The sticky note is on the front page of my file of this content so I'll automatically see it next time I review the notes in preparation to teach this lesson. The sticky note begins with big red letters saying "Telling is necessary but not sufficient"!

Student Examples

Reading Comprehension Test Item

The content in paragraph 3 of this essay indicates that the writer's belief was

a. The first stage of the civil rights movement was a failure.
b. Supreme Court decisions do not have as much influence on society as actions by the Congress.
c. Social movements are able to influence the political process.
d. The costs of civil disobedience sometimes outweigh the benefits.

Error Analysis of Item

1. What I got wrong and what the right answer is.

I thought the answer was (a): The first stage of the civil rights movement was a failure. Now I know the answer is (c): Social movements are able to influence the political process.

2. Why I got it wrong.

I confused my beliefs with what was actually in the text. I thought of what the author called "the first stage" as a failure, but the author didn't say or imply that. The author was really trying to make a different point.

3. How I will remember this and prevent future similar mistakes.

My teacher taught me to ask myself questions about what I read. So I'll ask myself a question like, "Is this what I think or is this what the author is really saying?" Then I'll look back at the text to make sure it was something that the author actually said or implied instead of something based on my own ideas.

I'll remember to ask myself questions while taking a test by tying a string around my wrist before taking a test. I don't usually wear a string so seeing it will remind me to ask myself questions about my answers to the test questions.

Error Analysis of Essay

1. What I got wrong and what I should have done.

There were two major things wrong with my paper. First, I didn't elaborate on my ideas enough. I should have developed the ideas in my topic sentences more and given more examples to support my points.

The paper was not as well organized as it should have been. In some paragraphs the ideas I started off with were not related to later ideas in the paragraph. Then in the next paragraph I would pick up on ideas I started in the previous one. I should have followed through with related ideas in the same paragraph instead of jumping around.

2. Why I did this wrong.

I was so concerned about coming up with ideas and getting them on paper that I didn't pay that much attention to where the ideas were and how organized it was.

3. How I will prevent similar mistakes in the future.

I'm going to make a checklist to use when I revise and proofread my papers. One thing on the checklist will be Development of Ideas. Another thing will be Organization of Ideas.

Error Analysis of Research Report

1. What I got wrong and what I should have done.

I lost credit because I did not cite the sources of my information in the text. I should have put the authors' names and publication years at the end of the information I got from them.

2. Why I did this wrong.

In elementary school we didn't have to do this, so I didn't know it was the correct procedure. I didn't understand "plagiarism." I also didn't read the assignment sheet carefully enough to see this was required. I just read it to get a general idea of what was expected and missed some details.

3. How I will prevent similar mistakes in the future.

I'll remember to cite my sources in the text because I'll think about how I would feel if someone took my ideas and didn't give me credit for them. I'll also read my assignment sheets more carefully, looking for specific details instead of general ideas.

Math Problem

Subtract

$$
\begin{array}{r}
2668 \\
-1629 \\
\hline
1049
\end{array}
$$

Error Analysis of Item

1. What I got wrong and what the right answer is.

The answer 1049 is wrong. The correct answer is 1039.

2. Why I got it wrong.

I forgot to change the "6" in the tens column to a "5" after borrowing to subtract 9 from 18 in the ones column.

3. How I will prevent mistakes like this in the future.

From now on, instead of trying to remember I borrowed in my head, I will cross out the number I borrowed from, and write the new number above it. For example,

$$
\begin{array}{r}
5 \\
26\cancel{6}8 \\
-1629 \\
\hline
1039
\end{array}
$$

Biology Test Item

Which of the following is correct for the **resting** membrane potential of a typical neuron?

   a.   It is negative outside compared to inside.

   b.   It depends on high permeability of the membrane to sodium and potassium ions.

   c.   It carries impulses from one region to another.

   d.   It results from the unequal distribution of ions across the membrane.

Error Analysis of Item

1. What I got wrong and what the right answer is.

I thought the answer was (b): It depends on high permeability of the membrane to sodium and potassium ions. Now I know the answer is (d): It results from the unequal distribution of ions across the membrane.

2. Why I got it wrong.

I know there was high permeability to potassium but I forgot it was impermeable to sodium.

3. How I will remember this and prevent future similar mistakes.

I'll remember that the resting potential of a neuron depends on the imbalance. The unequal distribution of ions results from the difference in permeability between sodium and potassium. The membrane is highly permeable to potassium, but it is impermeable to sodium. This causes it to be negative inside compared to the outside.

I'll also try to use the process of elimination more so I can rule out some of the answer choices.

Both self-questioning and error analysis promote critical thinking about oneself and deeper understanding of personal successes and failures. The goal is to use these insights to increase personal awareness and self-control, thereby improving performance in future similar situations.

⚔ Technology

Earlier in this chapter videotaping your teaching was discussed, and an online rubric for assessing critical thinking was presented. Online authentic assessment resources were also identified. Numerous other technological resources are available on assessments that facilitate reflective and critical thinking, some of which have already been discussed in this chapter.

One Web site, About: Secondary School Educators, found at http://712educators.about.com/cs/ctassessment/index.htm, sponsors links to critical thinking skills assessment for teachers to assess their students' critical thinking and for students to assess their own critical thinking.

The Assessment Resource Center, at http://www.umuc.edu/odell/irahe/arc/4gen_ct.html, has links to a variety of tools for assessing general education skills, including critical thinking. This site gives a broad view of the critical thinking skills and dispositions your students will need in college so you can help prepare them before they get there. A site for free online tests of thinking, located at http://www.testingthinking.com/thinking/ns/, specifically addresses developing and assessing critical thinking for students in preschool, elementary school, middle school, high school, and higher education.

Summary

Assessment is more than feedback, and includes both reflection in action and reflection on action. It's important to do both formative and summative assessments. Many assessment techniques exist now so teachers are no longer limited to using tests to evaluate students' progress in learning. Recent work has emphasized use of alternative and authentic measurement strategies such as portfolios and rubrics. To be effective, assessment should be instrumental in aiding learning and not just judging it. Providing feedback and guidance based on assessment results are important dimensions of effective assessments. Having students reflect on their responses to test items, explaining and analyzing their answers, can improve teaching and learning. Numerous and varied assessment resources for teachers, peers, and students' self-assessment are available online.

Resources

Angleo, T.; and K. P. Cross. *Classroom Assessment Techniques: A Handbook for Faculty.* 2nd ed. San Francisco: Jossey-Bass, 1993.

Assessment to Promote Learning. *Educational Leadership* 63, no. 3, 2005. Whole issue.

Assessment Resource Center, Critical Thinking. General Education Skills Assessment. 2005. Retrieved August 2, 2007 from http://www.umuc.edu/odell/irahe/arc/4gen_ct.html.

Brown, S.; C. Rust; and G. Gibbs. *Strategies for Diversifying Assessment in Higher Education.* Oxford: Oxford Centre for Staff Development, 1994.

Bullock, A. A.; and P. Hawk. *Developing a Teaching Portfolio: A Guide for Preservice and Practicing Teachers.* Upper Saddle River, NJ: Prentice Hall, 2001.

Facione, P. A.; and N. C. Facione. Holistic Critical Thinking Rubric. 1994. Retrieved October 2, 2006 from http://social.chass.ncsu.edu/slatta/hi216/learning/pnf.htm.

Hartman, H. J. Developing Students' Metacognitive Knowledge and Skills. In *Metacognition in Learning and Instruction: Theory, Research & Practice,* ed. H. J. Hartman. Dordrecht: Springer, 2001.

Lyons, N. "How Portfolios Can Shape Emerging Practice." *Educational Leadership.* May 1999, pp. 63–65.

National Research Council. *How People Learn: Mind, Brain, Experience and School.* Washington, D.C.: National Academy Press, 2000.

National Research Council. *Knowing what Students Know: The Science and Design of Educational Assessment.* Washington, D.C.: National Academy Press, 2001.

Novak, J. *Learning, Creating and Using Knowledge: Concept Maps as Facilitative Tools in Schools and Corporations.* Mahwah, NJ: Erlbaum, 1998.

Schrock, K. Assessment and Rubric Information. 2007. Retrieved August 2, 2007 from http://school.discovery.com/schrockguide/assess.html.

Secondary School Educators. Critical Thinking Assessment. 2007. Retrieved August 2, 2007 from http://712educators.about.com/cs/ctassessment/index.htm.

TeacherVision. Pearson Education Development Group. 2007. Authentic Assessment Overview. Retrieved August 2, 2007 from http://www.teachervision.fen.com/teaching-methods-and-management/educational-testing/4911.html.

The Critical Thinking Company. Testing Thinking: Assess Critical Thinking Skills Online. 2005. Retrieved August 2, 2007 from http://www.testingthinking.com/thinking/ns/.

Wiggins, G. Assessment as Feedback. New Horizons for Learning. 2004. Retrieved August 13, 2007 from http://www.newhorizons.org/strategies/assess/wiggins.htm.

8

Teaching Strategies to Promote Reflection

This book explores a style of teaching that will enhance reflective and critical thinking abilities in both teachers and students. The goal is to promote meaningful learning, retention, application, and transfer of what is learned and to foster independent, reflective thinking and learning. Teaching reflectively requires reflecting in as well as on action. Teacher self-questions in particular subject areas can facilitate instructional management by stimulating your thinking about how to plan, monitor, and evaluate lessons in different content areas. The techniques outlined in this chapter will help students succeed academically by making learning more meaningful and thinking more reflective.

Reflective thinking, critical thinking, and meaningfulness each require thought. Sometimes students resist thinking because it can be hard work! The techniques introduced here are intended to prevent memorization without understanding, often referred to as "rote learning." Minimize this type of learning.

Techniques covered here include questioning strategies, thinking aloud, problem solving, and cooperative learning. Other chapters in the book explain the teaching strategies of self-questioning, reciprocal teaching, graphic organizers, mental imagery, role playing, scaffolding, learning cycle, and structured controversy.

A majority of teaching techniques explored in this book promote students' active involvement in and responsibility for their own learning. Sometimes students try to manipulate teachers into letting them learn the easy way, by simply *telling* students the material they need to know so they can produce correct answers even if they don't understand them. "Spoon-feeding" is only efficient in the short run, like the famous old Chinese proverb about being given a fish rather than being taught to fish. Research has shown that when teachers apply the instructional techniques in this chapter, students become more active, reflective, and independent learners.

❧ Questioning

Why is questioning one of the most effective teaching techniques? Think about and record all of the types and functions you can think of regarding the use of questions in teaching. Think about questioning very broadly, both from the point of view of you asking your students questions and your students asking you questions. What do you see as the functions of questions?

Questions are powerful teaching, thinking, and learning tools that have a broad range of potential applications. They are especially useful for developing reflective and critical thinking, which is why they are used so extensively in this chapter and throughout the book. Question functions include checking understanding, clarifying assignments, making students talk, diagnosing students' problems, helping students understand their own strengths and weaknesses, narrowing a topic, obtaining information, making students think, helping students organize their thoughts, increasing students' interest, generating alternate approaches, putting events into larger perspectives, and summarizing.

Research on classroom instruction shows that most of it consists of information transmission. Students' minds are treated as glasses to be filled with the vintage wisdom of authority. Relatively little questioning occurs, and when it does, most of it requires relatively low-level responses. There is evidence that when teachers ask mainly low-level questions (What is the name of . . . ?, How would you describe . . . ?) student achievement does not reach levels as high as it does when students are asked mostly higher-level questions (What do you think is the most important . . . ?, How would you approach . . . ?).

When during instruction are learners' questions most useful for comprehension? Research tells us that questions most effectively aid understanding when answered while students are in the process of using the knowledge they have acquired. This is because clarification of confusing content is more likely to occur while students are **applying** knowledge and skills than while **acquiring** them.

Leading Discussions

Discussing assignments, concepts, skills, attitudes, and strategies is a common occurrence in teaching. Wilbert McKeachie, a prominent expert on teaching, identifies several types of questions that can be used to skillfully stimulate and guide discussions. Although it is better for most discussions to have a problem solving type of orientation, periodically it is necessary to ask factual questions to check students' background knowledge. For example, What is the definition of the "cold war"?

Following are types of discussion questions.

- Interpretation and application questions can help improve students' understanding of the material they are learning. For example, What do you think were the causes of the "cold war"? These types of questions are more effective for stimulating discussions than factual questions.
- Problem questions are those that emerge from problems or particular cases to be solved. They help students with problem solving. For example, What might be a good way to approach that problem?
- Connective, comparative, and causal questions are good for helping students see relationships in material or concepts. For example, How is this problem similar to the last one?

- Evaluative questions require judgment. For example, Why do you think this other way of organizing your paper would be better than the way it is organized now?
- Critical questions can help students learn to challenge assumptions and conclusions and think for themselves. For example, Do you think the author presented enough convincing evidence to support her conclusion?

Reflecting on your own teaching style, which types of these questions do you tend to ask most often? Which might you ask more of?

In addition to improving your own questioning skills, you can also help your students learn to ask better questions by following guidelines — knowing what, when/why, and how to use them. Only knowing **what** question to ask is not nearly as useful as also knowing **when and why** to ask various questions and **how** to ask them. The following guidelines can be applied to questioning in general and to particular types of questions.

> **What:** Evoke information from students rather than telling it to them. Ask questions, elicit answers, and encourage students to think out loud.
>
> **When:** Asking questions is an excellent way to determine what students know and/or understand. Once the knowledge base is determined, more questions can be used to build progressively more knowledge and understanding or to guide solving a problem.
>
> **Why:** Students learn best when they are actively engaged with the material and when material to be learned is built on their own knowledge and experience. Starting from what students know provides the basis for building a more solid foundation. Eliciting helps you provoke students into thinking their way toward understanding. It also enables you to test students' knowledge without first reciting a great deal of material. Students thus become more self-directed learners.
>
> **How:** Don't tell; elicit. Ask questions. Turn students' questions around. Refuse to give out information; if possible, draw it out instead. Emphasize intermediate- and high-level questions because they promote more complex thinking and thorough understanding than low-level questions.

Listen more than you speak. Listen to students' answers/thoughts to determine what they do and don't know or understand. Students will make better progress through a questioning approach than with a lecture or telling approach. Table 8.1 lists some examples of eliciting information by questioning and compares them to examples of telling.

A major tension that exists between teachers and students is caused by the difference in their ways of organizing knowledge. Rather than teaching separate pieces of information, teach the organization of the material emphasizing the importance of the big picture. One approach for introducing students to the idea of forming their own knowledge structures (organizations) is the technique of teaching students to use questioning techniques. In the beginning, teachers ask the questions, but the long-term objective is to teach students the skills of

TABLE 8.1 Stimulate Reflection by Asking Instead of Telling	
Eliciting (Do)	**Telling (Don't Do)**
What are the most important ideas in that section of the story?	The most important ideas in that section of the story are that the inventor developed a new type of airplane and that someone was interfering with her getting a patent for it.
What could you infer about a cause of pollution based on this paragraph?	Based on this paragraph, mercury is one cause of pollution.
What is an element?	An element is a basic unit of matter.
What were some of the long-lasting effects of the French Revolution?	Long-lasting effects of the French Revolution were increasing the values of liberty and equality.
What are the important things to consider for solving this problem?	Important things to consider for solving this problem include identifying what is given and what is to be found.
Which tense should you use in this paragraph? Why?	In this paragraph, use the future tense because the events discussed will occur a year from now.
How would you produce a constant level of acceleration if you decreased the force?	To produce a constant level of acceleration, mass must change in direct proportion to the force.

self-questioning. Self-questioning has been demonstrated to be an effective instructional technique because it requires

- active processing;
- reflecting on one's own thinking;
- recalling prior knowledge.

Teaching students how to manage their work by planning, monitoring, and evaluating helps develop their critical thinking skills. Management strategies for academic work are discussed in Chapter 6 on Students' Reflective and Critical Thinking. The "I DREAM of A" approaches to writing and math/science, which also emphasize these processes, are discussed in the chapters on English and Mathematics.

Question Types and Levels

One difficulty teachers have with using questioning techniques is not recognizing that some types of questions are better than others. For example, open-ended questions are usually better than closed questions and intermediate- and higher-level questions are generally better than lower-level questions. Although students learn most when you ask intermediate- and higher-level questions, lower-level questions can be used to build to these higher levels.

Bloom's (1958) taxonomy of cognitive objectives is often used by teachers to formulate different types and levels of questions. Bloom identified six types of questions and arranged them in a hierarchy. The hierarchy is knowledge (demonstrate ability to identify facts), comprehension (demonstrate understanding), application (show how to use an idea or skill), analysis (break a problem or concept into parts), synthesis (combine parts into a whole), and evaluation (make a judgment). The hierarchy assumes that as you move from low to high level (from knowledge to evaluation), each of the lower levels is assumed to be required for the next higher level. For example, knowledge is required for answering comprehension questions, and knowledge and comprehension are both required for answering application questions, and so forth. Recently, "create" has been added to the end of this taxonomy, after evaluate, thus making it the highest level. Details are available online at http://www.nwrel.org/scpd/sslc/institutes_2007/documents/forum_4/holden/bloomrevised.pdf.

Research shows that most questioning by teachers occurs at the low end of the taxonomy, with knowledge and comprehension questions, which results in lower levels of student achievement than when instructors ask mostly high-level questions. Higher-level questions help students

- think abstractly;
- experience and resolve discrepancies, thereby promoting reorganization and development of thought;
- manipulate information acquired;
- think about material more deeply and thoroughly.

A different questioning taxonomy consists of low-, intermediate-, and higher-level thinking.

TABLE 8.2   Question Levels, Types, Examples

Question Level	Sample Words or Directions	Examples
Low	label demonstrate define give attributes describe	What's the author's name? What is the topic of your paper? What is an asymptote? What is a recessive trait? What is the law of chemical equilibrium?
Intermediate	sequence classify enumerate synthesize reproduce compare contrast	What type of novel is this? Which point in your paper does that example illustrate? In what order will you perform those operations? How is the heart like a pump?
High	evaluate transform conclude predict generalize propose alternatives resolve conflict infer affect or cause plan verify	How do you think the story will end? What do you usually include in an opening paragraph? How can you make sure you don't have any spelling mistakes? How do you usually prepare for a multiple-choice test? How else could you solve this problem? What conclusions can you draw about the best approach to use for this type of problem?

Each of the subject-specific chapters in this book has examples of these categories of low-, intermediate-, and high-level questions.

Open versus Closed Questions

One method for achieving better questions is to make them open-ended. Examples of open-ended questions are

- How do you go about taking notes in a math class?
- What's your plan for getting ready for the unit test?
- Why did you use that equation to solve the problem?

Examples of less effective, closed questions are

- Do you take notes in the art history class?
- Are you getting ready for the midterm?
- Did you use the right equation to solve the problem?

How do open-ended questions differ from the less effective closed questions? Open-ended questions require students to think more deeply about and elaborate on the information, whereas closed questions can be answered with short, even one word, responses. Open-ended questions, which often start with "how, what, or why," are frequently used to start conversations and find out how students study.

Teachers can use questioning techniques in numerous ways, including asking students questions, answering students' questions, having students predict test questions, having students ask and answer each other's questions, modeling good questions for students, teaching students to self-question, and using questions to help students analyze, organize, connect, and apply material they have learned.

Prior Knowledge

Students usually come to class with more knowledge and skills than they or their teachers realize. The knowledge and skills students bring with them are critical building blocks because they hold the keys to meaningful learning. When instruction emphasizes meaningful learning, students are more likely to understand and retain what they learn. Throughout this book you will find questions designed to activate your prior knowledge of topics covered. These are intended to help make what you are learning here more meaningful by encouraging reflection and making connections with new material.

One of the first things to do when teaching is to assess the quantity and quality of the students' background information in the area targeted for instruction. If you just assume that students have minimal prior knowledge about a topic, and give them a lecture covering important content, you risk boring students with what they already know as well as losing valuable instructional time.

"Why" questions, which require students to elaborate on ideas, have been demonstrated to be effective both when students do have prior knowledge about a topic and when students do not have prior knowledge. When students do not have substantial prior knowledge, "why" questions help focus their attention on the information to be learned. When students do have prior knowledge, why questions help them connect the new material to their existing knowledge.

A key feature that separates young children from older learners is that older learners have a greater need to have their prior knowledge and experience validated. Sometimes prior knowledge reflects a correct understanding of concepts and sometimes it contains preconceptions. Some of these are caused by limited past experience and some are due to misinterpretations of previous experience.

One common naïve theory that many low-achieving students have is that "learning always comes easy" to students who do well. They don't realize academic success is often borne out of struggle. So these erroneous understandings can occur both with ideas about **how** students learn as well as with **what** ideas they learn. Preconceptions can form the basis of strongly held beliefs that are resistant to conventional instruction. By identifying and addressing students' prior knowledge, you can help them learn to use the correct ideas as building blocks and to eliminate the incorrect ideas that interfere with learning. Research shows that the best way to overcome preconceptions is to provide students with experiences that allow them to confront the erroneous ideas and have them discover for themselves why those ideas are not valid.

Another reason for eliciting students' prior knowledge before teaching new material is that if the existing information is activated during learning, it will be easier for students to remember the new material because it will be stored with the prior knowledge. Otherwise, students tend to treat new material in isolation, not connecting it to what they already know. Storing new material with prior knowledge makes the new material easier to understand, remember, and use.

The 6PQ Method of Discovery Learning described next offers a reasonable way to find out what students already know about a subject and, at the same time, credits them for that prior knowledge. The 6PQ method systematically uses students' prior knowledge as a stepping-stone for discovery.

6PQ Method of Discovery Learning

The 6PQ Method is a six-step question process that was developed in a tutoring context at Oregon's Chemeketa Community College. It has been adapted successfully for use in many teaching situations. It is a questioning procedure for guiding students' thinking while avoiding telling or lecturing. The goal of guiding the students is for them to arrive at the answer rather than be given the answer. Each of the types of questions can be described by one of six words, each beginning with the letter P. As a student responds to each question, the teacher enhances the process by frequently paraphrasing the response to verify that the teacher understands what the student has said.

At the end of a 6PQ sequence it is helpful to have the student summarize what was learned. This has the potential of greatly improving the student's understanding and retention of the information. It will also help you assess what was learned. Sometimes it's surprising to discover that students' summaries don't match your expectations.

The 6PQ Method becomes more valuable with each use. It does not have to be used in its complete form at all times. The only steps that should always

TABLE 8.3   6PQ Method of Discovery Learning

Stage in Process	Action	Examples
1. Preface	Establish rapport and determine the topic.	How did your homework go last night? Is there some way I can help you today? What did you have trouble with?
2. Pace	Determine what the student already knows. Elicit relevant prior knowledge and experience.	What do you know about...? What do you already know about writing a persuasive essay? Have you ever been persuaded by something you read? What can you tell me about that experience? Because you did the first part of this problem right, what can you tell me about factoring polynomials? What do you already know about mitosis?
3. Probe	Investigate the limits of the student's knowledge by seeking more detailed information.	How do you know that? Why do you think the author chose that particular setting for the crisis? What are the goals of a persuasive essay? What do you mean by "evidence," when you say you "need evidence to back up your argument"? How could you change that paragraph to make it more persuasive? What type of problem is this? What else can you tell me about quadratic equations? Those are the right names of the phases of mitosis; now, in what order do they occur? What happens during telophase? What does it look like?
4. Prod	Have the student make an educated guess about what the answer could be.	Ask, "What do you think the answer might be?" If you had to guess, what would you say? What might be the author's reason for choosing that setting? What do you estimate the answer to be? What do you feel may happen during telophase?
5. Prompt	Give the student a hint. You can provide simple examples of the answer in the form of a question, solve a simpler version of the same problem, or give part of an answer and have the student provide the rest.	Do you remember what you did on the last problem? It starts with the letter T. Telophase has something to do with the new nuclei.
6. Process	Have the student apply the content/skill. Help the student to see other applications for the information or help to make connections to larger issues.	How could you use the skills of persuasion in your everyday life—with your family, friends, and at work? How does your understanding of mitosis help you learn about meiosis?

occur are 1 (preface), 2 (pace), and 6 (process). It's recommended that you paraphrase frequently, but not continuously, as it can get tedious and lose effectiveness if overdone. Use your intuition about how often to paraphrase depending on the particular students and situation.

As with all procedures, reflective teaching requires wise use and adaptation where needed. Initial uses of the 6PQ method should attempt to follow the procedure closely, but with experience, you'll find ways of adapting the process to each new situation. Avoid the temptation to give hints too early in the process. The following dialogue is an example.

1. PREFACE

Teacher: Celeste, is there something I can do to help you with last night's homework?

Student: I'm stuck on one of the problems.

Teacher: So you want me to help you with a specific problem? (PARAPHRASE)

Student: Yeah, I figured out some of it, but now I'm stuck.

Teacher: What problem are you working on?

Student: A factoring problem, #4: Factor $(6x^3 + 12x^2 + 6x)$.

Teacher: So you only need help solving part of the problem? (PARAPHRASE)

Student: Yeah.

2. PACE

Teacher: What do you know about this problem so far?

Student: I think this is called a polynomial.

Teacher: Yes, that's right.

Student: And I know I have to pull out what the parts have in common. So first I pulled out a six from each part. That left me with $6(x^3 + 2x^2 + x)$. Is that right?

Teacher: That's good so far. What else do you know?

Student: Next I saw that all parts have an "x" so I pulled that out.

Teacher: What did that leave you with?

Student: I got: $6x(x^2 + 2x + 1)$ Am I OK so far?

Teacher: Yeah, you're doing fine. What comes next?

Student: I don't know. This is where I get stuck.

Teacher: OK. So you know you can factor out $6x$ from the polynomial, but that's where you run into trouble, is that right?

Student: Yes.

3. PROBE

Teacher: Can you tell me more about the trinomial you have left, $(x^2 + 2x + 1)$?

Student: I remember something about two sets of parentheses, but I can't remember what numbers to put in them.

Teacher: Do you know the name for the trinomial?

Student: What do you mean by a name?

Teacher: There's a specific equation the trinomial is associated with.

Student: Is that the quadratic equation?

Teacher: That's right. What else can you tell me?

Student: Nothing. Nothing at all.

Teacher: OK, so you know that you arrange numbers in two sets of parentheses and that somehow this is connected with the quadratic equation, but that's it.

Student: Yes.

Teacher: How are the parentheses set up?

Student: They are next to each other.

Teacher: And what does that mean?

Student: That you multiply what's inside each of the parentheses. Oh! So I can put an "x" inside each parenthesis and multiply them to get x^2. Is that right?

Teacher: Yes, good! When you multiply the "x"s in the parentheses, it results in the first term of the quadratic equation.

Student: I guess I knew more than I thought!

4. PROD

Teacher: OK, now look at the problem again and make an educated guess about how to fill in the rest of the quantities.

Student: Hum . . . I'm getting a little clearer about it. I've got to put the numbers and "x"s into the parentheses so that when they are multiplied together I get the trinomial ($x^2 + 2x + 1$). But I don't know what to do to get it—what else to put where.

5. PROMPT

Teacher: I'll give you a little hint. Remember what function you used to get the x^2 from the "x"s in the parentheses?

Student: I multiplied.

Teacher: Right, so what function will you use to get the $2x + 1$?

Student: I guess I have to multiply to get the last term, oh yeah, and then I add to get the one in the middle! I have to find numbers that when multiplied you get one and when added you get $2x$. So what would that be? Let's see. . . . One times one equals one, and one plus one equals two. That must be it! Is it?

Teacher: Sounds like you got it! So what does it all look like?

Student: It must be $6x(x + 1)(x + 1)$.

Teacher: Great, that's it! But can you take it one step more? Isn't there a simpler way of representing the information in the two sets of parentheses?

Student: Oh, I see, $(x + 1)(x + 1)$ can be changed to $(x + 1)^2$. So that means it ends up as $6x(x + 1)^2$. Is that it?

Teacher: Alright, now you got it!

6. PROCESS

Teacher: How can you use what you learned to solve other problems?

Student: Well I was stuck on homework problems #7, 24, and 30, because I think they are similar problems that I got stuck on the same general way.

Teacher: Yes they're similar. So do you think that you can solve problems 7, 24, and 30 now based on what you have learned? (PARAPHRASE)

Student: I think so. Thank you for the help!

Teacher: Will you summarize what you learned before you try those other problems?

SUMMARY

Student: I started with the problem: Factor $(6x^3 + 12x^2 + 6x)$. I saw that I could pull out the 6 as a common factor, and that I could also pull out the x, but then I got stuck. Now I know to arrange the numbers in parentheses side by side so when they're multiplied they give me the end terms in the trinomial and when added they give me the middle term.

In this method, telling or showing how to solve the problem is used only as a last resort. Through 6PQ, students learn that they know more than they think they do, which helps build their confidence and willingness to persist.

Fill out Table 8.4, Questioning Self-Analysis, by circling the letter in the appropriate column. This questionnaire is designed to stimulate your thinking about your prior knowledge and experience with familiar components of the 6PQ model.

Guided Questioning

Questioning helps students elaborate on information they are learning by enabling them to add details, explain relationships, clarify ideas, make inferences, visualize information, and connect what they are learning with their prior knowledge and experience. It also aids comprehension and long-term memory of new material to be learned. Students can be guided to generate their own questions, which research shows aid learning more than teacher-generated questions.

Guided questioning is an approach to teach students to ask and answer their own questions about lesson content. It revolves around giving students generic question stems to use as prompts. Examples include: What do you think causes . . . ? Why is . . . important? How does . . . tie in with what we learned before? By providing these question stems, the teacher can control the quality of student-generated questions.

TABLE 8.4 Questioning Self-Analysis				
Component of Process and Question	**Yes**	**No**	**Sometimes**	**Not Sure**
1. Preface: I establish rapport with students and identify teaching objectives at the beginning of each lesson.				
2. Pace: I ask about and build from what the students already know.				
3. Probe A. I test the limits of students' knowledge and understanding.				
B. I guide students' thinking and learning through questioning.				
C. Most of the time I ask intermediate- or high-level questions.				
4. Prod: I encourage students to make an educated guess when they say they don't know something.				
5. Prompt: I give students hints about the right answer or right thing to do only after I have tried all the strategies listed above.				
6. Process: I have students apply what they have learned to new situations.				
7. Summarize: At the end of a lesson I ask students to summarize what they learned.				
8. Paraphrase: I restate students' comments in my own words to verify that I have understood what they said.				

This approach to developing students' questioning skills can be done individually, as guided self-questioning, or in groups, as guided peer-questioning. In guided self-questioning, students formulate and then write answers to their own questions. In guided peer-questioning, students formulate their own questions and then take turns answering each other's questions in a small group using a reciprocal questioning procedure.

This questioning technique helps students think critically about material they are learning and further extends high-level thinking. Research indicates that while both self- and peer questioning improve performance when compared to discussion and review techniques, sometimes peer-questioning is even more effective than self-questioning.

⚔ Subject-Specific Teacher Self-Questions

Table 8.5 summarizes reflective thinking teacher self-questions to stimulate your thinking about managing instruction in particular content areas.

TABLE 8.5 Self-Questions for Reflective Thinking: Subject Specific			
Reflective Thinking Process	Planning	Monitoring	Evaluating
Reading	How can I find out what students already know about this topic? What do I want students to learn from this text? How long is it likely to take students to read this?	What are students having difficulty understanding? How are students clarifying what they don't understand? How well are they remembering what they are reading?	Did students connect their prior knowledge with what they read? Is there anything students still don't understand? What reading strategies did they use?
Writing	What do I want students to learn from writing their reports? Which parts of the essay are likely to be most difficult? What grammar rules should I teach them and how?	Are students elaborating enough on their ideas? How well are they planning the order of ideas they're writing about? Are students considering alternative ways of expressing ideas?	What did students do best in their papers? What types of grammar mistakes were most common? What feedback should I give students to improve their future writing?
Mathematics	How I can teach students to recognize problem types? What kinds of difficulties do students usually have with this type of problem? What mathematical concepts and procedures do students need to learn for this type of problem?	Are students making appropriate representations of the problem? Are students using the correct formula? Are students making any careless mistakes?	Did students consider whether their answer made sense? What methods did students use to solve the problem? What kinds of mistakes were made?

(*continued*)

TABLE 8.5 *(Continued)*

Reflective Thinking Process	Planning	Monitoring	Evaluating
Science	How can I determine what preconceptions students have that might impede their learning? How should I teach students to formulate hypotheses? What data do students need to collect?	How well do their research designs fit the hypotheses they are testing? How accurately are students recording their observations? Should they be trying a different approach?	How well did students control for important variables? Were students' conclusions justified based on their results? What did students learn about how scientists think in these types of situations?
History	What do I want students to learn about the Civil War? How can I find out what preconceptions students might have about the Civil War? How should I help students learn the causes of World War II?	How well do students understand the implications of the law of supply and demand? How well are they learning differences between political, social, and economic causes of the war? What are they doing to keep up-to-date on current events?	To what extent have students been able to apply what they learned in history to their understanding of current events? What's a better way to teach the differences between political, social, and economic causes of war? How well did students remember important dates?
Foreign Language	What first language features might interfere with students learning the new language? How much time should I allocate to each of conversation, reading, and writing? Which grammar rules are most important?	How well do students understand me when I speak in the foreign language? Are their readings too complex or do they have too much new vocabulary? What writing problems are most prevalent?	How can I remind myself not to speak so quickly? What's a better way to teach the differences in verb tenses? What were the strengths and weaknesses of their Internet communications with native speakers?

✄ Pair Problem Solving

Another method that can be used successfully in most teaching relationships is for one person to approach a situation and talk constantly about the thoughts that are going through his/her mind as the work progresses. The thinker-talker can be either the teacher or a student. You can teach students how to think aloud by first modeling the process. Gradually increase the difficulty of think-aloud tasks you assign as students gain experience. Consider discussing alternative approaches once students have completed the task.

Whimbey and Lochhead (1982) describe this technique as a thinker and listener pair working on problems and switching roles. Pair problem solving has become a popular way of helping students think about their own problem solving. Students take turns serving as thinkers (problem solvers), who externalize their thought processes by thinking aloud, while analytical listeners track and guide the problem solving process as needed.

It is a higher-level thinking (sometimes called metacognitive), self-monitoring strategy that gives students feedback on what is understood and what is still unclear. It helps students identify what parts of a problem they understand and where they get stuck. This method makes problems more engaging, teaches communication skills, and fosters cooperation. It encourages the skill of reflecting on beginning and later thoughts. Pair problem solving facilitates self-checking and evaluating. It encourages the formation of study and support groups, and exposes teachers and students to various solution approaches. By listening to his or her own thoughts, the student gains awareness and control over his or her problem solving. Externalizing thoughts enables them to be seen from a fresh perspective.

Think Aloud

What Is Think Aloud?

One person will say out loud all the steps and all the mental work done when performing an academic task (solving problem, answering a question, conducting an experiment, reading through lecture/textbook notes, etc.) There are at least three different ways to use the Think Aloud process.

1. When the thinker-talker is the subject matter expert, the process allows the expert to model his or her own thinking for students. This modeling shows how to think about the material (knowledge, skills, procedures). It lets students hear what goes on in an expert's head when a text is read, a homework assignment is attacked, study for a test is planned, an essay is written, an error is found, or a problem is solved. It also should include statements from the expert that externalize her/his feelings so that students can learn how to self-regulate their own emotions.

2. When the thinker-talker is a student, the process is valuable even when the student is alone. The student becomes more aware of what goes on in his/her head when doing an academic task. Frequently, this provides real insight into improving performance. Students will not, however, learn this process just by having it suggested. You can model the Think Aloud process as a learner would perform it, thereby providing students with an opportunity to hear what is going on in the learner's mind.

3. There is real value to using the Think Aloud process with two students—one serves as the THINKER while the other serves as the analytical LISTENER. This approach is known as "pair problem solving" and has been demonstrated to be an effective approach for helping students learn. The thinker verbalizes out loud ALL the thoughts that arise in the process of completing an academic task. The listener actively attends to what the thinker says, examines the accuracy, points out errors, and keeps the thinker talking aloud. Together, the students can discover errors and identify naïve theories, disorganizations, and other impediments to academic performance. The teacher needs to observe each pair, monitor progress, and provide feedback on the process.

When Should the Think Aloud Process Be Applied?
- To diagnose a problem and hear what the student thinks, knows, studies.
- To demonstrate to the student what and how to think about academic content/strategies.
- To help guide the student in learning what and how to think about academic material/tasks.
- To see what and how the student thinks for assessment purposes.
- To help the student to become more thorough, precise, and systematic when doing academic tasks.
- To help the student to become more aware of and in control of his/her own knowledge, skills, and attitudes.

Why Should Think Aloud Be Used?
- To prevent passivity and rote learning.
- To help students communicate what they know and how they approach academic tasks. This helps the teacher identify/diagnose misunderstood/misused concepts, rules, facts, important omissions, and inadequate/incomplete knowledge, approaches, or skills. It helps students think more precisely, carefully, and systematically. It helps students examine their own knowledge, skills, and attitudes.
- To become more aware of their strengths and weaknesses by hearing themselves think.
- To check up on their own performance and make appropriate changes as needed through combining this self-awareness with feedback from the listener.
- To help achieve the ultimate goal of students being their own thinkers and listeners.
- To increase students' control over themselves as learners and to improve their academic (and nonacademic) performance.

How Does the Think Aloud Process Work?
Problem Solver's Task
- Translate your thoughts (ideas, images, etc.) into words and recite them aloud.
- Verbalize aloud all the steps you go through when solving problems. Don't censor. No thought or step is too small, easy, obvious, or unimportant to verbalize.

- Verbalize all the thinking you do before you start to solve the problem (what you are going to do, when, why, and how). Even second-guessing yourself is important to verbalize aloud: "I think I should use that long, complicated formula we were using a couple weeks ago. What was it called, the quadratic equation? No, maybe not. Maybe I'm supposed to use the formula we did in class yesterday."
- Verbalize all thoughts during problem solving. "OK, I'm almost through with this division problem. Now that I have my answer, all I have to do is multiply to check and see if my answer is right," Verbalize *ALL* the thinking done before, during, and after work. The verbalization must include plans of what to do, when certain steps are taken, why steps are used (or not used), and how to proceed with each thought.

Listener's Task
- Think along with the problem solver. Follow carefully and make sure you understand every step. If not, ask a question. Have the problem solver identify and define important terms, variables, rules, procedures, etc. Make sure the problem solver vocalizes all the steps and does all the work. If the problem solver skips over a step without thinking aloud, ask her/him to explain the missing thought.
- Do NOT work on the problem independently. Listen to and work along with the problem solver.
- Never let the problem solver get ahead of you. If the problem solver is working too fast, slow him or her down so you can follow carefully, analytically, and accurately. Whenever necessary, ask the problem solver to wait so you can check a procedure or computation and catch up.
- Check the problem solver at every step. Don't wait for the answer. Check everything—each computation, diagram, procedure, etc. In the back of your mind, constantly ask yourself, "Is that right? Did I check that?" To promote precise thinking, have the thinker carefully define important terms and variables.
- If you find an error, avoid correcting it. Point it out and try to get the problem solver to self-correct. If he/she gets stuck, ask questions to guide thinking in the right direction. If necessary, give suggestions, hints, or partial answers. Give the answer as a last resort. Let the problem solver know that you are not trying to be difficult, you are trying to help him/her become an independent problem solver. If no amount of suggestion helps the thinker and you must give information or demonstrate a procedure, assign a similar task as follow-up and require the thinker to do it aloud.

To make sure listeners really do their job, teachers should periodically ask listeners to summarize the steps the problem solvers used. The following activities were suggested by Larcombe to help student pairs in elementary grades or remedial high school students learn to externalize their mathematical thought processes.

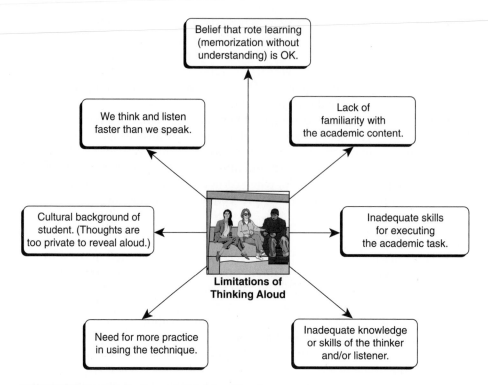

FIGURE 8.1 *Limitations of Thinking Aloud*

1. Students take turns describing the rules they use.
2. Students describe to each other how the parts fit together when doing a construction task.
3. Working with concrete objects at first, students can describe operations used when calculating.
4. One student must guess an object, mathematical representation, or graphic based on another student's description.

Limitations of Thinking Aloud

The factors summarized in Figure 8.1 may cause some students problems in terms of using this technique.

⋇ Reflective Use of Teaching Strategies

This chapter supplements information on how to use questioning, thinking aloud, and cooperative learning, which are discussed throughout this book. Table 8.6 provides specific information for "reflection on action," to help you consider and decide which strategies to apply in your lessons. It promotes reflection in action as you monitor a lesson while it is progressing and consider alternative teaching strategies that might be more effective.

TABLE 8.6	Key Information about Teaching Strategies		
Teaching Strategy	**What Is It?**	**When and Why to Use It?**	**How to Use it?**
Structured Controversy	Method of debating	To help students learn to develop arguments and see issues from different points of view. Develops critical thinking.	Students take and defend a position to partner. Then they reverse roles in the positions they defend. Finally they try to synthesize their perspectives.
Graphic Organizer	External visual representation summarizing information	Visually provide a big picture and make connections between ideas. Add to or replace verbal information.	Make concept maps, charts, cycles, tree diagrams, semantic webs, flow charts, Venn diagrams, continuum, or learner's own graphics.
Mental Imagery	Internal representation of information using any of the senses	Aids thinking about material to be learned by concretizing information.	Have students make visual, auditory, olfactory, tactile-kinesthetic, and/or gustatory representations of information.
Role Playing	Dramatization of material to be learned	Engages students in learning from a new, meaningful perspective.	Students become the material to be learned, from planets to cells, word problems, or literary/historical characters.
Think-Pair-Share	Reflection-based individual and cooperative learning	Provides opportunity for reflection, communication, and understanding from different perspectives.	Individuals write their own ideas and then share what they wrote with their partner and discuss both sets of ideas. The partner then presents the other person's ideas to the class.
Inquiry	Discovery-oriented learning whereby students pose problems, conduct research, and find solutions	Engages learners in authentic activities. Pursuing own interests increases motivation to learn and boosts self-directed learning abilities.	Have students formulate their own questions about a curricular topic. Guide to appropriate resources. Construct avenue for sharing learning outcomes with others.

(continued)

TABLE 8.6   (Continued)

Teaching Strategy	What Is It?	When and Why to Use It?	How to Use it?
Problem-Based Learning	Realistic problem situations form basis of learning and applying curricular content and skills.	Active, authentic learning in meaningful context. Promotes development from novice to expert.	Choose problem that will interest and challenge students, who usually work in groups to acquire information and construct solutions.
Reciprocal Teaching	Cooperative learning and scaffolding method of improving reading comprehension through skill-based dialogues about text.	Temporary support as students learn to independently use four reading comprehension skills: predict, clarify, question, and summarize.	Model strategies. Teach when, why, and how to use them. Teacher–student groups provide repeated modeling and feedback on strategy use. Student-student strategy practice groups work until they can use the skills independently.
Tutoring	Assistance learning material already covered in class.	Provides different approach, more individualized attention, more time on-task.	Peers, older students, professionals, or computers ask questions, monitor comprehension, provide learning activities, present information, and assess progress in achieving learning objectives.

How else can teachers help their students become better critical thinkers? As previously discussed, strategies include encouraging them to think aloud and to make graphic representations of their work, such as papers they are writing or problems they are solving. These strategies are effective because they externalize the students' thinking processes, making it easier for students to evaluate their own thinking objectively.

Self-questioning is another powerful technique that promotes critical thinking. By asking and answering questions such as "How can I state this in my own words?" the student is directed toward reflecting on and critically evaluating what is understood and what is unclear and what is and isn't known. In the process of answering such questions, students sometimes discover that their initial understanding was incomplete or incorrect. This discovery can reveal some important preconceptions that interfere with learning.

There is a Learning Cycle Model based on Piaget's theory of intellectual development. It involves a constructivist approach to teaching and is intended to help students progress from concrete to abstract thinking about content (i.e., from concrete to formal operations). A learning cycle comprises three stages: exploration, concept introduction/development, and application. This model is illustrated in the chapter on Science.

⚔ Cooperative Learning

Cooperative learning is an excellent way to help students reflect on and critically evaluate their thinking and learning because it requires them to communicate their knowledge and understanding to their peers. The processes of deciding what to say, how to express it, and getting feedback from peers, as well as learning about their peers' knowledge and understandings, heighten students' awareness of their strengths and weaknesses in their own thinking and learning. The following information on cooperative learning will help you reflect on the nature of the teaching strategy so that you can critically evaluate when, why, and how to use it so that it meets your students' needs. Use this type of reflective thinking whenever you are considering the application of a particular teaching strategy. Such knowledge about teaching strategies, illustrated with scaffolding, is discussed in Chapter 2 on Managing Teaching Reflectively.

What Is Cooperative Learning?

Cooperative learning involves students working together toward a common goal in a teaching–learning situation. There are three basic forms of cooperative learning: tutoring (peer or cross-age), in which one student teaches another; pairs, who work and learn with each other; and small groups of students teaching and learning together. Not all group work is cooperative learning. Criteria for cooperative learning include positive interdependence, so that students "sink or swim together," responsibility for each other, and individual and group accountability.

Why Is Cooperative Learning a Useful Teaching Strategy?

Cooperative learning increases students' motivation to learn. Academic work is usually much more fun and exciting to students when they work together cooperatively. Research has shown that cooperative learning increases students' confidence in their own abilities, their self-esteem, and their feelings of competence in specific subjects. There are good reasons for the old saying, "The best way to learn something is to teach it." Teaching requires considerable depth of knowledge, understanding, organization, and memory of important concepts and skills. Cooperative learning provides situations for students to teach each other. When students explain and teach concepts to each other, retention of these concepts improves. Explaining also helps students connect their prior knowledge with new information. Research has also documented the positive effects of cooperative learning on improving social relations with students of different ethnicities and cultural backgrounds.

Cooperative learning can be used as a strategy to help a student move from other-centered (teacher) direction and control to self-regulation. Research indicates that cooperative learning can activate and enhance higher-level skills of reflective and critical thinking. There is an increasing amount of ethnic and linguistic diversity in classrooms in the United States of America. Cooperative learning has been demonstrated to be an especially effective method of teaching in settings characterized by such diversity. Cooperative learning can be done at almost any age and often with teachers' existing instructional materials. It helps improve achievement from elementary grades through graduate school.

How Is Cooperative Learning Conducted?

Your role in cooperative learning is different from whole class instruction. In cooperative learning, you are more of a manager and facilitator of learning, or a coach, than a transmitter of knowledge. Major teacher responsibilities include training students for cooperation, structuring groups, deciding whether/how to assign roles, selecting and preparing instructional materials (planning), and monitoring and evaluating student performance. You can develop personal action plans to design learning lessons that meet the needs of your specific students and curriculum. Resources are available for cooperative learning lessons in many subjects. (See Technology for some excellent sites on the Internet.)

There are numerous approaches to conducting cooperative learning lessons. Some, such as Learning Together and Jigsaw, can be used across subject areas. Other methods are more subject specific, such as Group Investigation for social studies, Groups of Four and Team-Assisted Instruction for math, and Reciprocal Teaching for reading. Think-Pair-Share and Pair Problem Solving are methods of cooperative learning that involve pairs of students working together, sharing their thoughts about a problem or task.

Other than pair activities, most forms of cooperative learning involve groups of four to eight students. Many proponents of cooperative learning emphasize the importance of setting up heterogeneous groups. Variables to use in heterogeneous grouping include achievement level, gender, and ethnicity. To set up such groups and effective cooperative learning lessons requires careful management by the teacher.

When used effectively, cooperative learning methods can be powerful strategies for improving social relationships, maintaining a high level of student engagement, promoting content mastery, increasing motivation, and developing higher-level thinking skills, including reflective and critical thinking. When not used effectively, cooperative learning can be disastrous, undermining each of these outcomes.

Do you use cooperative learning in your classroom? If so, how do you plan, monitor, and evaluate your lessons? Regardless of your specific approach, it's vital for teachers using cooperative learning to think reflectively about it before, during, and after the lessons. This essentially corresponds to planning, monitoring, and evaluating your instruction.

Part of planning entails making sure that appropriate resource materials are readily available for completing the task. Before conducting cooperative learning, it's advisable to carefully structure group composition instead of letting students choose their groups or grouping students who sit near each other. It's usually best to maximize the diversity or heterogeneity in a group, but sometimes homogeneous groups are more effective. Conceptualizing individual roles and responsibilities for each member of the group often helps the groups function more cooperatively as they have to depend on each other to complete the assigned task. When needed, provide training in **cooperative skills** so that students can work together more effectively. For example, students may need training in helping skills such as how to give each other feedback without hurting feelings or how to explain ideas to another student, or they may need training in how to be active, analytical listeners.

What do you do while the cooperative learning groups are working on their tasks? This is not the time to grade papers, fill out school forms, or prepare for another lesson. Teaching reflectively while using cooperative learning methods requires continuous vigilance: carefully checking up on what groups are doing, noting how well the group members are working together, and monitoring their comprehension of what's expected, their understanding of subject content, how well they are mastering the content, and their progress in completing the group assignment.

Without careful, ongoing oversight and supervision, cooperative learning can break down into individual work or off-task discussions about music, movies, or TV. Also, groups are likely to focus more on completing the assignment than learning the material. Finally, tensions can arise in a group if there is an imbalance in participation, from a dominant person to a non-contributor. Both of these participation extremes can undermine cooperative learning and breed resentment. One of the advantages of cooperative learning is that it gives teachers opportunities to work with small groups of students, meeting their specific needs, instead of having to work with the entire class at once.

Structuring Student Participation in Groups

Cooperative learning has been demonstrated to be an effective way to develop students' social skills and to improve relationships between culturally diverse students. However, students' different needs can make it hard for a group to feel unified. Research indicates groups tend to split into two distinct camps. Anticipate a possibility of such a division in advance, and be prepared to split the group in two and rotate individuals between the new groups, if necessary. A hostile group member, who attacks other members of a group, interferes with accomplishing academic objectives. Also, students may compete to speak and resist listening and learning from each other. When students have personal or role conflicts, the group tends to have less time to focus on academics than when students' group roles complement each other.

When there is an imbalance in the group—for example, someone is dominating the discussion—others won't participate much or at all. A good way to handle this is to assign each group member a specific role to fulfill. Assign a student who monopolizes the discussion to be the encourager of participation or the observer to sensitize the student to the issue of balanced participation.

Ask questions of less talkative group members; assign them specific tasks or roles that require communicating with other group members and emphasize the importance of effective listening and sharing the floor.

"Reciprocal teaching" and other cooperative learning roles described in this book can help teachers systematically achieve active and balanced involvement in groupwork. These models are presented to stimulate your thinking about different ways of helping students take an active role in their own learning. Experiment with these and your own and/or others' ideas.

How effectively do groups use the time allotted for cooperative learning activities? Without reflecting on how groups use their time, a considerable amount of it can be wasted with students being off task, gossiping, or discussing extracurricular activities. Jumpstarting refers to the problem of getting the group moving—either getting it off the ground to begin with or redirecting it after it has drifted away. One strategy is to create the role of timekeeper in a group to promote effective use of time. Or make timekeeping a responsibility of a more general role on monitoring progress the group is making and monitoring each student's contribution to the group activity so that no one dominates too much and no one slacks off. What do you do if you notice that a group isn't using time effectively? How effective is cooperative learning in your classroom? How do you keep groups on track and refocus them when needed?

Group Processing

To maximize the effectiveness of cooperative learning, after the learning activity ask yourself questions to evaluate how the groups functioned, what the outcomes were, and what plan could be developed that would contribute to future improvements. In addition, teach your students to engage in group processing, whereby they evaluate their group's functioning and make a plan for future improvements. This involves the group reflecting on how well it worked in specific ways, such as listening without interrupting and using time effectively. Group processing after a group has finished a task helps the group to function more effectively in the future. The reflective thinking cycle of planning, monitoring, and evaluating always leads back to planning.

✸ Technology

The Internet has a wealth of information on teaching strategies that promote reflective thinking. Examples of these resource sites are ten Regional Educational Laboratories, which have a central Web site at http://www.relnetwork.org/, with links to other online resources including the "What Works Clearinghouse," support for comprehensive school reform, and support for implementing No Child Left Behind. The Teaching Tips Index has excellent materials for virtually all teachers, regardless of school level, at http://honolulu.hawaii.edu/intranet/committees/FacDevCom/guidebk/teachtip/teachtip.htm.

A Google search of the web on "Reflective Teaching" identified 178,000 results! Narrowing the search to mathematics yielded 49,400 results, history 67,600, science 81,300, and English 89,700. Although some of these teaching resources are for elementary- and college-level teachers, many are very useful for middle and high school teachers.

The InTime lesson plan resource site (http://www.intime.uni.edu) includes videotapes of technology-rich, pedagogically sound lessons for middle and high school teachers in many subjects. Its model, Technology as Facilitator of Quality Education, identifies eight principles of good learning:

1. Active Involvement
2. Patterns and Connections
3. Informal Learning
4. Direct Experience
5. Compelling Situation
6. Reflection
7. Frequent Feedback
8. Enjoyable Setting

The model, at http://www.intime.uni.edu/model/modelarticle.html, also includes attention to critical thinking, information processing, making meaning, content standards, teacher knowledge, and teacher behavior. (See Figure 8.2.)

Another excellent online resource on teaching is TappedIn, a multifaceted professional development site for educators (http://tappedin.org/tappedin/).

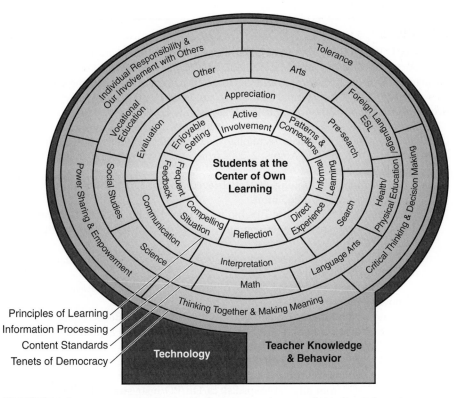

FIGURE 8.2 *InTime's Model: Technology as Facilitator of Quality Education*

As a teacher you can set up your own online office to meet privately with students online in audio- or text-based chats, participate in online conferences, network with peers, and engage in threaded discussions. Perhaps the most innovative teaching site is Active Worlds Educational Universe, a multi-user virtual environment with fascinating educational applications in history, science, mathematics, language arts, and other subjects. Visit http://www.activeworlds.com/edu/index.asp.

Summary

Reflective teaching includes both reflection on action and reflection in action. To reflect on action it's best to consider what teaching strategies you might use, and when, why, and how to use them. To reflect in action, consider how well a lesson is succeeding in meeting your objectives and change your strategies during the lesson as needed. Many different teaching methods can promote reflective and critical thinking. To use them effectively, you need to know what each strategy is and when, why, and how to use it. Choices will depend on the particular students and situation. You also need to plan, monitor, and evaluate your use of teaching strategies to use them reflectively. Numerous technology-based resources are available for teaching reflectively.

Resources

Anderson, L. W.; and D. R. Krathwohl, eds. *A Taxonomy for Learning, Teaching, and Assessing: A Revision of Bloom's Taxonomy of Educational Objectives.* New York: Longman, 2001.

Barman, C.; R. Benz; J. Haywood; and G. Houk. "Science and the Learning Cycle." *Perspectives in Education and Deafness* 11, no. 1 (1992), pp. 18–21.

Bruald, A. Classroom Questions. ERIC/AE Digest, ED 422407. 1998. Retrieved September 16, 2006 from http://www.ericdigests.org/1999-2/questions.htm.

Callahan, W. P.; and T. J. Switzer. Technology as Facilitator of Quality Education: A Model. 2001. Retrieved August 2, 2007 from http://www.intime.uni.edu/model/modelarticle.html.

Cotton, K. Classroom Questioning. 2001. Retrieved August 2, 2007 from http://www.nwrel.org/scpd/sirs/3/cu5.html.

Faculty Guidebook.(n.d.) Teaching Tips Index. Retrieved August 2, 2007 from http://honolulu.hawaii.edu/intranet/committees/FacDevCom/guidebk/teachtip/teachtip.htm.

Johnson, R.; and D. Johnson. *Cooperation and Competition: Theory and Research.* Edina, MN: Interaction Book Company, 1992.

Karplus, R. "Teaching for the Development of Reasoning." *Research in Science Education* 10, no. 1 (1980), pp. 1–9.

King, A. "Guiding Knowledge Construction in the Classroom: Effects of Teaching Children How to Question and How to Explain." *American Educational Research Journal* 31, no. 2 (1994), pp. 338–68.

McKeachie, W. *Teaching Tips,* 11th ed. Boston: Houghton Mifflin Co., 2001.

Saskatoon Public School Division. Instructional Strategies Online. 2004. Retrieved August 2, 2007 from http://olc.spsd.sk.ca/DE/PD/instr/strats/structuredcon/index.html.

Schon, D. *Educating the Reflective Practitioner.* San Francisco: Jossey-Bass, 1987.

Slavin, R. *Cooperative Learning: Theory, Research and Practice,* 2nd ed. Englewood Cliffs, NJ: Prentice Hall, 1995.

Tonjes, M. J. *Teaching Reading, Thinking, Study Skills in Content Classrooms,* 2nd ed. Dubuque, Iowa: Wm. C. Brown Publishers, 1987.

Whimbey, A.; and J. Lochhead. *Problem Solving and Comprehension.* Philadelphia: Franklin Institute Press, 1982.

Wilen, W.; M. Ishler; J. Hutchison; and R. Kindsvatter. *Dynamics of Effective Teaching,* 4th ed. New York: Longman, 2000.

Reflective and Critical Reading

Reading is probably the most important academic skill for students because it plays a fundamental role in learning virtually all academic subjects. Reading reflectively and critically can help students make sure they really understand what they're learning. Regardless of what subject you teach, you can help your students learn to read better by focusing on reading actively, reflectively, and critically in your content area and sharing your reading strategies with your students.

Students with severe reading difficulties are likely to fail until those problems are corrected. Although most students will not have severe problems, many will have reading skills that can and should be improved. This situation exists because reading is not a single skill, but a complex web of skills that needs to be used selectively, automatically, and in a coordinated fashion.

✖ Reading Skills

The basic, lower-level, cognitive skills of reading include letter and word recognition, comprehension, finding the main idea, identifying supporting details, making inferences, and drawing conclusions. Even for students who have some degree of competence with these skills, ongoing assessment, instruction, practice, and feedback can effectively improve them.

The higher-level, metacognitive skills of reading include skimming, activating relevant prior knowledge, forming mental images, predicting the direction of the text, self-questioning about content, checking up on comprehension, clarifying, reviewing, summarizing, and connecting new material with prior knowledge. Critical thinking skills for reading include questioning assumptions, recognizing contradictions and inconsistencies, and considering the quality of sources, evidence, and conclusions.

Don't expect students to be competent with these skills, because they are rarely taught and not everyone develops them independently. They need to be continually addressed, practiced, and polished. Strategies are skills in the process of development. Improvements in these skills can lead to dramatic improvements in academic achievement. Students who are aware and in control of their reading strategies are at a distinct advantage because many of the strategies involve monitoring comprehension, taking steps to clarify difficulties, and restoring the comprehension process when it has broken down.

Reciprocal teaching, discussed later in this chapter, is specifically designed to develop some of these skills. Effective instruction in reflective, critical reading skills requires describing the skills or strategies; modeling them for students; giving examples; explaining when, why, and how to use them; emphasizing the value of flexibility in selecting specific skills to fit the particular context; providing guided practice on a range of texts; giving corrective feedback; and scaffolding skill development.

Students who are not good readers often have preconceptions about students who are good readers. One major preconception is that good readers automatically understand everything they read the first time they read it. Often students don't realize that good readers actually work at making sense of what they read. Good readers are more mentally active while reading than poor readers. Good readers engage in mental activities with the text, such as visualizing, self-questioning, and inferring. Although poor readers engage in some of the same reading strategies (for example, skimming, rereading, and pointing to keywords), they do not coordinate them to achieve understanding.

Look at the Table 9.1 chart of critical reading strategies. Define each term, use the self-questions as a guide, then look back at what you have read so far in this chapter. Reflect on and analyze your use of reading strategies. Indicate (Yes/No) for each of the chart strategies you used when reading this material. Indicate your general use of each of them as yes, no, or sometimes. Do this same exercise with your students.

TABLE 9.1 Critical Reading Strategies

Strategy	Definition	Sample Self-Questions	Used Here: yes or no.	Generally Use: yes, no, or sometimes.
1. Skim		What is in this chapter?		
2. Activate prior knowledge		What do I already know about this?		
3. Predict		What might be discussed next?		
4. Image		How can I picture what I'm reading?		
5. Check comprehension		Is there anything important that doesn't make sense?		
6. Clarify		How can I clarify what I don't understand?		

(continued)

			Used	Generally
		Sample	Here:	Use: yes, no,
Strategy	Definition	Self-Questions	yes or no.	or sometimes.
7. Self-question/ test on content		What did the text say about the preconception poor readers had about good readers?		
8. Review		What has been discussed?		
9. Summarize		What were the most important ideas?		
10. Connect prior knowledge		How can I connect what I already knew with the new ideas in the text?		

TABLE 9.1 (*Continued*)

⚔ Preconceptions about Reading

A preconception that teachers often have about reading is the invalid assumption that the texts students read are "considerate" or "friendly" to readers and have explicitly stated main ideas, clear organization, appropriate density, and instructional devices that promote effective information processing. To what extent do you make those assumptions about what your students are reading? Students need to learn strategies for reading difficult and poorly written books. Think out loud while reading difficult text so that students can see and hear your processing strategies.

Another preconception is that using good reading strategies ensures comprehension. However, just using a good reading strategy does not guarantee understanding. Research suggests that both high and low comprehending readers use the same strategies, but use them differently. The key to successful reading comprehension is knowing **how to use** the strategies and how to apply them **in combination** with other reading strategies.

⚔ Reading a Textbook

The following four steps have been recommended for helping students get more out of what they read: Preview, Read, Outline, and Review/Recite. Have your students reflect on whether and how they use reading strategies such as these.

When reading a textbook, read it differently than other books. Four steps may seem like extra work, but they actually save time in the long run. Use this information as diagnostic tools to identify types of reading problems your students might have and to recommend effective strategies to overcome these problems. For example, if you realize that students are not checking up on their comprehension, recommend asking self-questions such as "Is there anything I don't understand? Can I say this in my own words?"

The following are general principles for reading a textbook. Allocate sufficient time for reading—avoid overload. Read reflectively, checking carefully and critically for meaning. Make connections within and between reading materials, class notes, prior knowledge, and everyday life experience. Also separate relevant from irrelevant information, concepts from examples, main points from details, and fact from opinion or assumption. Periodically review. Analyze and integrate maps and illustrations with written material. Plan to remember: what, why, and how. These principles and the following four steps can help students get more out of what they read.

Step 1: Previewing

Before playing a game you must know the general rules—how it starts, finishes, etc. Likewise, when reading a chapter, get a general picture of the main points. This enables more "goal directed" reading, knowing what to look for. These steps will help:

- If they are included, read the chapter outline and summary to reinforce major points.
- Read the first and last paragraphs of the chapters, again; the main theme should be presented to create a general picture.
- Flip through the entire chapter, observing headings, subheadings, and illustrations. Note italics, bold print, underlined words. What does the organization tell you? Mentally create an overview (image) of the information.
- Plan reading time. Consider the length, complexity, and familiarity of the material; decide how long it will take to read and understand (always overestimate).

Step 2: Reading

General principles. Set a general purpose for reading the material. Establish specific learning objectives. Approach chapters one paragraph or section at a time. Identify key concepts and terms. Note any questions, problems, or issues raised. Translate concepts into your own words.

- Convert any subheading into a question. For example, if the subheading of a paragraph reads "The Causes of Nuclear Accidents," read with the question in mind "What are the causes of nuclear accidents?" The answers to these questions will be the main points of the paragraphs.

If highlighting, underline only keywords. Avoid "coloring the whole page," which defeats the purpose of highlighting.

- Create personal examples. Knowing something specific aids memory of a main idea. Write them down in chapter notes or outlines.
- Look up unfamiliar words or use the context to figure them out. Although it may seem time consuming to do this, if vocabulary interferes with comprehension, the time spent reading is wasted. Have a dictionary on hand in case internal clarification doesn't work.
- Don't continue without understanding. Be alert to the possibilities of vagueness, ambiguity, contradictions, and/or inconsistencies. Not all texts are well-written. Take the time to go back and clarify what was read before proceeding, or again, time spent reading will be wasted.
- Read with a purpose and ask questions such as
  What information is relevant and important?
  What is the central idea or concept in this section?
  What keywords should I clarify?
- Use text digestion techniques: underlining, making notes in the margins, outlining, and creating graphic organizers.

Step 3: Outlines and Graphic Representations

Teach students to use a selective and concise skeleton outline to show major topics, subtopics, and their relationships. Help them learn to turn outlined sections into questions to self-test learning, understanding, and memory of important information. They should leave room for additions and modifications of the outline. This is a very effective way of studying because it's active, actually writing instead of passively looking at a page. These strategies can help students reflect on what they're learning and determine what they should study more.

- Use the subheadings of paragraphs as a skeleton outline to organize the information. Make an outline using these main ideas, but paraphrase to facilitate memory.
- Fill in the outline with diagrams, examples, etc. This provides an effective study guide for test preparation. Students can critically evaluate their learning.
- Graphic organizer techniques can help students analyze text and see how it is structured. Several organizer techniques have been found to be especially useful for reading text. Many graphic organizers have a specific function, such as flow charts showing sequences, but all help convey the "big picture" of important parts and how they are related to the whole. Some graphic organizers found to be useful for reading text include network tree, fishbone map, cycle, spider web, continuum scale, series of events chain, compare/contrast matrix, and a problem/solution outline. Examples of these from the North Central Regional Educational Laboratory can be found online at http://www.ncrel.org/sdrs/areas/issues/students/learning/lr2grap.htm.

Constructing graphic organizers from text is an excellent way of enhancing understanding relationships between ideas. Sample graphic organizers are presented later in this chapter. Relationships can be coded and added to notes. For example, use "P" to show a part–whole relationship, such as the heart is part of the circulatory system. Use "E" to show an example, such as Orion is an example of a constellation.

Most of what students have to learn in school involves organized bodies of knowledge rather than discrete pieces of information. When students understand how that knowledge is organized, the information is more meaningful, easier to understand, and easier to remember. However, they are seldom taught to make those connections while reading.

If students know in advance what kinds of relationships to look for, and remember to look for them while reading, they should find it easier to identify important relationships in the material they read. Understanding how ideas are related is often needed for successful performance on tests. Many exam questions are considered "tricky" by students because they require students to think of higher-order relationships rather than simple associations.

How can students identify relationships? Teach students relationships such as those in Table 9.2 and teach them to recognize keywords that identify these relationships. Also teach them to ask themselves questions about relationships between ideas, such as "What type of relationship is described in this paragraph? Is it a cause–effect relationship? Is it making a comparison? contrast?" Questioning while reading helps students interrelate information and connect it with what they already know.

Networks of related ideas that the reader brings to the text set up expectations that influence understanding and interpretations of what is read. If there is a mismatch between reader's and writer's ideas, comprehension can break down. Learning to understand the structure of ideas in a text can improve comprehension. For example, teaching students "story grammars" such as that a novel usually has a protagonist, antagonist, climax, and denouement helps the reader set up appropriate expectations that make the text easier to understand. The literary web graphic organizer in Chapter 12 on English is an excellent story grammar learning tool. What other types of relationships and corresponding questions can you think of?

Table 9.3 is a graphic organizer that identifies and builds on students' prior knowledge, the KWL chart, which has three columns: K = What students already know about a topic, W = What students want to learn about the topic, and L = What they have learned about the topic. Students record their prior knowledge in the K section, they pose questions in the W section, and report on what they learned in the L section.

Additional examples of graphic organizers are included in many chapters in this book. All may be adapted for use in reading. See the chapter on English for a graphic organizer used in reading literature and a complete list of Language Arts templates from Inspiration Software. Figure 9.1 shows an Inspiration template for analyzing poetry.

TABLE 9.2   Reading for Relationships

Type of Relationships	Keywords and Descriptions	Questions
Part	part of, portion of, segment of piece—one thing is part of another (object, idea, process, concept)	What is _____ part of? How does this part relate to the big picture of _____ ?
Type/Example	type of, category, examples of, kind of—one thing is a member of a class, or an example of a class, category, process, concept, object, or instance	What is an example of _____? What category does _____ fit into?
Cause–Effect	leads to, results in, causes, is used for, produces, outcome	What caused _____? What did _____ lead to?
Analogy	similar to, analogous to, like, corresponds to, in common	What did _____ compare to? What do ____ and ____ have in common?
Characteristics	has, characterized by, feature, property, trait, aspect, quality, detail	How is _____ described? What makes _____ unique?
Evidence	indicates, illustrates, demonstrates, supports, documents, proves, shows, confirms, facts, data	What does the evidence suggest? How good is the evidence?

TABLE 9.3   KWL Chart

K (Already know)	W (Want to Know)	L (Learned about topic)

Mental Imagery

Graphic organizers are external mental representations. Mental imagery involves internal mental representations. To what extent do you use mental imagery when reading? What types of images do you construct? What do you know about your students' use of images? Imagery is a promising, relatively under-utilized tool

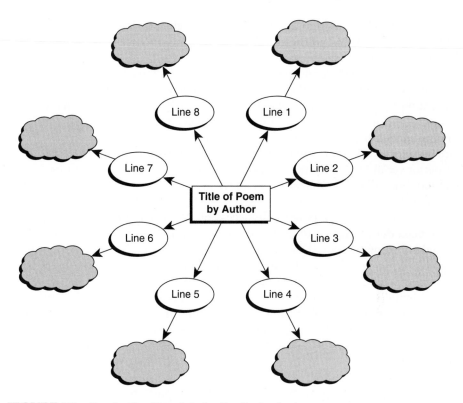

FIGURE 9.1   *Inspiration Template for Poetic Analysis*

for facilitating thinking and learning. However, some students are ashamed of using visual images to mediate their solution of reasoning problems. They have preconceptions about images and often view them as "intellectual crutches." Yet research shows that the construction of visual images facilitates reasoning with transitive inferences. Imagery strategies include forming mental pictures (internal representations) and drawing pictures or diagrams (external representations) to help encode or clarify information.

Teach students to construct images utilizing each of the senses. For example, auditory images, such as the sound of Martin Luther King making his "I Have a Dream" speech, can be useful for remembering what is read in history. Olfactory images, such as the smell of sulfur, are useful for learning what is read about chemical reactions. Tactile-kinesthetic images can be used for learning Newton's Third Law of Motion. Research on the effect of teacher-induced image generation on students' recall and transfer of scientific rules shows that it had a significant effect. Imagery training, where you explicitly teach students how to form images, is very helpful.

Merely encouraging students to create images during a learning situation may not be enough. Students do not always use what they have been asked to, even if they have been trained. Much information students have stored remains inert, and they need to be prompted to use it until they can do so on their own.

Why is it that students may not apply potentially useful strategies, such as visual images, that are in their repertoire? There are many potential variables operating to influence strategy use. Students' beliefs about their own competence to perform tasks can profoundly influence their motivation to perform, their acquisition of specific strategies, and their use of acquired strategies. There are individual differences in imagery—people with vivid imagery tend to have superior recall to those who had poor visual images. Impulsive students may act too quickly and haphazardly to allow the processing required for effective strategy use.

Visual images are potentially accessible knowledge representations that have been demonstrated to improve reading comprehension by systematizing initial encoding of textual material and facilitating later retrieval of that information. When people operate on their mental images, they apparently undergo a process analogous to operating on the physical object itself.

Mental representations of information to be learned or used in problem solving are important determinants of whether and how learning will occur. Research shows the benefit of using multiple representations, including internal representations, such as mental images, and external representations, such as charts or tables.

Research on combining visual imagery strategies with mnemonic (memory) techniques has provided evidence to support the idea that multiple encodings have a more positive effect on recalling information than do single encodings. In one study, 10th-grade students were trained to use graphic organizers and outlines to help comprehend history text. Training included teacher prompting to use the graphic organizer on multiple-choice quizzes. This prompting was phased out on the sixth quiz. One of the graphic organizer groups had prior training in question-generation and summarization techniques. This group significantly outperformed the others.

Research on using concrete, visual models to facilitate understanding of scientific information suggests that there was a consistent pattern of such models helping lower aptitude learners think systematically about scientific material they have to learn. Research identified seven characteristics of effective models. The good models were complete, concise, coherent, concrete, conceptual, correct, and "considerate" (using vocabulary and organization appropriate for the learner). The effectiveness of models depends on the student's instructional goals. See Mayer's research on guidelines for application of concrete models, including when and where they should be used, why to use them, and who models are good for.

A related study looked at use of a diagram in learning from social science texts, and found that a diagram was better than a verbal explanation in representing spatial and hierarchical relations. In the same study, the researcher found that a combination of nonverbal information—diagrams and explicit verbal explanations of them—was more effective than diagrams without explanations. The main contribution of this study was its integration of verbal with nonverbal information, with each facilitating processing of the other.

Step 4: Review and Recite

Reviewing your work is the best tool for remembering. Summarize and compare your summary to the book's, checking to ensure you recalled and understood all the main points. Think about how what you read links up with class notes and other readings. Decide what you will try to remember, why it's worth remembering, and how you're going to remember it (such as what you already know that you can connect it with). Test yourself.

- Find interesting ways of remembering facts. Give meaning to what you have read by applying memorable events, words, etc. to each idea. Use memory devices—they are excellent if you need to memorize a list, for example.
- Distribute study time. If someone doesn't like a subject, they shouldn't try to study it for hours at a time. One hour per subject is usually enough to do at one sitting and doesn't put an overwhelming burden on memory. Although time must be invested to really master a chapter, it's best to space it over time and not cram before exams. Much information is presented in textbooks. Teach students to look for ways to tie together what you cover and what your students read.

⚔ Reciprocal Teaching

Reciprocal teaching is a cooperative learning method of improving reading comprehension that has been used successfully from first grade through graduate school. In reciprocal teaching a teacher and a group of students take turns leading discussions about specific segments of text using reading strategies of questioning, clarifying, summarizing, and predicting. Instructional techniques involved are demonstration, modeling and explaining, practicing with feedback, dialogue or "simple conversation with a purpose," scaffolding or providing students with temporary support, and taking turns leading text dialogues. The combination of these techniques leads to student self-regulation or self-management of reading comprehension.

Reciprocal teaching is based on four principles.

1. The purpose of reciprocal teaching is to improve reading comprehension by equipping students with strategies needed to monitor comprehension and construct meaning.
2. Teacher and students share responsibility for acquiring the reading strategies. After initially assuming major responsibility for teaching these strategies, the teacher gradually shifts responsibility to the students.
3. Every student is expected to participate in discussions. The teacher provides assistance as needed to support student participation.
4. The teacher regularly tries to turn control of the dialogues over to students.

Advantages of reciprocal teaching include students being actively engaged in learning; reading strategies used in an integrated, coordinated way in a meaningful context; students enjoying working together and being "teacher"; students able to learn with the benefit of repeated modeling and learn to take responsibility for their own and each other's learning.

Stages of Reciprocal Teaching

An overview of five stages of reciprocal teaching is shown in Figure 9.2. The stages are teacher demonstration, student learning and guided practice in using the four comprehension strategies, coordinated practice using the strategies with segments of text in small groups led by the teacher, practice in small groups of students, and student competence and self-regulation.

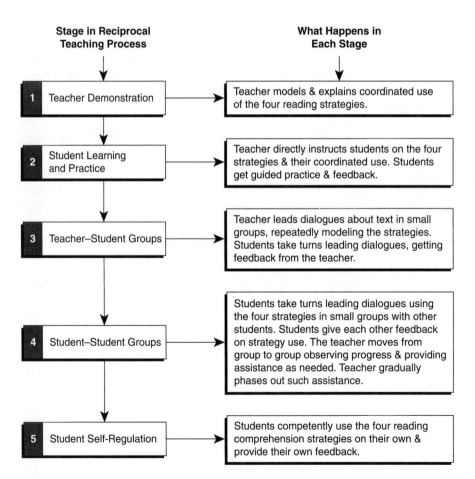

FIGURE 9.2 *Reciprocal Teaching Stages*

Sample Dialogue

Teacher: Today let's use that reading method where we take turns teaching.
Do you remember which reading strategies we use?

Student 1:   I remember three of them: questioning, predicting, and clarifying.

Teacher: That's right, are there any more?

Student 1:   I think there's at least one more, but I don't know what it is.

Student 2:   There definitely is one more. Is it summarizing?

Teacher: That's it. Do you remember why we use these strategies and this method?

Student 2:   The strategies are supposed to improve our reading comprehension and the method is supposed to help us learn to use the strategies on our own.

Teacher: Let's all read the article on page 25. Looking at the title "New York's Big Ditch," I **predict** it's an article about a giant pothole in the heart of New York City. Who has another prediction?

Student 1:   I think it's going to be about a gutter where homeless people sleep.

Teacher: OK. now let's all read the story silently. I have something that needs **clarifying.** What do they mean by an "Indian portage"?

Student 2:   I think it means an area where Native Americans used to trade.

Teacher: That makes sense. Like a port of entry. Does anyone else have something they'd like to clarify?

Student 1:   I didn't know what portage meant either, but I think I understood everything else.

Student 2:   I didn't understand a few things in the last article, but this one I didn't have any problems with. OK. One **question** that could be asked about this story is "What is New York's Big Ditch?"

Student 1:   Well, I was wrong. It's not about homeless people. It turns out the big ditch was the Erie Canal!

Teacher: OK, now I'll **summarize** what we read. The story tells how the Erie Canal was built on an old land route between Albany and Buffalo. It tells about the history of the land and how it used to be an Indian trading post where Native Americans met to exchange goods and services. Does anyone want to add anything to my summary?

Students 1 & 2:   No. What you said gets all the main points.

Teacher: OK, now let's read the article on page 40 and this time you lead the dialogue.

Reading Comprehension Strategies in Reciprocal Teaching

Four specific strategies are used as the basis of reciprocal teaching dialogues about text. They are questioning, clarifying, predicting, and summarizing.

Questioning

Teachers can teach students to formulate and ask questions about a reading, a task to perform, how someone feels, or about a problem to solve. In reading, questions are usually better if they focus on important information in the text rather than unimportant details. A leader or facilitator may ask questions that are answered by others in the group, or everyone may be expected to ask questions.

Questioning is important because it improves comprehension and helps students integrate information. Students can practice writing "where, when, why, and how" questions and get feedback from their peers and the teacher. Teachers should help students evaluate their own questions (To what extent are they about important ideas?), and then see whether students can answer their own questions. Modeling good questions can help students learn to identify good questions. Good questions require reflecting on and critically evaluating what is read.

Clarifying

Clarifying involves the reflective and critical thinking processes of checking up on and recognizing when something is unclear (comprehension monitoring) and taking steps to achieve comprehension (clarification). Seeking clarification promotes both comprehension monitoring and text reprocessing strategies, such as reading and searching for relevant content.

When comprehension breaks down, students reread the parts before and after the unclear section to get contextual clues to its meaning. Students look for signals to word meanings, such as "or" signifying a definition/synonym, and search for referents of potentially vague terms such as "them" and "it." When students cannot figure out the meaning on their own (internally clarify), they often seek outside help (externally clarify) by asking someone else a clarifying question ("What does this mean? Does it mean . . . ?") or checking a dictionary. See Chapter 3, Communication, for more information on clarifying.

Predicting

Predicting involves finding structure and/or clues about what might come next when reading a text. Thus it requires reflecting on the text. Making predictions activates prior knowledge and creates expectations, which makes information more meaningful and easier to remember. It encourages students to think about what they already know and compare that to what they are now learning, doing, or planning.

These processes establish **expectations** about what students will encounter while they work, which motivates students to persist and continue to work to see if their predictions are correct. It doesn't matter whether the predictions are right or wrong. What's important is the expectation established in the reader.

Initially, predictions may come from several sources, including clues in a title and students' prior knowledge or experience. Later predictions come from clues within the body of the text. For nonfiction, students may underline clues such as main concepts, examples, and connections to other things the class has discussed. For fiction, clues include the main character, when and where the story takes place, and what happens. Questions and clues are related and used to make predictions based on students' prior knowledge and past experiences. Model predicting for students and provide them with practice and feedback on their predictions.

Summarizing

Summarizing involves making a few sentences state the most important ideas. The length depends on the particular material. It can be as short as a sentence or two. Good summaries do not include details or unimportant information. **Selecting** information (main ideas and very important details) and **reducing** it to its essentials (eliminating redundancy, substituting general ideas for specific details) are the most fundamental processes in summarizing. Both selecting and reducing require critical thinking about what has been read. Summarizing aids comprehension and memory because it encourages one to analyze and to differentiate between relevant and irrelevant information. It can also promote comprehension monitoring and clarifying unclear material, because it is hard to summarize without understanding and remembering.

When students summarize, they develop a simplified representation of the major focus of the material. They judge the importance of ideas/information in the text. (It may help to ask students to rate the importance of each idea on a four-point scale, from least to most important.) Students select or construct sentences that reflect the main topic of the text. Students condense text by getting rid of relatively unimportant and/or redundant information. Finally, they organize the material to be included in the summary.

Summarizing is easier for students when they have clear structures for organizing the material (cause/effect, similarity/difference, problem/solution, heading/subheadings) and can identify clues about what information is important. Reciprocal teaching and reading in general require reader-based summaries, not writer-based summaries.

Reader-Based vs. Writer-Based Summaries

Depending on the purpose of the summary, a student may choose to write a reader- or a writer-based summary. A **reader-based summary** is designed so that the reader gets an accurate picture of what the author considered most important. It is an objective representation of what the author wrote. Authors use signals when stressing the importance of an idea. Such devices include introductory statements/topic sentences (often the first sentence), summary statements (often the last sentence), italics, underlining, and repetition. The reader-based summary is produced for someone else to read. The summary writer must be very familiar with what the author said and meant in order to write an effective reader-based summary. In contrast, a **writer-based summary** is designed in any way that suits the writer. It is a subjective representation that helps the writer understand what was read, and it reflects what is personally meaningful to the summary writer rather than the author.

Reader- and writer-based summaries correspond to a distinction between reading in an extensive mode and reading in a reflexive mode. One study examined the characteristics of successful and less successful readers. Readers using a reflexive mode related emotionally and personally to the text, directing their attention toward themselves, their own thoughts and feelings, and away from information conveyed by the author. Readers using an extensive mode tried to focus on the author's message and understanding the author's ideas and did not relate the text to themselves.

Like the writer-based summary, the reflexive mode emphasizes a subjective interpretation of text, whereas the reader-based summary and extensive mode emphasize an objective interpretation of text. Research suggests that the readers who made the most progress in reading and had the most success in school after one semester tended to read in an extensive mode, were generally aware of text structure, monitored their understanding effectively and consistently, and integrated information in the text.

Following are research-based guidelines for effective reciprocal teaching:

1. Shift gradually. The shift from teacher control to student responsibility must be gradual.
2. Match demands to abilities. The difficulty of the reading material and the responsibility given to students must match the competencies of each student and grow as these competencies develop.
3. Diagnose thinking. Instructors should carefully observe the "teaching" of each student for clues about how the student is progressing in mastering the reading strategies and whether or what kind of follow-up instruction is needed.

Adapting Reciprocal Teaching

Reciprocal teaching has been adapted to improve students' reading and writing skills. Three teachers were trained in the conventional method of using reciprocal teaching but were encouraged to adapt the model as they saw fit for their particular students. When the four reading strategies were introduced to the students, some of them expressed appreciation for learning concrete tools for improving their reading comprehension.

The teachers reported that students had more difficulty with summarizing than any of the other reading strategies. One teacher devised a checklist so students could evaluate their own summaries based on specific criteria. Several students were frightened of questioning, but were relieved when they learned it is okay to be wrong. Errors were viewed as learning experiences. In one class reciprocal teaching was done occasionally as a form of whole class instruction, so all the students became resources for answering questions. Some students had trouble formulating questions about important ideas rather than unimportant details. Students were better at recognizing good and bad questions than generating good questions. Some students even found questioning exciting.

One effective adaptation involved students compiling questions as a group and giving them to other groups to answer. Each group wrote its questions and traded with another group. Clarifying was easier than questioning for students, but some only felt comfortable asking for clarification about words in bold print. Apparently these students felt it was acceptable to not know the meaning of words that were highlighted as important or new, but felt embarrassed about clarifying words in regular print because they felt they were supposed to already know them.

Some students expressed insecurity about their ability to use context clues to figure out the meaning of unfamiliar words. Teachers reported that predicting was the easiest of the four strategies for the students in this study. Teachers commented that they had to frequently remind students why and how to use the four strategies. Several students spontaneously commented that they had begun using the four reading strategies on their own. Teachers reported that the students especially enjoyed taking turns being the instructor and leading dialogues about the text through reciprocal teaching.

✄ Cultural Issues in Reading

The No Child Left Behind initiative is intended to help minority students, who tend to lag behind white students, close the gap in achievement. It is a controversial program, with mixed results to date. How else might you help minority students improve their reading?

Research on Latino learners shows that literacy in their native language, Spanish, can function as a bridge to reading comprehension in English. To successfully utilize this bridge, it's important to identify their specific needs and their strengths. Have they had gaps in their formal schooling experience? Are they literate in their native language? Research shows that Latino students who use reading comprehension skills such as skimming and context clues in Spanish tend to use these skills when reading in English. Another way to build on their strengths is to allow students to use their biculturalism by discussing English texts they read in Spanish with their Latino classmates. Although some teachers are uncomfortable with Spanish being spoken in their classrooms, research shows that such peer discussions can improve students' comprehension of texts written in English. Using multiple modalities—that is, print, verbal, and visual cues—can also help convey the meaning of what students read.

African-American adolescent males can also improve their reading by engaging in strategies that uniquely meet their needs and interests. Research shows that debating and culturally responsive literacy instruction that links classroom content to their everyday life experiences are especially beneficial approaches. Culturally responsive literacy instruction involves selecting texts by taking into account students' academic, cultural, social, and emotional needs. Examples include texts addressing economic advancement, resistance to oppression, intellectual development, and cultural uplift. Recommended books include *With Every Drop of Blood: A Novel of the Civil War* by Collier and

Collier for middle school students and *The Pact: Three Young Men Make a Promise and Fulfill a Dream*, by Jenkins, Davis and Hunt for high school students.

✻ Technology

Additional Adolescent Literacy resources are available online at a Web site sponsored by the International Reading Association (http://www.reading.org/resources/issues/focus_adolescent.html), which includes lesson plans for middle and high school classes and special materials for adolescent girls.

The American Federation of Teachers has many useful reading resources, including descriptions of successful programs, tips for parents, and teacher-to-teacher discussions. The English Language Arts homepage has resources grouped by school level, with elementary grades pre-K–5 and secondary grades 6–12. A page on reading strategies has hot links for more depth of information on each of 22 strategies with a checklist to highlight their use before, during, and/or after reading. In addition to information on teaching reading, it has tools such as videotapes, information on best practices, links to other useful sites, and resources for teaching literature, writing, and thinking.

The National Capital Language Resource Center has extensive information on language instruction, including Goals and Techniques for Teaching Reading, Strategies for Developing Reading Skills, Developing Reading Activities, Using Textbook Reading Activities, Assessing Reading Proficiency, and Resources. Although developed as a resource for college faculty, the ideas can easily be used by middle and high school teachers. Visit http://www.nclrc.org.

A description of Deshler's school-wide approach to adolescent literacy, using his research-validated **Strategic Instruction Model,** with its "content enhancement routines" and the **Content Literacy Continuum** framework, is available online at http://www.aasa.org/publications/saarticledetail.cfm?Item Number=5872&snItemNumber=950. This approach involves intervening with both teachers and students to use strategies that promote literacy in the content areas.

Summary

Reading is a complex set of skills that is fundamental to academic success across the curriculum. Students who are not good in reading often have preconceptions about good readers. Sometimes reading is difficult because the texts themselves are poorly written. To read effectively, reflectively, and critically in their school subjects, students can benefit from learning a variety of reading strategies and how to coordinate their use. Students often need for you to give them direct instruction in these strategies and to model or scaffold their use. It's also valuable for students to learn how texts are structured differently in the various subjects and to learn specific strategies for identifying their text structures. Various technological resources such as videos and Internet sites can help improve students' reading.

Resources

American Federation of Teachers. The Importance of High Quality Reading Instruction. Retrieved August 23, 2006 from http://www.aft.org/topics/reading/index.htm.

Anderson, V.; and S. Hidi. "Teaching Students to Summarize." *Educational Leadership* 46, no. 4 (1988/1989), pp. 26–28.

Collier, J.; and C. Collier. *With Every Drop of Blood: A Novel of the Civil War.* New York: Laurel Leaf, 1992.

Deshler, D.; and J. M. Tollefson. "Strategic Interventions: A Research-Validated Instructional Model That Makes Adolescent Literacy a Schoolwide Priority." *School Administrator.* April 2006. Retrieved July 18, 2007 from http://www.aasa .org/publications/saarticledetail.cfm?ItemNumber=5872&snItemNumber=950.

Greece Central School District (n.d.). Reading Strategies: Scaffolding Students' Interactions with Texts. Retrieved August 3, 2007 from http://www.greece .k12.ny.us/instruction/ela/6-12/Reading/Reading%20Strategies/reading% 20strategies%20index.htm.

Hare, C. V.; and K. M. Borchardt. "Direct Instruction of Summarization Skills." *Reading Research Quarterly* 20, no. 1 (1984), pp. 62–78.

Hartman, H. J. "Reciprocal Teaching to Reciprocal Education." *Journal of Developmental Education* 18, no. 1 (1994), pp. 2–6, 8, 32.

International Reading Association. Focus on Adolescent Literacy. 2007. Retrieved August 3, 2007 from http://www.reading.org/resources/issues/focus_adolescent .html.

Jenkins, G.; S. Davis; and R. Hunt. *The Pact: Three Young Men Make a Promise and Fulfill a Dream.* New York: Riverhead Books, 2002.

Jones, B. F.; J. Pierce; and B. Hunter. "Teaching Students to Construct Graphic Representations." *Educational Leadership.* December/January 1988/89, pp. 27–31.

Mayer, R. E. "Models for Understanding." *Review of Educational Research* 59, no. 1 (1989), pp. 43–64.

North Central Regional Educational Laboratory. Graphic Organizers. Learning Point Associates. 1988. Retrieved August 26, 2006 from http://www.ncrel.org/sdrs/ areas/issues/students/learning/lr2grap.htm.

Palincsar, A.; K. Ransom; and S. Derber. "Collaborative Research and Development of Reciprocal Teaching." *Educational Leadership* (1988/1989), pp. 37–40.

Rosenshine, B.; and C. Meister. "Reciprocal Teaching: A Review of the Research." *Review of Educational Research* 64 (1994), pp. 479–531.

Rubenstein-Avila, E. "Connecting with Latino Learners." *Educational Leadership,* February 2006, pp. 38–43.

Tatum, A. W. "Engaging African American Males in Reading." *Educational Leadership,* February 2006, pp. 44–48.

The Essentials of Language Teaching: Teaching Reading. The National Capital Language Resource Center, Washington, DC. 2004. Retrieved August 3, 2007 from http://www.nclrc.org/essentials/reading/reindex.htm.

Reflective Teaching of Mathematics

How do you conceptualize mathematics? How do your knowledge and beliefs about mathematics influence your teaching? Because research shows that teachers' knowledge, beliefs, and attitudes about mathematics affect their instructional decision making regarding what to teach, why, and how, it is important to reflect on your own ideas and feelings about mathematics and consider how they affect your teaching.

In the past it was considered acceptable to just emphasize students' abilities to get the right answers to math problems. Now there is consensus that students need to *understand* mathematics. To what extent do your students try to make sense of mathematics? What strategies do you use to promote their understanding? How do you assess their comprehension of mathematical principles and procedures?

⚔ Preconceptions

Making connections between new information and prior knowledge is one of the keys to meaningful learning. How and to what extent do you elicit and use what your students already know about mathematics? Some prior knowledge is valid and can be used as building blocks, though some is invalid and can interfere with learning new ideas. The issue of students' naïve theories about mathematics has been a major topic at the four national conferences of the Misconceptions Seminar, "From Misconceptions to Constructed Understanding." Abstracts from all four are available at http://www2.ucsc.edu/mlrg/mlrgarticles.html. How do you identify and address students' naïve theories about mathematical concepts and procedures?

How do your students conceptualize mathematics? Many students have erroneous beliefs about mathematics: what it's all about, why they have to learn it, and how it is best learned. The most pervasive general preconception about mathematics might be its characterization as computation. Mathematicians and expert mathematics teachers view computation not as an end in itself, but as a tool for problem solving, identifying structures and patterns and understanding, explaining, and verifying them. Many people learn mathematics by memorizing facts and procedures rather than through conceptual understanding. A resource book identifying mathematics misconceptions is identified at the end of this chapter.

186

Low-achieving math students often think that high-achieving math students get correct answers to problems easily and don't make mistakes. They don't realize that good math students know when their approach to solving a problem isn't working and try a different strategy. Low achievers think about mathematics as answer or product driven and don't understand or appreciate mathematics as a process. Teach them the value of and strategies for estimating answers to problems.

One way to identify and overcome students' problematic ideas about mathematics is to use a three-step questioning process designed to challenge different aspects of students' understanding. Consider how students would represent the statement "There are ten times as many students as teachers in this school."

1. Question their qualitative understanding by asking a question such as "According to this statement, which are there more of in this school, teachers or students?" Determine whether the language in the statement is confusing the students.
2. Question their quantitative understanding by asking a question such as "If there were 20 teachers in the school, how many students would there be, based on this statement?" Determine whether students understand the implications of quantitative aspects of the statement.
3. Question their conceptual understanding by asking a question such as "How would you write an equation for that statement?" Many students write: 10 S = T. Look for patterns such as this one. Then induce conflict by asking "If you substitute S = 100 in your equation, would you get T = 20 as before?"

This inductive approach is intended to provoke students' awareness of their naïve theories.

Another common naïve theory students tend to have is the belief that there is only one way to solve a problem. For each type of problem, teach students alternative solution strategies and encourage them to evaluate which ones make the most sense to them.

Reflective learning in mathematics can also be facilitated by teaching students to conceptualize, visualize, and recognize problem types and corresponding solution strategies.

⚔ Visualizing Mathematics

Students often find it easier to solve mathematical problems if they are more concrete and less abstract. To what extent do your students visualize the problems they solve? How effectively do they construct and use visual representations? Visualization strategies include making mental pictures of a problem and using graphic representations to organize parts of a problem, in order to see relationships between parts of the problem and the whole. Find out about the mental representations and models students use to understand problems they

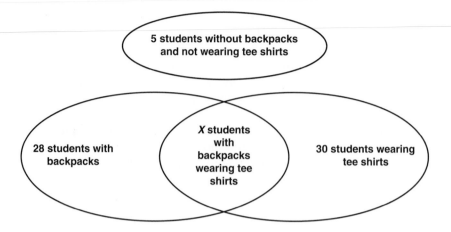

FIGURE 10.1   *Venn Diagram to Visualize Problem*

are solving. Provide them with a variety of mental representations and models so that they can understand them from different perspectives.

See The Adventures of Jasper Woodbury in the Technology section for examples of using real-life video situations to concretize problems and facilitate problem solving.

Venn diagrams and tables are examples of effective graphic organizers that can aid problem solving and learning mathematics. However, you need to model for and teach students how to make such diagrams and how to use images and representations when solving problems and learning mathematics.

Consider this problem: In a room of 45 students, 28 have a backpack, 30 are wearing a tee shirt, and 5 are not wearing a tee shirt and do not have a backpack. How many students have a backpack and are wearing a tee shirt?

$$\text{Total} = 45 \text{ Students in the Class}$$

To find the value of x, students need to add the contents of each region of the diagram, leading to a total of 45, and use the following equation: $(28 - x) + (30 - x) + x + 5 = 45$. The solution is $x = 18$. Using this Venn diagram to represent the parts of this problem in relationship to the whole can help students visualize and solve the problem.

The concept map in Figure 10.2 illustrates how a graphic organizer can help students understand and remember the different types of triangles. It is organized into two major categories: angles and sides. Give students this graphic organizer and then have them create their own drawings of each type of triangle. You can use their drawings to assess their understanding and provide them with corrective feedback. Teach students to cover up the definitions alternatively with their drawings to self-test their understanding and memory so they can critically evaluate and reflect on what they have mastered and what they still need to learn. As a quiz or test, give them a partially complete concept map and have them fill in the missing information.

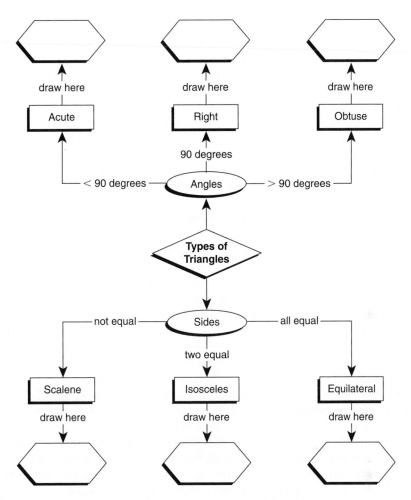

FIGURE 10.2 *Visualizing Information on Types of Triangles*

⋈ Effective Mathematics Teaching

How do your students feel about learning mathematics? What are your goals for teaching them? Research suggests that effective mathematics teaching, which results in students understanding mathematics, depends on thinking about students' perspectives and using student-centered instructional practices. Reflective mathematics teaching includes examining content standards such as those specified by the National Council of Teachers of Mathematics and those specified by state departments of education, and using these standards to formulate instructional goals. After identifying goals, reflective teachers consider their own assumptions, knowledge, and beliefs about how best to design lessons and plan instructional activities.

Reflective mathematics teaching entails considering students' assumptions, prior knowledge, beliefs, and attitudes toward the content. It requires examining your own thoughts about teaching before, during, and after lessons. Teachers' reflective thinking about mathematics instruction starts with the **preactive** stage, which involves planning your lesson before it takes place. The **interactive** stage of reflective thinking involves monitoring or checking up on how a lesson is progressing and self-regulating while it's being conducted. After the lesson, the **postactive** stage of reflective thinking involves assessing the lesson's success and revising lesson plans to make them more effective in the future. To what extent do you engage in these types of thinking? Reflective mathematics teaching also involves thinking about your own experiences as a student of mathematics. What practices were most successful in helping you learn mathematics? How might these insights help you work more effectively with your students?

Model-based reasoning in mathematics is a cyclical process of constructing, evaluating, and revising models based on such activities as inventing or selecting a model for a particular problem, exploring the qualities of a model, and applying a model to the process of problem solving. Evaluating and revising models after application helps students construct better models next time they have to solve similar problems, thereby continuing the cycle. Show students alternative ways of solving problems, while emphasizing important mathematical ideas.

Many students have anxiety about learning mathematics and believe they aren't capable of truly understanding it. For such students, memorizing approaches and getting the right answer becomes their mathematics learning goal. Teachers who aren't reflective about their mathematics teaching are likely using strategies that perpetuate such attitudes in their students. How willing are you to look back on your lessons and criticize them?

By looking at mathematics from students' perspectives, and thinking about past learning difficulties, you can develop insights into reasons for learning problems and consider alternative approaches. The ultimate instructional goal is for students to develop mathematical concepts and skills and achieve a positive attitude toward mathematics. Many mathematics teachers have had personal experience with math anxiety at some point in their schooling or careers. Reflecting on your own experiences and sharing them with students can help demystify mathematics and make it more accessible to a wider range of students.

✵ Writing in Mathematics

How often do your students write about mathematics? Writing in mathematics is an excellent way to promote reflective thinking and conceptual understanding. It's also a good way to find out about students' naïve theories. One strategy is to have students write an estimate of what they expect the answer to a problem to be and explain why. Then once the answer has been obtained, have them compare, in writing, the actual to the estimated answer and explain any discrepancies. Finally, have them write an explanation of how they could make a better estimation in the future on a similar problem.

A second strategy is to have students write a plan for how they will solve a problem, or to have them describe the steps they took to arrive at an answer, with the reasons for each step in the solution process. One math teacher did an exercise with her high school students to assess their understanding of how they were to approach a related rates problem and to help them with the solution process. Before solving the following problem, they were asked to create a list of questions that would guide their thinking about how to solve the problem.

"A boat is pulled in to a dock by means of a rope with one end attached to the bow of the boat, the other end passing through a ring attached to the dock at a point 4 ft. higher than the bow of the boat. If the rope is pulled in at the rate of 2 ft/sec, how fast is the boat approaching the dock when 10 ft of rope are out?"

Although her students first thought she was crazy for wanting them to write down questions, once she explained the three phases of planning, monitoring, and evaluating the problem solving process and gave a few examples, they got into the exercise. After the students generated their questions, the teacher asked them to use their questions to solve the problem. Some students did not write very effective questions and got stuck, so the teacher decided the class should develop a master list of questions for them all to follow. Their list appears in Table 10.1.

Students who solved the problem using this list were asked to help a student who had not. Afterward the teacher led the class in a discussion about how each question related to part of the solution. Some students reported that in the past they had been so focused on getting the answer that they had never given much thought to the thinking process and found this exercise to be very useful in guiding their thinking.

A third method of writing in mathematics is to have students keep a journal. It can include what goes on during class and what they find confusing or difficult to understand. Students can also identify any preconceptions they have discovered and describe how their knowledge and beliefs about mathematics changed during a lesson. In their journals, students can write about their problem solving, including what steps they took at each stage of the problem solving

TABLE 10.1 Class Generated Self-Questions		
Planning	Monitoring	Evaluating
Does this problem resemble a problem already done?	Is my algebra correct?	Does the answer make sense?
How should I diagram this problem?	Am I using the correct formula?	Did I find what I was supposed to find?
What do I have to find out?	Is my diagram labeled correctly?	Did I make any careless mistakes?
What equation must I differentiate?		

process and why, and assess their comprehension of mathematical concepts and procedures. Finally, students can write about their feelings when learning mathematics so that they can develop awareness of what causes them to feel confident and what causes them to feel anxious. Periodically collect and review these journals to develop insights into your own teaching and their learning, and provide them with individualized feedback and support.

⚔ Math Anxiety

What makes your students most anxious? Many students have trouble solving word problems. What do your students find easiest? Most difficult? How anxious are they when taking math tests? For some students, math anxiety may be compounded with more-general test anxiety. What strategies, if any, do they use to alleviate their anxiety and relax? You can teach them a variety of relaxation techniques. Creative visualization, as used by Olympic athletes, involves visualizing yourself succeeding at the tasks you're anxious about, and can be very helpful. So can deep breathing or progressive relaxation. Another successful visualization technique is the "safe place," where you picture yourself at a location you find calming, such as the beach. Encourage your students to experiment with various anxiety reduction techniques and find out what works best for them.

Helping students become more reflective about their mathematics learning can be the first step in overcoming anxiety and developing positive attitudes. Sometimes students are strong in one area of mathematics and weak in another. For example, some students find algebra relatively easy but have great difficulty with geometry. For other students, the opposite might occur.

Do your students feel they have to solve problems quickly? Another naïve theory that many students have is that speed is an important feature in solving a problem. Although speed in problem solving may be needed for some standardized tests, in actuality mathematicians are often slow and deliberative in problem solving, taking considerable time just to clearly identify and define what the problem is before attempting to solve it, and then considering a variety of potential solution strategies and deciding what methods to use and in what order. Knowing that speed isn't very important can make some students feel less anxious about solving mathematics problems, except on timed tests where speed very well might be an issue.

⚔ Additional Mathematics Teaching Strategies and Issues

One successful approach a teacher has used to think reflectively about her students' mathematical thinking involves finding out what her students know, building on their knowledge, and using this information to guide instruction. This includes

- forming hypotheses about what students do and don't understand;
- using these hypotheses to decide on appropriate instructional activities;

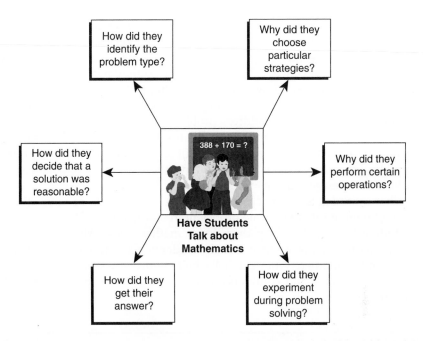

FIGURE 10.3 *Ideas for Student Discussions about Mathematical Problem Solving*

- gathering additional information about students' thinking while implementing these activities;
- diagnosing individual students' levels of understanding;
- modifying instruction based on this new information;
- making sure that instruction is consistent with what students need to learn about mathematics by taking into consideration both individual students' needs and what is mathematically important.

See Figure 10.3 for ideas on having students discuss mathematics with each other. Listen to these explanations to assess students' understanding of mathematical concepts and procedures and their use of technical terms.

What activities could excite your students about learning mathematics? Find out about your students' interests and construct learning activities accordingly. For example, if they like rides at amusement parks, use lessons on roller coasters to teach them how mathematical concepts like slope apply to the design process. To teach them how to analyze data and draw conclusions, have them do research or conduct surveys on topics that interest them, such as how much it would cost to build a playground in their neighborhood, who is likely to win the next election for mayor of their town, or how successful their favorite band is in selling its music. The technology-based series The Adventures of Jasper Woodbury, discussed in the Technology section of this chapter, contains excellent math problem solving scenarios that students tend to find very motivating and meaningful.

Another important aspect of teaching mathematics reflectively is evaluating your textbooks. Recent research shows that even very widely used algebra books have many weaknesses. How good are your textbooks at explaining abstract mathematical concepts? To what extent to they relate mathematics to everyday life experiences? How would you evaluate the teaching methods they use, including examples and step-by-step descriptions of procedures? To what extent and how well do they address problematic beliefs about mathematics? Two of the most important limitations identified were that algebra textbooks did not build on students' prior knowledge of mathematics and didn't promote mathematical thinking. If your textbooks have these limitations, what steps do you take to compensate for them?

What attitudes and what expectations do the parents of your students have about their ability to become proficient in mathematics? How can you get your students' parents to help them learn mathematics? Although in many cases parents might not be able to help students actually solve problems in geometry or trigonometry, they can help their children by simply communicating their expectations and confidence that their children can be successful in mathematics.

✷ Gender Stereotypes

To what extent do gender stereotypes affect your students? Many girls and women are good in math, but some might have a fear of success in math because of gender stereotypes! Gender stereotypes about females and mathematics tend to increase adolescent girls' (and even college women's) anxiety and decrease their mathematics self-concepts, especially while taking tests. The idea that math is a subject for boys and men but not girls and women to excel in can create a self-fulfilling prophecy.

Invite female mathematicians to speak to the class. Have students do research on successful women in math to break down such stereotypes. Educate your students' parents so that they don't perpetuate this negative and invalid stereotype. Few people know that the concept of squaring, used by Einstein in his famous equation $E = mc^2$, was developed by the female French mathematician the Marquise Du Chatelet in the early 1700s, or that Einstein's first wife used to check his mathematical calculations for him!

✷ Questioning

Because asking questions is such an important strategy for helping your students think about mathematics, reflective teaching requires you to think about the types of questions your students need at particular times. Table 10.2 gives examples of low-, intermediate-, and high-level questions to ask about mathematics. Research suggests that students learn more when you minimize lower-level questions, reserving them as building blocks, and spend most of your time questioning at intermediate and higher levels. The intermediate- and higher-level questions in Table 10.2 can help you make class more interesting by helping

TABLE 10.2 Low-, Intermediate-, and High-Level Questions: Mathematics	
Question Level and Type	**Example of Question Type**
LOW LEVEL	
Label	What is the name for the ratio of the opposite side of a triangle divided by the hypotenuse on a right triangle?
Define	What is an asymptote?
Describe	What is the law of sines and cosines?
INTERMEDIATE	
Sequence	In what order would you perform the operations to solve that problem?
Reproduce	How could you graph the following equation: $$Y = f(x) = \frac{x^2 - 1}{x^2 - 9}$$
Describe Similarities/Differences	How does the product of two positive numbers compare to the product of a positive and negative number?
Estimate	Approximately what do you expect the answer to be?
Enumerate	What are the eight fundamental trigonometric identities?
Infer Similarities/Differences	How does this approach to the problem compare with the last one we tried?
Classify	What type of problem is this?
Synthesize	Now that you've solved each of the parts of the problem, what will be your final answer?
Apply	How can you use algebra in everyday life?
Analyze	How could you break that problem into parts?
HIGH	
Evaluate	What is the best method of solving that problem?
Causal Relation	How did you get that answer?
Generalize	How do you usually approach quadratic equation problems?

(continued)

TABLE 10.2   (*Continued*)

Question Level and Type	Example of Question Type
Predict Outcome	If you don't reverse operations to check your answers, what is the potential result?
Transform	If we change the factoring problem from $4x^2 - 9$ to $4x^2 - 7$, how will that affect your answer?
Plan	What steps will you take to solve that problem?
Verify	How can you check your answer?
Conclude	Now that you've identified the type of problem it is, and what is given, what is your conclusion about what must be found?
Propose Alternatives	What other approaches could you use to solve that problem?
Resolve Conflict	Both times you solved that problem you got different answers. What do you do now?

you reflect on the range of questions you tend to ask in class and by giving you ideas for varying your questions. What types of questions do you ask students most often? What types of questions do they ask themselves? Which might you and they do more of?

I DREAM of A

The I DREAM of A method helps students learn to be reflective when solving math problems by teaching them to ask themselves questions and to think aloud to guide their planning, monitoring, and evaluating. It is also intended to help students think about their attitudes when solving problems.

I DREAM of A is a technique for developing mathematical problem solving skills that synthesizes thinking aloud and questioning. It is a math-specific adaptation of Bransford's IDEAL problem solver. Each capitalized letter stands for a component of the problem solving process, so the acronym represents a systematic approach to guide problem solving. These components involve critical thinking skills for planning, monitoring, and evaluating the problem solving process, as in the related rates problem discussed earlier in this chapter. The first four letters are all planning steps, which may be performed in different sequences. Problem solving often begins with "D," diagramming the problem, which sets the stage for "I," identifying the problem.

The I DREAM of A approach is not a rigid, cookbook, rote formula. It should be personally adapted by the problem solver to fit the needs of each problem solving situation. The teacher can serve as an expert model, demonstrating how to use I DREAM of A by thinking aloud and self-questioning while solving problems. Then two students work together, as in the pair-problem solving method previously described. One student is the questioner, who guides the problem solving process by questioning the other student and by having the problem solver think aloud periodically while problem solving. The problem solver answers questions and thinks aloud, as prompted by the questioner. Questions are asked for each of the seven components "I DREAM" and "A."

Although most questions focus on knowledge and strategies needed to solve a problem, the questioner occasionally asks about the problem solver's feelings to establish and maintain a positive attitude. The questioner decides what questions to ask, when to ask the problem solver to think aloud, and when to ask about the problem solver's attitudes. An illustration of the model follows. Table 10.3 illustrates questions by others and student self-questions that could be asked when problem solving. Remember that questions should be constructive for each individual problem rather than always using a prescribed set of questions.

TABLE 10.3 I DREAM of A in Math	
Stage in Problem Solving Process	**Sample questions for others to ask and self-questions**
Identify and define	What type of problem is this? What is given/to be found? How could you state the problem in your own words? What do you know about this type of problem? Does anything seem confusing? What information is relevant? What isn't? How do you feel about your ability to solve this problem?
Diagram	How would you sketch or draw a picture of that problem? What symbols or notation should be in your diagram? Are you sure you have all the important parts? Are you sure they are in accurate relationship to each other? How does your diagram help you identify and define the problem?
Recall important concepts and approaches	Have you solved problems like this before? How? Do you have an example of how to solve this type of problem in your text or notes? What definitions, rules, concepts, procedures, equations might you need to solve this problem? Why? When would you use them? Is there anything you should review? Are there any mistakes you tend to make on these problems? What formulas do you need?

(continued)

TABLE 10.3   (*Continued*)

Stage in Problem Solving Process	Sample questions for others to ask and self-questions
Examine alternative approaches	How else could I solve this problem? Think out loud about how you might solve this problem. What approaches could you use? Are there any general strategies, like working backward or trying extreme values, that might be useful? Which is best? Why? What would you estimate the answer to be? What difficulties might arise while solving the problem? How could you break the problem into parts? What would you do first, second, . . . ? Which is the best way?
Apply your plan	What is your plan for solving this problem? Think out loud as you apply your problem solving plan. How should I begin? Am I thinking aloud as I work? How confident am I about what I'm doing?
Monitor the process	How are you doing so far? Is your approach leading you where you need to go? How can you tell? Should you try another approach? How have you been checking to make sure you haven't forgotten anything and haven't made any careless mistakes? Are you keeping a positive outlook? Does everything make sense? Is there anything I don't understand? Is my approach heading in the right direction?
Assess the process and outcome	Are you sure you have answered the problem completely? Looking back at the problem statement, does your answer make sense? How can you verify your answer? What did you learn from solving this problem that could help you in the future? How well did I do? Did I make any careless mistakes? What could I do better next time?

In a pair learning situation or cooperative learning context, students take turns performing the roles of questioner and problem solver. To become independent problem solvers, students can learn to ask themselves such questions when working on their own and internalize the components of the problem solving process. The sample questions are presented to stimulate thinking about appropriate types of questions to ask. Each situation will require somewhat different questions. Research shows that **student-generated self-questions are more effective than teacher-imposed questions.** Teacher-imposed questions are good building blocks or scaffolds to temporarily guide students through problem solving until they can independently self-question, maintain a positive attitude, and guide their own problem solving.

✕ Technology

Technology provides many opportunities for mathematics teachers to use innovative and effective approaches to teaching and learning. How can technology, such as videotapes and CDs, computer software such as spreadsheets and The Geometer's Sketchpad®, online tutorials, WebQuests, and graphing calculators help students become more reflective learners?

Videotapes of cross-cultural eighth-grade mathematics teaching were a major source of data for the classic TIMSS 1999 study, which enabled examination of teaching and learning from alternative points of view, including the perspectives representing each of the seven participating countries. In each country in the TIMSS study, most mathematics teaching and learning was characterized by students **independently** solving mathematics problems. How were you taught to solve mathematical problems? To what extent do your students solve math problems **cooperatively**? What are the advantages and disadvantages of each?

One pattern revealed in TIMSS across cultures was that teachers spoke more than students in class at a ratio of 8:1. How much do you talk in class compared to your students? Another pattern was that lesson content included both review of previously learned material and coverage of new material: introducing it and having students practice it. Do your lessons reflect this pattern? Which do you emphasize more, review or new material? How do you allocate time when covering new material?

Have you ever seen yourself conducting a mathematics lesson? Videotapes of your own teaching can be a major stimulus to your ability to reflectively teach mathematics. Often teachers are unaware of some of the ways they come across to students, for example, how a look on their faces can discourage students. Videotapes preserve classroom activities so that they can be analyzed in detail and viewed by others to obtain additional feedback. Novice teachers can benefit from experts providing them with specific comments and recommendations about their teaching when having students work independently and cooperatively on solving problems.

The Jasper Woodbury series is an excellent example of how technology can demystify mathematics, and make it exciting and meaningful for students grades 5 and above. Using the series can improve solving multi-step word problems and decrease math anxiety. Originally on videotapes, now on interactive video-disks, a series of real-life adventure stories show students how mathematics is vital for solving important, realistic problems in everyday life. Students become motivated to learn mathematics as they are engaged in authentic problem solving situations. Reflection is promoted by Jasper's problem-based approach to problem solving, which emphasizes the importance of identifying the problem, communicating with other students about the problem, and making connections to other subjects in the curriculum, including history, literature, and science. Mathematical topics include algebra, geometry, and statistics.

The Algebra Project, created by Bob Moses, a civil rights activist, is designed to promote mathematical literacy in urban and rural students. It begins with students having an experience, such as a field trip, then informally developing a model of it or pictures of it, next formalizing their experience with language, and finally creating symbolic representations of it using mathematical concepts. Thus mathematics is constructed out of students' reflections on their own experiences, so students understand the role of mathematics in their everyday lives. To see videotapes of the approach, visit the National Headquarters Web site at http://www.ncrel.org/sdrs/areas/issues/content/cntareas/math/ma1algeb.htm.

Another videotape series for mathematics teaching is Project Mathematics, an animated video approach to teaching basic topics in high school mathematics that can't be taught as effectively with traditional teaching methods using a textbook and blackboard. It also includes material on the history of mathematics. Color, motion, and sound are used to demonstrate mathematical concepts, which are connected to actions in everyday life experience. Each module has an associated workbook. Although developed in the U.S.A., it is now used in other countries around the world and is appreciated by both teachers and students.

Geometer's Sketchpad allows students to explore and discover geometric characteristics and properties in ways that are not possible without technology. By using the mouse to manipulate figures, students can visualize and analyze them from different perspectives, which greatly improves their understanding. Another advantage is that it helps students become more reflective about mathematics by promoting awareness of how geometry is related to algebra and trigonometry.

Graphing calculators are now available online so students do not necessarily have to purchase hand-held versions of them. They are especially useful in promoting reflective learning of algebra because they promote deeper understanding of equations and how they are plotted, which enables students to solve algebraic problems by reasoning instead of memorization. The Cool-math Web site, which has a free, online graphing calculator, has a link to Webgraphing.com, which shows how graphing calculators promote learning in pre-calculus and calculus in addition to algebra.

The Internet has voluminous and diverse resources for mathematics teaching and learning. One comprehensive site is Mathematics Archives. It has a database that is searchable by topic and has K–12 teaching materials, plus it recommends software and sponsors contests and competitions. There are numerous free online tutorials to help middle and high school students learn mathematics. Topics include fractions, decimals, units of conversion, quadratic equations, factorization, polynomials, geometry proofs, sines and cosines, logarithms, linear equations, and differential equations. Students who have computers and Internet access at home can be assigned specific tutorials for homework. Students who don't have Internet access at home might access these tutorials from school computers with Internet connections. Alternatively, for nominal prices teachers can purchase CDs so that students can use these computer-based tutorials without having to access the Internet. Web-based tutorials for algebra and math fundamentals are available at mathpower.com (http://www.mathpower.com/).

WebQuests

Table 10.4 was copied from the Internet to show some of the possibilities of using this Internet-based inquiry learning approach in middle school mathematics instruction.

TABLE 10.4	Grades 6–8 Math WebQuests
Aerodynamic Adventure	Activities built around a simulation about plane flight and math.
Creative Encounter of the Numerical Kind	After researching place value and numeration systems, students create a base-4 numeration system for a primitive alien tribe.
Design a Dream Vacation	Given a $2000 per person budget, design a vacation from a list of destinations. Use a spreadsheet. Decide on sights and activities.
Designing a Home	Design a house using plans, considering costs, energy use, etc.
Dilemma of the Dangerous Meatloaf, The	Students determine and defend a position on the healthfulness of a food through analysis/research.
Dream A Dream, Reach A Goal	Create a realistic fiction story with information about a musher, his dog team, the trail, the weather, and the checkpoints along the Iditarod Race.
Evaluating Math Games	Play and evaluate math games.
Franchise	Convince your classmates to invest in the franchise business you've selected.
Geometry Meets Poetry	Take a concept from geometry and portray it as a poem and an animated graphic.
Harry Potter WebQuest	Harry Potter has challenged your school to a Quidditich Match . . . but first you need a field and the supplies. Review concepts of decimals, percent, measurement, perimeter, area, circumference, and money management.
Hockey Salary Creator	Use mathematical concepts to evaluate the hockey players of National Hockey League teams.
Home Improvement	You are being hired as interior decorators to design newly remodeled rooms.
King of Tides, The	Analyze real-time data to try to prove a causal relationship between the moon and tides.
Let's Have a Field Day!	Plan a day in the park and figure out how much it will cost.
March Madness	Analyze the statistics leading up to the NCAA Basketball championship games.

(continued)

TABLE 10.4 (Continued)	
Math-Scape	This WebQuest has students create a landscape design.
Personal Budget WebQuest	Set up a budget and a lifestyle.
Pizza Family Reunion, A	Use spreadsheets to modify a recipe and develop a shopping list for a large party.
Rising Cost of Colleges, The	Research 3 colleges of choice. Investigate tuition rates and other expenses. Find scholarships.
Roller Coaster Madness	Design a roller coaster.
Roller Coaster Statistics	Research eight roller coasters and decide which roller coaster offers the best thrill based on height, length, and maximum speed.
Searching for Solutions	Solve real-life problems involving Internet research and higher-level math skills. New URL.
Sports Night	Collect data about athletes, scatter graph the data, and make predictions about future performance.
Teaching Tessellations	Write a book explaining tessellations to 4th, 5th, and 6th graders at a neighboring elementary school.
Titanic: What Can Numbers Tell Us?	Create a spreadsheet and examine statistics about the voyage.
Vacation Anyone?	The students use the Internet to take an imaginary vacation somewhere in the U.S. and then present it.
Weekend@Bernie's	Make a budget for a given (yet strangely familiar) family.
Who Wants to be a Millionaire?	Analyze career paths and investment habits needed to become a millionaire in one lifetime.
Your Opinion Sells	Design, conduct, analyze, and write up a student opinion poll.
	Last updated 5/6/2003 at 15:42:49.

Table 10.5 is a similar chart from the Internet for using WebQuests in high school mathematics.

Do you ever feel stuck about how best to teach a topic? One online environment where you can receive expert advice from "Dr. Math" is The Math Forum. The Math Forum is an important and popular site for mathematics teachers, K–12, found at http://mathforum.org/. In addition to providing expert advice to particular questions, you can meet with other teachers to

TABLE 10.5 Grades 9–12 Math WebQuests	
Best Mathematicians You've Never Heard Of, The	Find out information about a mathematician then create a presentation.
Buying Your First Car	What one may incur when buying car for the first time.
Call Me	What's the story behind those 10–10 numbers advertised on TV? Use linear systems to compare one 10–10 plan to a regular long-distance plan. Write an essay to persuade your family to use a particular long-distance plan.
Cavern World	Interdisciplinary unit where students create their own world using science, math, government, economics, and English.
Charts and Graphs	Use Internet sites to gather data to create bar and line graphs and pie charts
Evaluating Math Games	Play and evaluate math games.
Great Pyramid, The	Build a scale model of the pyramids at Giza and compare them mathematically with each other and with some present-day structure.
Hockey Salary Creator	Use mathematical concepts to evaluate the hockey players of National Hockey League teams.
In Pursuit of Mice with Math	Plan and budget a class trip to DisneyWorld. Appropriate for an Applied Math class.
Major Leagues	Baseball has gotten rid of long-term contracts and pay is based on the performance of the player the year before.
Make It Beautiful	Students will design a landscape project, estimate its cost, sell the project to their fellow students, and plant it.
Math Models & Economics	A compilation of WebQuests designed to fulfill most of the one-semester requirement for Math Models and Economics courses for high schools. It includes: Buying/Leasing a vehicle; Buying/Renting a house; Budget and Career; and Investment.
Mathart: Connecting Math and Art	Design and teach a lesson that integrates art and math.
My First Car	Can you buy your own car? Where do you buy it? What about insurance? How will you pay for it?

(continued)

TABLE 10.5   *(Continued)*

Personal Budget WebQuest	Set up a budget and a lifestyle.
Road Block	Study averages, data analysis, data manipulation, trends, and graphing while analyzing car insurance.
Space Station Phyve	Research and design a rotating space station or colony.
Take Me Out to the Ball Game	Using statistical data, you will determine the best ten years for various famous baseball hitters. Based on your statistical information, you will come to a conclusion, WHO IS THE BEST BASEBALL HITTER OF ALL TIME?
Titanic: What Can Numbers Tell Us?	Create a spreadsheet and examine statistics about the voyage.
Trilingual Packaging Dilemma	Design a sturdy, attractive box for a game using triangles.
What's in a Line?	Visit the Internet and see how linear equations come up in real life.
What's Your Favorite Proof of the Pythagorean Theorem?	Students present one of the proofs of the Pythagorean Theorem, develop their own proof, and grapple with related questions. They compare research done in Pythagoras's day to research done today, and contrast the treatment of the Pythagorean Society to treatment of other groups in more recent times.
When Will I Ever Use This?	The most common complaint that students have about mathematics and algebra in particular is "When am I ever going to use this?" Today algebra is ON TRIAL.
Who Wants to be a Millionaire?	Analyze career paths and investment habits needed to become a millionaire in one lifetime.
Yellowstone Caldera Webquest	Make predictions about volcanic activity and damage based on historical data.
Your Opinion Sells	Design, conduct, analyze, and write up a student opinion poll.
	Last updated 5/6/2003 at 15:43:03.

discuss mathematics teaching in a Teachers Lounge at "Teacher2Teacher (T2T)." This site also provides information for parents interested in mathematics teaching. Help is available for specific math problems and for mathematics teaching and learning in general.

TERC, another online resource for mathematics teaching from pre-kindergarten through college, currently has projects in 249 schools. Their work includes curriculum and professional development for teachers for the goals of helping students become lifelong learners in mathematics and science. To promote this goal, they sponsor online learning communities where you can collaborate remotely with other teachers (http://www.terc.edu/).

Extensive resources on using technology for mathematics teaching are available at the online virtual library, http://www.math.fsu.edu/Virtual/, which includes links to many high school level programs across the U.S.A. and in other countries including Canada, the United Kingdom, and Hong Kong.

Summary

Students', teachers', and even parents' knowledge, beliefs, and attitudes toward mathematics can have profound effects on learning and instruction. Recent trends have emphasized learning mathematics for understanding instead of just getting the right answer. Anxiety and gender stereotypes can negatively impact on students' achievement in mathematics, so apply strategies to help students overcome them. Questioning and self-questioning are effective strategies for learning mathematics and solving problems. It's also very helpful to connect mathematics learning and problem solving with everyday life experience. Many teaching strategies, including technology-based approaches, now help students reflect on the meaning of mathematics in everyday life.

Resources

Agnes Scott College. *Biographies of Women Mathematicians*. 2007. Retrieved August 3, 2007 from http://www.agnesscott.edu/Lriddle/WOMEN/women.htm.

Ameis, J. A.; and J. V. Ebenezer. *Mathematics on the Internet: A Resource for K–12 Teachers*. Upper Saddle River, NJ: Merrill/Prentice Hall, 2000.

Apostol, T. (n.d.). Project Mathematics. Retrieved August 3, 2007 from http://www.projectmathematics.com/index.html.

Artzt, A.; and E. Armour-Thomas. *Becoming a Reflective Mathematics Teacher: A Guide for Observations and Self-Assessment*. Mahwah, NJ: Lawrence Erlbaum Associates, 2002.

Bernander, L.; and J. Clement. *Catalogue of Error Patterns Observed in Courses on Basic Mathematics* (Internal Report No. 115). Amherst: University of Massachusetts. Scientific Reasoning Research Institute, Hasbrouck Laboratory, 1985. (ERIC Document Reproduction Services No. ED 287 762).

Coolmath 4 Kids. *Coolmath's Graphing Calculator*. 2007. Retrieved August 3, 2007 from http://www.coolmath.com/graphit/index.html.

Dodge, B. *Math WebQuests* for grades 6–8 & grades 9–12. 2007. Retrieved August 3, 2007 from http://webquest.sdsu.edu/matrix/9-12-Mat.htm.

Drexel University. The Math Forum. 2007. Retrieved August 3, 2007 from http://mathforum.org/.

Edge, D.; and E. Freedman. *Math Teachers' Ten Commandments*. 1992. Retrieved August 3, 2007 from http://www.mathpower.com/tencomm.htm.

Fennema, E.; T. Carpenter; and S. Lamon. *Integrating Research on Teaching and Learning Mathematics*. Albany, NY: State University of New York Press, 1991.

Hyde, J. S.; E. Fennema; and S. J. Lamon. "Gender Differences in Mathematics Performance." *Psychological Bulletin* 107 (1990), pp. 139–55.

InspireData: *Giving Students the Power to Visualize, Investigate, and Understand Data*. TERC. 2006. Retrieved August 6, 2006 from http://www.terc.edu/newsroom/880.html.

Jackson, C. D.; and R. J. Leffingwell. "The Role of Instructors in Creating Math Anxiety in Students from Kindergarten through College." *The Mathematics Teacher* 92, no. 7 (1999), pp. 583–86.

Livingston, C.; and H. Borko. "High School Mathematics Review Lessons: Expert–Novice Distinction." *Journal for Research in Mathematics Education* 21 (1990), pp. 372–87.

Lochhead, J.; and J. Mestre. "From Words to Algebra: Mending Misconceptions." In *The Ideas of Algebra, K–12*, ed. A. Coxford and A. Schulte. Reston, VA: National Council of Mathematics Teachers, 1988.

MathMedics. SOS MATHematics. 2007. Retrieved August 3, 2007 from http://www.sosmath.com/.

Moses, R. *Radical Equations: Civil Rights from Mississippi to the Algebra Project*. Boston: Beacon Press, 2001.

National Council of Teachers of Mathematics. *Principles and Standards for School Mathematics*. Reston, VA: National Council of Teachers of Mathematics, 2000.

National Research Council. *How People Learn: Mind, Brain, Experience and School*, expanded ed. Washington, D.C.: National Academy Press, 2000.

North Central Regional Educational Laboratory. The Algebra Project. 2004. Retrieved August 3, 2007 from http://www.ncrel.org/sdrs/areas/issues/content/cntareas/math/ma1algeb.htm.

Posamentier, A.; H. Hartman; and C. Kaiser. *Tips for the Mathematics Teacher: Research-Based Strategies to Help Students Learn*. Thousand Oaks, CA: Corwin Press, 1998.

Schoenfeld, A. *Mathematical Problem Solving*. New York: Academic Press, 1985.

Trends in International Mathematics and Science Study. 2003, 1999. Retrieved July 3, 2006 from http://nces.ed.gov/timss/.

University of Tennessee, Knoxville. *Math Archives*. 2001. Retrieved August 3, 2007 from http://archives.math.utk.edu/.

Zinsser, J. *La Dame D'Esprit: A Biography of the Marquise Du Chatelet*. New York: Viking, 2006.

Teaching Science Reflectively

Students often consider science to be one of their most difficult subjects, whether in middle school, high school, or college. As a result, many students develop science phobias, much as they tend to do with mathematics. How do your students feel about learning science? It's also common for students to have preconceptions (misconceptions) about science that can undermine learning important concepts. To what extent are you aware of these problematic ideas? How do you address them?

It's important to reflect on the content you teach, and to think reflectively and critically about the pedagogy you use to teach specific scientific concepts and skills. This includes considering what, why, and how you teach so that it meets the needs of your students. Also, how and how often do you help your students to think reflectively and critically about science so that they learn to think like scientists? Do you help them gain awareness and control over themselves as learners so that they become independent, self-directed learners? How and to what extent do you help both boys and girls feel motivated and confident about learning science?

Two major themes in science education today are teaching to national standards and overcoming students' preconceptions (misconceptions) that inhibit learning. Reflective science teaching includes awareness of science standards and planning to meet them. It also includes monitoring students' comprehension and progress, and evaluating the extent to which they are meeting the established standards.

⚔ Standards

National Science Education Standards, including content standards for students learning science, professional development standards for teachers instructing science, and assessment in science, are presented in detail in a book free online at http://www.nap.edu/readingroom/books/nses/html/.

Reflective and critical thinking are at the heart of scientific literacy, as conceptualized in the National Science Education Standards. In the section on Principles and Definitions, scientific literacy is characterized as follows:

> Scientific literacy means that a person can ask, find, or determine answers to questions derived from curiosity about everyday experiences. It means that a person has the ability to describe, explain, and predict natural phenomena.

Scientific literacy entails being able to read with understanding articles about science in the popular press and to engage in social conversation about the validity of the conclusions. Scientific literacy implies that a person can identify scientific issues underlying national and local decisions and express positions that are scientifically and technologically informed. A literate citizen should be able to evaluate the quality of scientific information on the basis of its source and the methods used to generate it. Scientific literacy also implies the capacity to pose and evaluate arguments based on evidence and to apply conclusions from such arguments appropriately.

A standardized tool to help teachers observe their own teaching and evaluate the extent to which they are meeting the standards in both science and mathematics is the Reformed Teaching Observation Protocol (RTOP). Items are organized into the following categories:

1. Lesson Design and Implementation
2. Content: Propositional Pedagogic Knowledge
3. Content: Procedural Pedagogic Knowledge
4. Classroom Culture: Communicative Interactions
5. Classroom Culture: Student/Teacher Relationships

RTOP is a measurement instrument designed to promote teacher self-reflection and the use of the results to improve teaching. Some teachers use it to analyze and evaluate videotapes of their own teaching with reform as the goal. Reflective science teaching benefits from videotaping your lessons and using such an observation form to self-test your meeting of the national standards, including use of science terms and concepts and attention to problem solving.

In addition to national standards, many states and even cities have their own standards and their own sets of standardized tests. Research suggests that in science teaching it is especially useful for students to struggle with interesting, meaningful problems that can stimulate discussion about competing approaches. One recommended approach involves building on what students know or can do independently and providing students with temporary support until they can perform tasks on their own. This is known as *scaffolding*. However, reflective and critical thinking are needed to use scaffolding effectively, as you consider what types of support to provide, what order to sequence supports in, and how to decide when it is time to reduce or withdraw support from students.

You need extensive knowledge for excellent teaching. This includes pedagogical content knowledge, such as how to overcome common learning difficulties; subject-specific content knowledge and pedagogical knowledge, such as which teaching strategies work best for whom and in what contexts. How do you decide which teaching methods to use? The chapter on teaching strategies summarizes knowledge about what specific strategies are, why to use them, and how to use them. Research shows that "activity-based" science teaching is especially beneficial for students with lower achievement, ability, and socioeconomic status. Effective activity-based methods include scaffolding, cooperative learning, model-based reasoning, inquiry, and the learning cycle.

⚔ Science Learning Problems and Solutions

How well do you prepare your students for college science courses? Research suggests that introductory college science courses often are characterized by negative features such as failure to motivate student interest, passive learning, emphasis on competitive rather than cooperative learning, and reliance on algorithms rather than understanding. These features sometimes steer students away from careers in the sciences. Recent research suggests that the mismatch between teaching practices and students' learning styles may account for many of these problems.

One model of learning styles is especially appealing because it conceptualizes the dimensions (sensing/intuiting, visual/verbal, inductive/deductive, active/reflective, and global/sequential) as a continuum rather than as dichotomous. To guide instruction for each of these styles, systematically use a few teaching methods that overlap learning styles and help meet the needs of all students.

1. Give students experience with problems before giving them tools to solve them.
2. Balance concrete with conceptual (abstract) information.
3. Liberally use graphic representations, physical analogies, and demonstrations.
4. Show students how concepts are connected within and between subjects and to everyday life experience.

Teaching science reflectively can help you improve the alignment between your teaching practices and students' learning styles.

Preconceptions about Science and Gender

There is a well-known low ratio of women to men in science careers. Misconceptions or preconceptions about gender differences in the ability to succeed in science contribute to this imbalance. Do you have such preconceptions about your students' potential science achievement based on their gender? To what extent do your students and/or their parents have these beliefs? Such attitudes can also promote debilitating science anxiety in girls. Reflective and critical thinking about this issue can help address the problem. This issue is especially important now that the United States of America is in jeopardy of losing its edge in science because of our relatively low rank of ninth in high school science achievement compared to other countries, based on the TIMSS 2003 report.

Madame Curie's discovery of radioactivity is usually the only important contribution of a woman in science that students learn about. To help students overcome these stereotypes, have them do research on famous women in science, both historically and today. For example, the Marquise Du Chatelet, who lived in the 1700s, was the first woman published by major Science Academies in Paris and Bologna. Although neglected by Watson, Crick, and the

Nobel Prize committee for her breakthrough in the discovery of the double helix, Rosalind Franklin is recognized as having played a major role in determining the structure of DNA. Today, Lisa Randall, a physicist at Harvard, has made important contributions to our understanding of hidden dimensions of the universe. Bring women scientists to your school or classroom to help overcome preconceptions!

Minorities and Science Education

Ethnic and racial stereotypes occur alongside gender stereotypes in science. Often the only African-American scientist students learn about is George Washington Carver and his work with peanuts. Several web resources provide a more comprehensive approach to recognizing minority scientists and inventors. One site, http://www.infoplease.com/spot/bhmscientists1.html, has charts of 10 African-American scientists from 1731 to 1950 and 10 African-American inventors from 1791 to 1976.

An especially comprehensive site, The Faces of Science: African Americans in the Sciences (https://webfiles.uci.edu/mcbrown/display/faces.html), has hot links to information on male and female scientists in each of the following categories: biochemists, biologists, chemists, physicists, engineers, entomologists, geneticists, inventors, mathematicians, computer scientists, meteorologists, medical doctors, veterinarians, geologists, oceanographers, protozoologists, and zoologists.

Lisa Yount profiles twelve Asian-American scientists in the categories of physics, computer science, medicine, and superconductivity technology in her book *Asian-American Scientists* (1998).

The National Atomic Museum has a web page dedicated to a recent exhibit on the contributions of Hispanic leaders in science and technology. See http://www.atomicmuseum.com/tour/scientists.cfm. Another resource is a directory featuring Hispanic, Latina, and Chicana women in science: http://telusplanet .net/public/ecade/hispanic-women.html.

Such resources can help minority students realize that they can excel in science and have successful careers in a variety of sciences.

There tends to be an achievement gap between white and some minority students in science education. Stress on Analytical Reasoning (SOAR) is a program at Xavier University in New Orleans with a record of success teaching science to minority students interested in health sciences, physics, engineering, or mathematics. To help close the achievement gap, one particularly useful teaching strategy SOAR has used is Pair Problem Solving. This technique has a thinker and listener pair work on problems and rotate roles. Students take turns serving as thinkers who externalize their thought processes by thinking aloud and analytical listeners who track and guide the problem solving process as needed. For more details on this approach, see Chapter 8, on Teaching Strategies to Promote Reflection.

As with the problem of gender stereotypes in science, it's recommended that you bring minority scientists to your school or classroom to overcome stereotypes and preconceptions based on race or ethnicity. Also, recommend that students watch the PBS series NOVA Science Now, which is hosted by

Dr. Neil deGrasse Tyson, the African-American Director of the Hayden Planetarium at the Natural History Museum in New York City. A Web site on this program has a whole section of resources for teachers at http://www.pbs.org/wgbh/nova/sciencenow/.

Preconceptions

Although you may be unaware of them, preconceptions enter classrooms in a variety of ways and from various sources. They often prevent or inhibit students' ability to construct accurate understandings of scientific concepts. Students are not blank slates who simply acquire information provided by teachers and books. They usually come to class with at least some prior knowledge, beliefs, values, attitudes, and experiences that influence what and how they think and learn. Some background information provides a foundation to build on. Some of what they bring is an emerging foundation, parts of which can be built on, parts of which must be revised, and parts of which must be discarded. Some of what they bring creates obstacles to, inhibits, or prevents learning. Some problematic beliefs don't really have much of an impact on what students learn in their science classes.

Preconceptions, or misconceptions, about science are preexisting faulty ideas about science, based on false or incomplete information, limited experience, incorrect generalizations, or misinterpretations. They may be false, but they are consistent with the student's basic understanding. Some problematic conceptions result from cultural myths or scientifically out-of-date information. Others may arise from vague, ambiguous, or discrepant information.

Recently, researchers and educators have objected calling these faulty ideas misconceptions and prefer the terms "naïve theories," "alternative frameworks," "faulty knowledge," or "preconceptions," which emphasize the emergent nature of structures of knowledge. Some researchers conclude that all these terms are appropriate given the specific context in which they are used. Consequently, it may be more useful to think of them as complementary instead of competing views of inaccurate scientific conceptions.

Teachers often err in assuming students come to their classes with accurate prior knowledge of specific concepts. Many teachers and students fail to realize that students have private theories that contradict what they are taught in their science classes. Often students' misconceptions go unrecognized and unaddressed, so they remain in the student's knowledge base, and over time form deep roots that are hard to eradicate.

Scientific textbooks sometimes contain misconceptions and alternative conceptions about science, so reading them can interfere with learning unless the teacher filters conceptual problems before students read them and treat them as valid knowledge. One study of a biology textbook found 117 misconceptions and 37 alternative conceptions, which were distributed through 18 of the 22 chapters. One type of misconception is using wrong or out-of-date words to represent concepts. For example, "semi-permeable, membrane" has been replaced with "selectively permeable" or "differentially permeable," so it is not misunderstood as partially permeable or partially impermeable. (Some scholars treat the term "misconception" as one of these out-of-date terms and argue that "preconception" should be used instead!)

Another type of misconception is statements that are wrong. For example, "Oxygen is produced as a waste product" is erroneous because in the context of nutrition and photosynthesis, where it appeared in the text, oxygen is really a useful end product of photosynthesis because it oxidizes food to release energy. An example of an alternative conception is defining dentition by the number and type of teeth, without including that dentition also includes the arrangement of teeth.

Research suggests you should consider the number of misconceptions, faulty knowledge, and alternative conceptions when selecting among science textbooks and select the one with the fewest. Reflective science teaching includes **awareness** of how commonplace problematic concepts are in standard science texts, and **control** over textbook selection to avoid those with false statements.

Learners must have extensive and deep, meaningful learning for the new, correct knowledge to come to mind and be applied instead of the old, naïve idea. This is because research shows that preconceptions are deeply entrenched and enduring, even after students learn new information that is inconsistent with their prior knowledge. Just because teachers have given students correct scientific information does not ensure students will use it to replace the old, faulty information. Sometimes students' prior knowledge is so strong that they won't even believe what they see! Even if a student can repeat a teacher's correct explanation about a concept he or she previously misconceived, probing the student may reveal that the preconception still persists. Prior knowledge affects students' observations, guiding them to information that is consistent with their own perspectives. Students attend to information selectively, seeking to confirm what they already "know."

According to research, multiple knowledge levels (or domains) of misunderstandings are involved in any given misconception. Pay attention to each level and the relationships between them. Each domain or level contains a variety of kinds of knowledge. Research supports an integrative model of misconceptions, in which deep understanding involves four interlocked levels of knowledge, and you need to address all four to help students overcome invalid prior knowledge. These levels are

1. *Content:* recalling facts, using vocabulary;
2. *Problem Solving:* strategies, self-regulation;
3. *Epistemic:* explaining rationales, providing evidence;
4. *Inquiry:* critical thinking—extending and challenging domain-specific knowledge.

To teach reflectively, develop plans to identify your students' types of faulty prior knowledge and select, adapt, or develop procedures to overcome them.

Research suggests there are many possible sources of faulty conceptions students have about anatomy and physiology. (See Figure 11.1.)

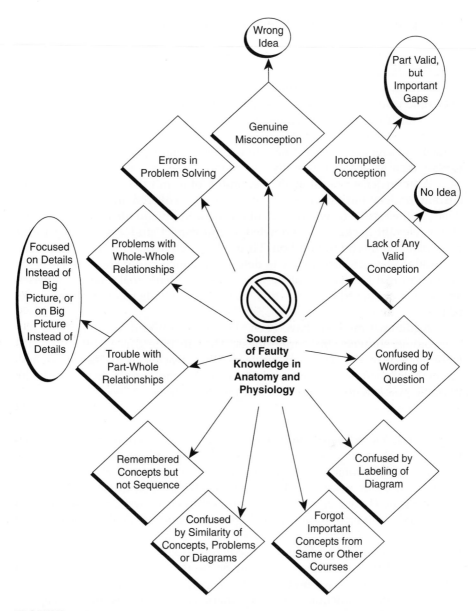

FIGURE 11.1   *Sources of Faulty Knowledge in Anatomy and Physiology*

Overcoming Preconceptions or Faulty Knowledge

Many researchers believe that students overcome problematic ideas by recognizing and replacing them. Some propose that awareness of these erroneous beliefs is necessary before students can overcome them. Awareness creates cognitive conflict, which motivates conflict resolution to accommodate current beliefs or cognitive structures. Accommodation may lead to modifying existing structures and/or creating new ones. One position is that earlier ideas are seldom pulled out and replaced. According to this perspective, it is more effective for teachers to help students differentiate between their present ideas and those of scientists and to help them integrate their ideas into conceptual beliefs more like those of scientists.

Active, meaningful learning activities are needed to help identify and overcome students' naïve theories. There are many instructional tools and resources for teachers to help students identify and overcome scientific misconceptions. Some include making analogies, experimenting, stimulating conflict, inducing discrepancy, teacher modeling, using technology, and having students explain their naïve theories orally and/or in writing.

Administer a pretest at the beginning of a unit that assesses students' current understanding of important concepts covered in the curriculum. Analyze the results to assess students' valid and invalid ideas. Ask questions about relevant background knowledge you expect students to bring to the class that you intend to build on. Through objective questions on the pretest or through class discussion, try to determine which faulty ideas are based on having no real knowledge of the content so students make wrong guesses, and which are based on erroneous ideas that students suspect or believe to be true.

Additional methods have been shown to be useful for identifying and overcoming students' inaccurate ideas. They include concept mapping, the learning cycle model, and cooperative learning. Teachers can benefit from having in their repertoire a variety of instructional techniques to deal with the intractable problem of preconceptions or misconceptions.

Conceptual Change Instruction   Underlying the success of several approaches for overcoming preconceptions is the concept of conceptual change and use of methods that promote conceptual change. The conceptual-change approach to science learning involves helping learners change their existing conceptions instead of merely adding new information to their knowledge bases. For example, in the unit on digestion, have high school students do their own concept maps of body fluid compartments and compare them to an expert model to induce awareness of discrepancies. (See Figure 11.2.)

Direct hands-on experiences can be used to help students develop a model of a concept based on their own observations, enabling them to make more accurate predictions and explanations. Conditions for conceptual change include dissatisfaction with a current concept, perceived plausibility of a new concept, and perceived usefulness of a new concept. Conceptual change models often emphasize confronting existing concepts and facts, pointing out contradictions, asking for consistency, and making theory intelligible, plausible, and fruitful.

As you read Table 11.1's seven-stage conceptual change model, consider how you might apply or adapt it. Think about it in the context of a specific preconception from your experience with your students. Also try to relate it to your own experience identifying and overcoming faulty knowledge that was once

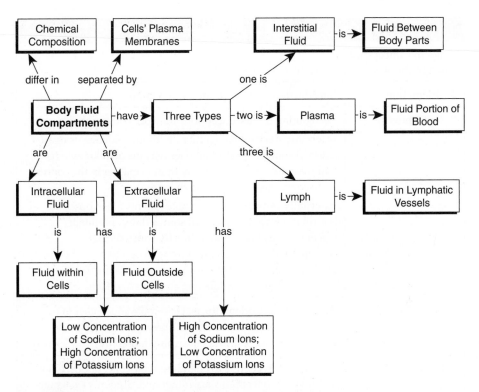

FIGURE 11.2   *Sample Concept Map of Body Fluid Compartments*

Copied from Chapter 9, H. J. Hartman, "Metacognition in Science Teaching and Learning," in H. J. Hartman 2001 (Ed.), *Metacognition in Learning and Instruction: Theory, Research and Practice*, p. 180 with permission from Springer.

part of your knowledge base. Reflecting on the model with reference to such specific experiences will make the model more meaningful and help you think more critically about its potential use.

Research on conceptual change teaching suggests that students can be taught active processing strategies (predict, explain) to help them notice and correct their preconceptions, thereby deepening scientific understanding. Students can learn to distinguish similar concepts from each other—for example, force, impulse, and work from properties of systems or objects.

To overcome faulty prior knowledge, try using cooperative learning activities in which students explain and illustrate scientific concepts and processes to each other. For example, have one student draw the "lock and key model" on the blackboard and discuss it with other students to answer a question you have asked. This kind of activity can provide a context for active processing that leads to conceptual change.

In one study, chemistry students ages 16–18 in a technical school were taught concept mapping to aid their visualization of knowledge structures and

TABLE 11.1   Conceptual Change Process Model

Stage in Conceptual Change Process	Activity
1. Orientation	Introduction to the topic and motivation.
2. Awareness	Recognition of misconceptions may occur through:
	Internally derived recognition: without feedback from an external source, the student uses her/his own knowledge and reasoning that interacts with information in the context to discover there is a misunderstanding.
	Externally induced recognition: students are exposed to information from an external source (lab experiment/teacher/tutor/book/) that directly contradicts their conceptions. Change occurs through cognitive conflict. Students are directly told their conception is invalid; they are confronted with conflicting concepts and facts.
3. Elicitation	Explication of student' ideas. Dissemble concepts into component parts—deconstruct. (Break component knowledge and skills into a learning hierarchy.)
4. Restructuring	Students are receptive to changing their conceptions. New and revised conceptions are integrated. Students exchange and clarify ideas after exposure to conflicting meanings, recursively expanding and reworking information.
5. Application	New or restructured ideas are consolidated by using them to solve problems or answer questions.
6. Explanation	Students engage in sense-making by discussing their solutions with other students and explaining orally or in writing why and how their conceptual understanding changed.
7. Review	Reflection on concepts, what they are, when, why, and how they are used; what they are related to—how they fit into the big picture.

to document and explore changes in students' knowledge structures as a result of learning. After four years of experience, the researchers found concept mapping to be a powerful tool for improving thinking and learning in chemistry. It helps teachers know what students know and how they relate concepts in their knowledge base, what naïve theories students have, and lets teachers see how students reorganize their thinking after a specific learning activity. Concept maps make learning new material meaningful through constructing, reconstructing, and deconstructing knowledge and understanding.

Teacher Self-Questions on Preconceptions in Science
- What prior knowledge do my students bring to class?
- How can I become aware of students' prior knowledge?
- What prior knowledge is valid and can be built on to promote meaningful learning?
- What prior knowledge is invalid and needs to be overcome and replaced with valid conceptions?
- How can I help students overcome their preconceptions?
- When should I implement different activities for overcoming students' preconceptions?

Multimedia Resources for Addressing Preconceptions

Multimedia resources for teachers interested in identifying and overcoming scientific preconceptions include videotapes, CD-ROMs, and Web sites. There are several online resources for lists of common science misconceptions. The Web site "Student Difficulties in Physics Information Center" (http://www.physics .montana.edu/physed/misconceptions/) has ideas identified by these categories: position, force acceleration, velocity, graphs, and problem solving. An astronomy Web site includes these categories of misconceptions: astronomy and astrology; moon, sun, earth, stars, and constellations; planets; telescopes; space flight; meteors, meteorites, and meteoroids; gravity; and relativity.

A page of chemistry misconceptions has a table of misconceptions and "proper" conceptions. Health education commonly includes information on eating and nutrition, which are especially important for teenage girls who might be prone to anorexia or bulimia. Duke University has a peer education program, ESTEEM, on misconceptions about eating, which could be adapted for middle and high school students. Preconceptions about cholesterol are prevalent throughout age spans and lists of them are available online.

The videotape or CD "A Private Universe" demonstrates the prevalence and persistence of scientific misconceptions (e.g., the change in seasons is due to the distance of the earth from the sun) from high school students through Harvard University professors. The CD-ROM series (for PC and MAC) "Misconceptions Seminar" contains conference proceedings from its annual International Seminar on Misconceptions in Science and Mathematics. A CD-ROM from the Second, Third, and Fourth International Misconception Seminars contains over 150 abstracts and complete conference papers. These abstracts are also available online.

An especially interesting Web site is from the Comprehensive Conceptual Curriculum for Physics (C3P). C3P, a Learning Cycle–based curriculum from the Physics Department of the University of Dallas (http://phys.udallas.edu/), is designed to apply research on physics education to high school physics teaching. The Web site provides information on high school students' alternate conceptions about physics, and has numerous resources for teachers, including a sample learning cycle lesson on kinematics.

Web sites of both the National Science Teachers Association (http://www.nsta.org) and the National Association for Research in Science Teaching (http://www.narst.org/NARST.html) have journals and conference proceedings (full text) with papers on scientific misconceptions and conceptual change.

Finally, the Overcoming Ecology Misconceptions Web site has a self-test to evaluate students' success in overcoming their misconceptions about ecology.

✄ Reading Scientific Texts

Students often complain about reading their science texts. Even otherwise competent readers may not be aware of the top-level structures underlying scientific texts. Top-down structures are important because they trigger higher-order ideas, which activate schemata that allow details to be inferred and attention to be allocated effectively. Research suggests that some students who don't understand the structure of scientific texts have problems representing the material, thereby impeding comprehension and retention.

One study found that students had difficulty sorting text into the text-structure categories of classification, comparison/contrast, enumeration, sequence, and generalization. In another study, after receiving eight hours of training in analyzing, recognizing, and organizing relevant information in scientific texts, experimental junior college chemistry students outperformed controls on measures of comprehension.

In this study, text structure instruction included modeling reading strategies, explicitly explaining how to identify a sequence (for example, how to put a sequence into one's own words), how to identify the keywords signaling a sequence, and how to identify supporting evidence. Thus, developing students' knowledge about how to read scientific texts can improve their comprehension by helping them focus on relevant information and use it to create internal connections and representations.

A related study focused on four of the same common science text structures—classification, enumeration, sequence, and generalization—and one different one, cause and effect. Students were taught to recognize these text structures and to construct graphic organizers of them after reading (post-organizers). Students who constructed post-organizers demonstrated superior memory on immediate and delayed posttests when compared to students who used rereading, highlighting, or underlining.

Research suggests it is important to provide students with information about what, when, why, and how to use learning strategies such as graphic organizers. To what extent do you regularly provide students with the knowledge needed to effectively and efficiently learn to use graphic organizers and other text digestion strategies?

When reading scientific texts, students often try to memorize big words, facts, diagrams, and details instead of trying to understand ideas. They learn so that they can "report back" information but not apply it. Some students, **conceptual change readers,** try to understand and accommodate their beliefs to the information in the text. They activate their prior knowledge and recognize when it was somewhat inconsistent with the meaning described in the text.

Conceptual change readers think about the meaning and work to resolve the discrepancy to refine their own thinking. This effort to clarify the misconception is described as a "conceptual change strategy." These students exhibit the self-awareness and self-regulation that are the essence of reflective learning.

✄ Learning Cycle

For over 30 years, Karplus's Learning Cycle has been used to structure science instruction in order to help students move from concrete experience to formal, abstract thinking about content. This constructivist approach has three teaching phases: Exploration, Concept Invention/Introduction, and Application. See Table 11.2, Sample Learning Cycle Lesson. Through this sequence students' thinking is expected to progress from concrete thinking about science concepts to being able to deal with these concepts on a formal, abstract level. Application often involves tasks or problems that relate to students' everyday lives. As previously mentioned, the CP3 project, described earlier and later in this chapter, makes extensive use of the Learning Cycle model.

Another Learning Cycle model was developed by Kolb. Like the Karplus model, **experience** in Kolb's Learning Cycle is the basis of learning and development. Kolb's model has four stages whereas Karplus's model has three. Kolb's stages are active experimentation, reflective observation, abstract conceptualization, and concrete experience. There are striking similarities in these approaches. Although the Karplus model has been used most extensively in science instruction, both of these learning cycle models can be used to promote

TABLE 11.2   Sample Learning Cycle Lesson

Stage in Learning Cycle	Exploration	Concept Introduction	Application
Topic: Digestion	Eat a handful of M & Ms. How does their digestion occur? What are the steps, processes, and parts of the body involved? Share your ideas with other students and develop a group answer to present to the rest of the class.	Students read about digestion in their textbooks. Students see a video on digestion. Teacher conducts a lesson on digestion.	Problem: Think about what happens when you eat a piece of pizza. How does digestion occur? What are the steps, processes, and parts of the body involved? How does your understanding of digestion now differ from your original conceptions? Share your ideas with other students and develop a group answer and diagram to present to the rest of the class.

reflective and critical thinking in science. Which of these two learning cycle models appeals more to you for use with your students? Please keep in mind, however, that a learning cycle might not always be the best approach. A study comparing the Karplus approach to **modeling** in urban, middle school science students found that although both the modeling and learning cycle groups outperformed the control students in their use of integrated science process skills, students who were taught by modeling developed better integrated science process skills than students who were taught by the learning cycle approach. Consequently, rather than just automatically using a commonly accepted approach, such as the learning cycle, carefully reflect on and critically evaluate the specific situation and what research shows about the advantages and disadvantages of a variety of instructional methods for your specific students and subject matter. A combination of the learning cycle and modeling approaches might be tested to see if it leads to even higher levels of integrated science process skills.

⚔ Representation Strategies

Mental representations of information to be learned or used in problem solving are important determinants of whether and how learning will occur. Representations can be internal, like mental images, or external, like flow charts, Venn diagrams, or tables. One study involved teaching ninth-grade physical science students to generate visual images to help them remember rules in science (e.g., Boyle's Law). Multiple intelligences research characterizes intelligent performance by the use of multiple representations. Multiple representations have a better effect on memory recall than do single representations. It is better to use both visual imagery and words to remember than to use either strategy alone.

A review of research on using concrete, visual models to facilitate understanding of scientific information found that such models consistently helped lower-aptitude learners think systematically about scientific material. Concrete models, which consist of words and/or diagrams, help students construct representations of the major objects, actions, and their causal relations in the scientific content being studied. Seven characteristics of effective models are complete, concise, coherent, concrete, conceptual, correct, and "considerate" (using vocabulary and organization appropriate for the learner). In short, models are "good" with respect to certain learners and certain instructional goals. The researcher also identified some guidelines for application of concrete models, including when and where they should be used, and why to use them.

Concept Maps

Concept maps help people learn how to learn. Procedures for creating them are in appendices of Novak's (1998) book, *Learning, Creating and Using Knowledge,* which describes his human constructivist theory. Concept maps are graphic representations of knowledge with the most general concept at the top, hierarchically leading to more specific concepts. Concepts are in boxes or circles, with labeled connecting lines identifying relationships. The labels are words that link one concept to another, and the label is placed in the middle of the linking line.

For example, in Figure 11.2 (see page 15) the concept *body fluid compartments* is in a box, with a line drawn from it to linking words, such as *are*, which has a line drawn from it to the more specific concepts *intracellular fluid* and *extracellular fluid*, which are also each in a box. The linking line coming from intracellular fluid, with the word *has*, leads to a more specific box containing the concepts *low concentration of sodium ions* and *high concentration of potassium ions*.

Concept maps empower learners by enhancing understanding, and reduce the need for rote learning. They can help you negotiate meaning with students and design better instruction. Concept maps can be used successfully with individuals or groups. They can be used with concepts, events, and social relationships; with young children and adults; with teachers and administrators; and in everyday life.

The benefits of concept maps include promoting meaningful learning (especially in science), understanding higher- and lower-level relationships, improving peer relationships and trust, resolving conflicts, and improving understanding of one's role in and contributions to team projects. They also help students and teachers differentiate preconceptions from valid conceptions, decrease anxiety, improve self-confidence, and more. Junior high school science students taught to use concept maps (and Venn diagrams) outperformed students who were not taught these strategies on tests of novel problem solving.

Research on using concept maps with high school biology students showed that students using concept maps had significantly better content mastery, better attitudes toward biology, and less anxiety than students who did not use concept maps. Earlier in this chapter a study was discussed on the benefits found for high school teachers and students who learned to use concept maps for chemistry.

Thinking reflectively and critically about conducting science lessons often includes selecting which representations or models to present to a class (flow charts, diagrams, concept maps), determining when to present them (order in the instructional sequence), and deciding how to present them (blackboard, transparency, computer). It also includes the teachers' self-assessment of the effectiveness of the representations selected, the timing of their implementation, the method of presentation, and a lesson improvement plan for more effective use of representations in the future.

✗ Inquiry Learning

Inquiry Learning is another effective strategy for developing and enhancing scientific thinking skills. Inquiry is how real scientists operate. They pose questions about topics that interest them, design methods to objectively answer their questions, defend their conclusions, and communicate them to the community. Online resources, including sample units and learning activities, are available at Science NetLinks (http://www.sciencenetlinks.com) and Teachnology (http://teach-nology.com/teacher/lesson_plans/science). The model in Figure 11.3 summarizes the strategy.

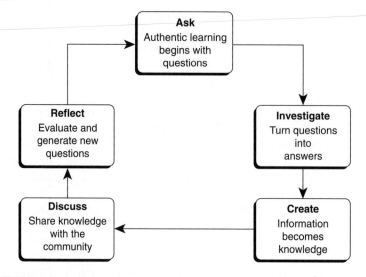

FIGURE 11.3 *Inquiry Learning Model*

Scientific inquiry is a national standard. According to The National Science Teachers Association (NSTA), inquiry refers to the many different ways scientists study the natural world, obtain evidence, and make explanations based on the evidence obtained from their investigations. It also includes activities students engage in to understand how scientists work and develop a deep understanding of scientific ideas. NSTA recommends scientific inquiry as "the centerpiece" of K–16 science education. In 2004 the NSTA created a list of three sets of recommendations for inquiry learning in science teaching. One set of recommendations focuses on how teachers should use inquiry as a **teaching approach.** The second set focuses on how teachers should help students develop their abilities to **conduct** scientific inquiry. The third set of recommendations focuses on how teachers can help students **understand** scientific inquiry. For more information, see their Web site at http://www.nsta.org/about/positions/inquiry.aspx.

✵ Questioning and Thinking Aloud

Science educators suggest that self-questioning and think-aloud processes are effective strategies to promote scientific thinking. A study designed to improve reflective learning of ninth-grade students studying science and eleventh graders learning biology involved seven learner objectives.

1. Increased knowledge of reflective thinking
2. Enhanced awareness of their learning styles
3. Greater awareness of tasks' purposes and natures
4. More control over learning through better decision making
5. More positive attitudes toward learning

6.   Higher standards for understanding and performance set by the students themselves, with more precise self-evaluation of their achievements

7.   Greater effectiveness as independent learners, planning thoughtfully, diagnosing learning difficulties and overcoming them, and using time more productively

Instructional materials included a question-asking checklist; an evaluation of learning behaviors; an outcomes notebook; and a techniques workbook, where students tried out concept mapping. This extensive study went through four phases and involved 15 methods of collecting data, including video and audiotapes, classroom observations, questionnaires, and tests. The results showed increased student control over learning and understanding of content.

Two previously discussed methods can advance the goal of teaching students to use the strategies of self-questioning, thinking aloud, planning, monitoring and evaluating, and maintaining a positive attitude while solving problems. Pair Problem Solving is discussed in Chapter 8, Teaching Strategies to Promote Reflection, and the I DREAM of A method, which uses questioning and thinking aloud to improve problem solving, is discussed in Chapter 10, Reflective Teaching of Mathematics.

Questioning is one of the most important methods of helping students think. Tables 11.3 and 11.4 include different types and levels of questions to ask in physics and biology.

TABLE 11.3   Low-, Intermediate-, and High-Level Questions: Physics

Question Level and Type	Example of Question Type
LOW LEVEL	
Label	What is the term for forces between stationary charges?
Define	What is acceleration?
Describe	What is the second law of thermodynamics?
INTERMEDIATE	
Sequence	In what order would you execute the steps needed to calculate the net electrical force on the charge as specified in the problem?
Reproduce	How could you demonstrate the existence of electrical charge and of charge transfer?
Describe Similarities/ Differences	How is the heart like a battery?

(continued)

TABLE 11.3   (*Continued*)

Question Level and Type	Example of Question Type
Estimate	A tiny drop of water has an excess of 50 electrons. If the drop stays stationary when placed in a 50-N/C downward electric field, approximately what is the mass of the drop?
Enumerate	What are the particles that make up atoms?
Infer Similarities/ Differences	How is your approach to this problem different from the last one you tried?
Classify	If one's hair stands on end, shooting way up in the air and out to the sides, what type of charge is there on one's body and hair?
Synthesize	How could you summarize all the things you learned about electric fields in this chapter?
Apply	How can you apply your knowledge of acceleration to explaining how roller coasters work?
Analyze	What principles were violated when you tried to design the electric circuit?
HIGH	
Evaluate	Which method of calculating an electric field at a point in space do you prefer? Why?
Causal Relation	Why do you get a shock when touching another person after walking in your shoes across a synthetic rug?
Generalize	What generalizations can we make about attracting and repelling electric charges?
Predict Outcome	What would happen if a dry paper plate were placed by itself in a microwave oven?
Transform	How could you prevent yourself from getting a shock when touching another person after walking across a synthetic rug?
Plan	What steps would you take to solve the following problem: Two charges, q and 6q, are separated by 1.0 m. What are the sign, magnitude, and position of a third charge, which causes all 3 charges to remain in equilibrium?
Verify	How could you check your answer to make sure it's correct?

Question Level and Type	Example of Question Type
Conclude	How could one reach the conclusion that the electrical force between ions, when in water, is less than when in the air?
Propose Alternatives	What are at least two ways to calculate the electric field at a point in space?
Resolve Conflict	Each time you solved the problem you got a different answer. How can you resolve the discrepancies?

TABLE 11.4 Low-, Intermediate-, and High-Level Questions: Biology

Question Level and Type	Example of Question Type
LOW LEVEL	
Label	What is the name of an expressed trait in Mendelian genetics?
Define	What is a recessive trait?
Describe	How does a Punnet Square work?
INTERMEDIATE	
Sequence	What is the order of the stages in meiosis?
Reproduce	How would you diagram the four phases of mitosis, prophase, metaphase, anaphase, and telophase?
Describe Similarities/ Differences	How is mitosis similar to meiosis?
Estimate	If two animals heterozygous for a single pair of genes are mated and have 276 offspring, about how many will have the dominant phenotype?
Enumerate	What are the phases of meiosis?
Infer Similarities/ Differences	How is a mass of jelly where eggs are deposited like a uterus?
Classify	Which type of life history is characteristic when the only individual in the life cycle is diploid?

(continued)

TABLE 11.4   *(Continued)*

Question Level and Type	Example of Question Type
Synthesize	What has research on various environmental cues shown about neural and biochemical control of reproductive behavior?
Apply	How can you use Mendelian genetics in agriculture?
Analyze	If you know that a person has blue eyes, what does that tell you about their genotype?
HIGH	
Evaluate	Which is more advantageous for species' adaptation to the environment, self- or cross-fertilization? Why?
Causal Relation	Under what conditions might you determine that crossing over took place?
Generalize	What generalization could you make about the relationship between one's genotype and phenotype for a trait?
Predict Outcome	If blue- and green-eyed persons mated, what would be the possible combination of genotypes among the offspring?
Transform	How does crossing over affect genetic variability?
Plan	If you wanted to produce an F2 generation with probable combination of 25% AA, 50% Aa, and 25% aa, what parents could you have?
Verify	How could you prove that those parents produce that probable composition in the F2 generation?
Conclude	If two brown-eyed people have a blue-eyed child, what can you conclude about the parents' genotypes?
Propose Alternatives	Other than X rays, what agents can produce mutations?
Resolve Conflict	If the offspring of parents does not reflect the parents' genotypic or phenotypic characteristics, how would you explain the offspring's genotype and phenotype?

⚹ Implications of Cognitive Science

A review of the literature on the implications of cognitive science for teaching physics identified four broad principles, each with corollaries, which help physics teachers think about their teaching. First is the **Construction**

Principle, which states that people organize their knowledge and experience into mental models and that people must build their own mental models. Second is the **Assimilation Principle,** which says that mental models control how we incorporate experiences and new information into our minds. Related prior knowledge and experience form mental models into which new knowledge and experience are incorporated. Third is the **Accommodation Principle,** which emphasizes that sometimes existing mental models must be changed for learning to occur. Fourth is the **Individuality Principle,** which highlights individual differences in students' mental models as a result of their personal constructions. Students have different mental models for learning and different mental models for physical phenomena.

These four principles provide a framework for reflective thinking in physics and other sciences. You can use them to help you plan, monitor, and evaluate your instruction, classroom activities, and learning assessments to maximize students' understanding of science. For example, research suggests that looking at the curriculum from the mental models perspective helps you establish the goals of identifying the mental models you want students to develop. It also promotes consideration of the character and implications of students' pre-existing mental models. Finally, it helps you realize the benefit of using touchstone problems to analyze and identify critical aspects of the curriculum.

An implication of the individuality principle is that you need to think about how students may arrive at the same answer but for very different reasons. To determine how students reason, listen to them thinking aloud without guiding them.

✁ Developing Scientific Thinking Skills

To what extent do your students have the thinking and reasoning skills they need to master science? To use thinking skills effectively, students need to know what they are and when, why, and how to use them. Table 11.5 is an example of knowledge given to science students about the critical thinking skill of justifying. Justifying is illustrated because it is important for scientists and science students to be able to defend the conclusions they reach from their observations and experiments.

Various teaching strategies can be used to develop intellectual skills, including building on prior knowledge, self-questioning, imagery, and graphic organizers such as concept maps, flow charts, and matrices. Scaffolding strategies, which involve providing temporary support, help students develop their cognitive skills so that they can ultimately self-regulate their use. Such strategies include a sequence such as providing students with models, conducting guided practice with feedback in groups, structuring individual guided practice with feedback, and students engaging in unguided individual practice with feedback. Through this type of sequence, students should finally be able to apply the strategies on their own.

TABLE 11.5 Critical Knowledge about Justifying			
Type of Knowledge	Knowing What	Knowing When/Why	Knowing How
Thinking Skill: Justifying	Justifying is explaining reasoning, providing evidence underlying conclusions/ reasoning; comparing obtained outcome with achieved outcome, and evaluating degree of difference.	Use justifying to establish a sound basis of support for beliefs, decisions, and/or actions.	To justify, one must understand the concept of evidence or support and its value in making decisions about what one does, knows, or believes. Procedures include finding evidence, weighing and comparing evidence to a standard or set of criteria, evaluating its strengths, weaknesses, and degrees of difference from the criteria, and looking at all possibilities. When there is strong support for one answer, interpretation, approach, etc., and weak support for all the others, justifying includes judging that one to be the best explanation, approach, answer-choice, etc. under the circumstances.

Adapted from Chapter 9, H. J. Hartman, "Metacognition in Science Teaching and Learning," in H. J. Hartman 2001 (Ed.), *Metacognition in Learning and Instruction: Theory, Research and Practice*, p. 189 with permission from Springer.

⚔ Technology

Increasingly, new technologies are supplementing and enhancing the learning process. These technologies can support new views of science teaching. A high school biology course characterized by "model-based reasoning" emphasized both the development of conceptual and strategic knowledge of classical genetics, as well as the development of insights regarding science as an intellectual activity. This nine-week course for seniors involved **model revising** problem solving in contrast with more common **model using** problem solving. In the model revising approach, students work in research groups sharing their observations of phenomena, building models, and defending their models to groups of students who critique each other's models. The critiques lead to model revising. The emergence of competing models increases student awareness of the need for models to explain existing data and predict additional observations. Students also get increased awareness that more than one model may be consistent with the data, and may predict and explain. The computer played an important role in the development of this course. Use of computers was guided by the perspective of students performing authentic activities like real scientists, including problem posing, probing deeply into a problem, solving problems, and communicating with others about the findings and conclusions. Software supplemented work with real organisms, and enabled students to learn genetics by engaging in activities like those of geneticists. This is a great way to use technology!

The InTime Web site has outstanding middle and high school lessons for using a variety of technologies in science teaching. These include **middle school** lessons such as

1. Aviation: includes use of a flight simulator, digital camera, computer, and projector;
2. The solar system: involves doing a WebQuest, and making PowerPoint slides;
3. Exercise that involves use of Polar Pacer Heart Rate Monitor, Polar Vantage XL Heart Rate Monitor;
4. Water quality: includes use of Vernier Probes, Computer, eProbe, and eMates.

InTime also includes **high school** science lessons such as

1. The ocean, which involves use of HyperStudio;
2. Biology lesson that involves use of the QX3 Computer Microscope;
3. Physics lesson on Newton's second law that includes use of Photogates, ULI interface, and a computer.

The Comprehensive, Conceptual Curriculum for Physics (C3P), discussed earlier in this chapter, also has useful resources at its Web site. Their Learning Cycle–based course topics and materials are summarized in Table 11.6. Hot links at the C3P Web site provide more detailed information on these topics and subtopics. The whole project is available on a CD-ROM, which includes curriculum materials and resources.

Other technology-based resources for learning science include online homework helpers and tutorials in physics such as http://www.physics247.com/, "Physics Homework Help from Experts." For assistance with chemistry, "The Science Page" (http://sciencepage.org/chem.htm) offers a variety of online resources for both teachers and students.

Free, online science resources for teachers, sponsored by the National Science Teachers Association, are available at http://science.nsta.org/enewsletter/2007-06/news_stories_high.htm. This site includes links to a variety of projects, such as "Urban Bird Studies," "Court TV" for forensic science, and "Project Oceanography."

The graphic organizer software, Inspiration, has science-specific templates that are easily modifiable for use by teachers and students. They are

1. Concept maps
2. Lab reports
3. Scientific method
4. Simple cycles

Figure 11.4 shows the basic structure of the Scientific Method template. Your school district might want to follow the lead of others and purchase a site license

TABLE 11.6 Course Topics (with Subtopics)
▪ Experiences, Observations, and Order; Inquiry; Logic; Gathering and Analyzing Data
▪ The Nature of Matter; Wave Particle Duality; The Fundamentals of Matter; Models of the Atom; Fusion and Fission of Atoms; The Universe from the Nuclear to the Galactic; Measurements of Matter; Space; Time
▪ Idea of Change in Time; Frames of Reference, Position, and Position vs. Time Graphs; Total Distance Traveled and Displacement; Velocities and Velocity-Time Graphs; Acceleration; Approaching the Speed of Light
▪ Classification of Forces; Force and Momentum; Resistance to Change in Velocity; Interactions; Gravitation; Forces Causing Two-Dimensional Motion; Threads to the Future
▪ Energy; Thermodynamics; Redistribution of Energy in Systems
▪ Electrostatics; Potential Difference, Current, and Resistance (Ohm's Law); Magnetism; Solid State Electronics
▪ General Wave Properties; Periodic Waves; Modeling Phenomena as Waves; Wave Behaviors; Simple Harmonic Motion; Matter as Waves and Particles
▪ Atomic Physics; Chaos and Fractals; Cosmology; Nuclear Physics; Particle Physics; Michelson-Morley Experiment; Special Relativity; General Relativity

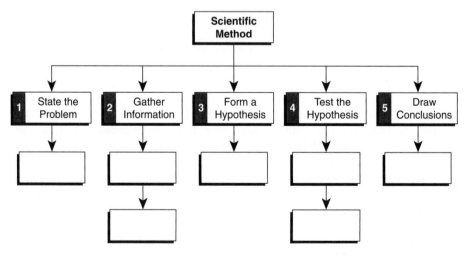

FIGURE 11.4 *Scientific Method Template*

for use in all schools, although a 30-day free trial version is available at the Inspiration Software Web site.

Summary

Important considerations for reflective and critical thinking in science teaching are standards, preconceptions or misconceptions students might bring to class; having a repertoire of active learning–based teaching methods for overcoming preconceptions (misconceptions); helping students learn to think authentically, reflectively, and critically like scientists; and students' motivation and attitudes about science. Some teaching strategies, such as the Learning Cycle, Concept Maps, Inquiry Learning, and Questioning, are especially recommended for science instruction. Numerous technology-based resources are available for science teaching.

Resources

Abimbola, I. O; and S. Baba. "Misconceptions and Alternative Conceptions in Science Textbooks: The Role of Teachers as Filters." *The American Biology Teacher* 58, no. 1 (1996), pp. 14–19.

American Heart Association. Common Misconceptions About Cholesterol. 2007. Retrieved July 17, 2007 from http://www.americanheart.org/presenter .jhtml?identifier=3006030.

ASD Planetarium (n.d.). Introduction to Astronomy: Popular Misconceptions in Astronomy. Retrieved August 5, 2007 from http://www.astronomy.org/ astronomy-survival/misconcp.html.

Baird, J. R. "Improving Learning Through Enhanced Metacognition: A Classroom Study." *European Journal of Science Education* 8, no. 3 (1992), pp. 263–282.

Binghamton University. Overcoming Ecology Misconceptions: Using the Power of Story. 2004. Retrieved August 5, 2007 from http://ecomisconceptions .binghamton.edu/intro.htm.

Brown, T.; and J. Crowder (n.d.). *Students' Difficulties in Physics Information Center.* Retrieved July 17, 2006 from http://www.physics.montana.edu/physed/ misconceptions/.

Comprehensive Conceptual Curriculum for Physics (C3P). 2007. Retrieved July 22, 2007 from http://phys.udallas.edu/.

Chemistry Misconceptions (n.d.). Retrieved August 5, 2007 from http://educ.queensu.ca/ ~science/main/concept/chem/c07/C07CDTL1.htm.

Cook, L.; and R. E. Mayer. "Teaching Readers about the Structure of Scientific Text." *Journal of Educational Psychology* 80, no. 4 (1988), pp. 448–56.

Elkin, L. O. "Rosalind Franklin and the Double Helix." *Physics Today.* February 2003, p. 61. Retrieved August 5, 2007 from http://www.aip.org/pt/vol-56/iss-3/ p42.html.

Eylon, B.; and M. Linn. "Learning and Instruction: An examination of four research perspectives in science education." *Review of Educational Research* 58 (1988), pp. 251–301.

Hartman, H. Metacognition in Science Teaching and Learning. In *Metacognition in Learning and Instruction,* ed. H. J. Hartman. Dordrecht: Springer, 2001.

Hartman, H.; and N. Glasgow. *Tips for the Science Teacher: Research-Based Strategies to Help Students Learn.* Thousand Oaks, CA: Corwin Press, 2002.

Inspiration Software (n.d.). Retrieved August 5, 2007 from http://www.inspiration.com.

InTime. Science Content Videos. 2002. Retrieved August 5, 2007 from http://www.intime.uni.edu/vidsearch/Display/Display_Content_Area.asp.

Karplus, R. *The Science Curriculum Improvement Study.* (SCIS) Lawrence Hall of Science, University of California, Berkeley, 1974.

Kolb, D. *Experiential Learning: Experience as the Sources of Learning and Development.* Upper Saddle River, NJ: Prentice Hall, 1984.

Lutz, A. (n.d.). Educating Students to Eliminate Eating Misconceptions. Retrieved August 5, 2007 from http://healthydevil.studentaffairs.duke.edu/peer_education/peer_groups/esteem.html.

Mayer, R. "Models for Understanding." *Review of Educational Research* 59, no. 1 (1989), pp. 43–64.

McDermott, L. "Millikan Lecture 1990: What We Teach and What Is Learned—Closing the Gap." *American Journal of Physics* 59, no. 4 (1991), pp. 301–15.

Meaningful Learning Group. (n.d.). Fourth Misconceptions Seminar. Ithaca, NY. Retrieved July 17, 2007 from http://www2.ucsc.edu/mlrg/proc4abstracts.html.

Mestre, J. *Problem Posing as a Tool for Probing Conceptual Development and Understanding in Physics.* 1994. Paper presented at the Annual Meeting of the American Educational Research Association, New Orleans.

Minstrell, J. "Teaching Science for Understanding." In *Toward the Thinking Curriculum: Current Cognitive Research,* ed. L. Resnick and L. Klopfer. Association for Supervision and Curriculum Development, Alexandria, VA, 1989.

Narode, R.; M. Heiman; J. Lochhead; and J. Slomianko. *Teaching Thinking Skills: Science.* Washington, D.C., National Educational Association, 1987.

National Academy of Science. National Science Education Standards. National Academy Press. 1995. Retrieved August 5, 2007 from http://www.nap.edu/readingroom/books/nses/html/.

Novak, J. *Learning, Creating and Using Knowledge.* Hillsdale, NJ: Lawrence Erlbaum Associates, 1998.

Randall, L. *Warped Passages: Unraveling the Mysteries of the Universe's Hidden Dimensions.* New York: Harper Perennial, 2005.

Reformed Teaching Observation Protocol (RTOP). 2002. Retrieved July 17, 2007 from http://physicsed.buffalostate.edu/AZTEC/RTOP/RTOP_full/.

Perkins, D.; and R. Simmons. "An Integrative Model of Misconceptions." *Review of Educational Research* 58, no. 3 (1988), pp. 303–26.

Regis, A.; and P. G. Albertazzi. "Concept Maps in Chemistry Education." *Journal of Chemical Education* 73, no. 11 (1996), pp. 1084–88.

Roth, K. "Reading Science for Conceptual Change." In *Science Learning: Processes and Applications,* ed. C. M. Santa and D. E. Alvermann. Newark, DE: International Reading Association, 1991, pp. 48–63.

Schneps, *A Private Universe.* Scientific Reasoning Research Institute. 1994. Retrieved July 17, 2007 from http://srri.nsm.umass.edu/.

Spiegel, G.; and J. Barufaldi. "The Effects of a Combination of Text Structure Awareness and Graphic Postorganizers on Recall and Retention of Science Knowledge." *Journal of Research in Science Teaching* 31, no. 9 (1994), pp. 913–19.

Tobias, S. "Peer Perspectives on the Teaching of Science." *Change.* March/April 1986, pp. 36–41.

Trends in International Mathematics and Science Study. 2003. Retrieved December 4, 2006 from http://isc.bc.edu/timss2003i/scienceD.html.

U. Massachusetts, Science, Technology, Engineering and Mathematics Teacher Education Collaborative (STEMTEC) 2007. Retrieved August 5, 2007 from http:// k12s.phast.umass.edu/%7Estemtec/.

Walberg, H. "Improving School Science in Advanced and Developing Countries." *Review of Educational Research* 61, no. 1 (1991), pp. 25–69.

Whimbey, A.; and J. Lochhead. *Problem Solving and Comprehension.* Philadelphia: Franklin Institute Press, 1982.

Yount, L. *Asian-American Scientists (American Profiles).* New York: Facts on Files, 1998.

Zinsser, J. *La Dame D'Esprit: A Biography of the Marquise Du Chatelet.* New York: Viking, 2006.

CHAPTER 12

Reflective Practice in Teaching English

This chapter has three main categories of information on teaching English reflectively and critically. First it focuses on teaching literature, next it addresses writing, and finally it takes on grammar. The chapter includes use of questioning and technology in teaching these aspects of English. Reading was addressed in Chapter 9, and writing for ESL students is a topic in Chapter 13, on Foreign Language Teaching.

Literature

The following questions are intended to prompt you to analyze and evaluate some characteristics of teaching and learning literature in your classroom. How do your students read literature? Do they relate literary work to their own experiences? How might you help them recognize and express relationships between themselves and what they read? What teaching strategies do you use to foster engagement in reading and responsiveness to text? How open are you to interpretations of literature that differ from your own? Reflective literature teaching involves taking a middle ground between viewing one interpretation as correct and accepting all interpretations as equally valid.

To what extent do your students become immersed in the literature they read and really connect with the characters and events? How do they think about what they read in relationship to a continuum of orientation from information to aesthetics? Do your students view literature as a tool for understanding themselves and their world in addition to understanding the author and the text? Are your students aware of how their individual characteristics and experiences impact on their interpretations of what they read? Each time you teach a piece of literature the results should be different because your students are different!

Unfortunately many students read literature relatively passively and take in information without actively thinking about it and making connections to their own experiences and culture. Many students don't realize how their cultural and regional origins, as well as their age, gender, socioeconomic status, and personal experiences, affect their roles as readers and the interpretations they construct.

Numerous techniques are available to help students become more reflective in their reading of literature. For example, see the Literary Web graphic organizer template in the Technology section.

Some literature teaching strategies are characterized as **rhetorically based writings** and depend on the logical structure of the text and context. These techniques include

1. Students assume the role of one character and write a letter to another character in the text.
2. Students write a letter to the author about their interpretation of the text.
3. Students act out the characters and events as a role play.
4. Students create an environment or set for the role play that is consistent with the author's characterization of it in the text.
5. Students write a letter to the audience about what they want them to get out of watching the role play.
6. Students write letters to each other comparing and contrasting the text with their own experiences with the world in which they live.

Each of these strategies requires students to carefully examine the text and reevaluate it from multiple perspectives. The reevaluations are likely to occur in several iterations, thereby enabling students to get broader and deeper perspectives on what they read and its meaningfulness to them.

Literature Reading Continuum

Most students and many teachers are unfamiliar with the idea that there is a literature reading continuum. At one end of the continuum is the orientation toward information acquisition and comprehension. At the other end of the continuum is the orientation toward aesthetic response and interpretation. What do you emphasize in your own teaching of literature? Many literature teachers are more interested in the latter than the former. What strategies best promote reading with an aesthetic orientation?

Literature Logs are informal writing tools that can help students use writing to think critically about literature. One approach emphasizes students analyzing and evaluating not just situations, events, or actions, but also making inferences and reflecting on implications. This approach also suggests that students compare belief systems or perspectives and reason about them independently, challenging invalid assumptions found in arguments. Prompt students to write about these issues by asking challenging questions.

Types and Levels of Literature Questions

Table 12.1 highlights three levels of questions that can be used in teaching literature. Within each level are different types of questions. Examples for teaching literature are given for each level and type. Research shows that students learn most when you spend the majority of your time questioning beyond the lowest level, which focuses on knowledge and comprehension. The intermediate and higher levels focus on more complex thinking so students learn more from these questions.

TABLE 12.1   Low-, Intermediate-, and High-Level Questions: Literature

Question Level and Type	Example of Question Type
LOW LEVEL	
Label	What is the term for a word with the same meaning as another word?
Define	What is an analogy?
Describe	What was the setting in which the novel took place?
INTERMEDIATE	
Sequence	What was the sequence of events that led to the discovery of the hidden treasure?
Reproduce	How would you diagram the location of the treasure?
Describe Similarities/Differences	How is this short story similar to/different from the other we read from the same author?
Estimate	About how long did it take them to dig up the hidden treasure?
Enumerate	What were all the places they looked for the treasure before finally finding it?
Infer Similarities/Differences	What moral was implicit in both of these stories?
Classify	What type of novel is this?
Synthesize	If we combine all the characteristics of our heroine, how would you describe her?
Apply	How could you use the reading strategy of imagery to help you remember this poem?
Analyze	What are all the feelings the poet is trying to evoke?
HIGH	
Evaluate	What do you think was the single most important clue that led to the discovery of the hidden treasure? Why?
Causal Relation	Why didn't the villain discover the treasure when he had so many clues?
Infer Affect	How do you think the villain felt when he discovered someone else beat him to the treasure?
Generalize	How do stories of good versus evil generally end?

TABLE 12.1 *(Continued)*	
Question Level and Type	**Example of Question Type**
Predict Outcome	How do you think the story will end?
Transform	How would the poem be different if it took place in winter rather than spring?
Plan	What steps would you take if you were to write a mystery like this one?
Verify	How could you determine the validity of the information in this critique of the novel?
Conclude	Now that you've examined all the narrator's arguments, to what conclusion do they lead you?
Resolve Conflict	Who should benefit from the treasure's discovery, the heroine who found it or the person who originally owned it?

Which levels and types of questions are most characteristic of your teaching of literature? Which might you use more of?

⚔ Writing

Writing is potentially a powerful tool for promoting reflective and critical thinking in English and virtually all other academic subjects and many aspects of everyday life. Many colleges and universities have recognized this potential and developed special programs and courses that emphasize writing in the various disciplines and writing across the curriculum.

You can help your students prepare for success in higher education by using writing to develop their reflective and critical thinking skills in all subjects through intensive and diverse writing assignments.

In addition to doing their own writing, have students analyze and critically evaluate their own writing as well as that of others. Topics for analysis include looking for inconsistencies and ambiguities, detecting implicit and explicit assumptions, differentiating fact from opinion, using reliable versus unreliable sources, presenting a more objective point of view versus a more biased one, and emphasizing relevant rather than irrelevant information. Have students use a checklist with these and other characteristics, as appropriate for the particular writing assignment, to assess their own writing before turning it in for a grade. Use a peer editing approach whereby students apply objective criteria to evaluating the writing of other students.

Building and defending arguments is an important feature of many disciplines. How effective are your students in constructing arguments? Do they provide sound evidence to support their arguments? The Structured Controversy approach to debating, briefly described in Chapter 8 on Teaching Strategies, is an excellent approach for developing critical thinking and the ability to construct a sound, well thought out, supported argument. It also helps students consider and understand issues from multiple points of view, thereby enhancing their recognition of and appreciation for complexity.

Sample Lesson on Developing a Persuasive Argument

How do you teach students to develop persuasive arguments? Following is a sample lesson and dialogue from a hypothetical middle school class learning to develop a persuasive argument. The teacher uses questioning to promote reflective and critical thinking about this type of writing.

Teacher: Today you're going to plan, develop, and write a persuasive argument while continuing to learn about America's involvement in the Vietnam War. What does that mean, "a persuasive argument"?

Alicia: That you're going to convince somebody of something.

Marika: That you're going to try to change somebody's mind.

Jeff: You are going to get somebody to think the same way you do.

Teacher: What would be an example of a persuasive argument?

Noah: We would try to persuade you to give us a party instead of a test on Thursday.

Teacher: What is it that makes an argument persuasive instead of just an argument?

Blank stares made Ms. Smart wonder if her students really understood the word "persuasive."

Teacher: Let's look at how the word "persuasive" is used in context. In our social studies book, in the chapter on Vietnam, find the section that discussed how the popular antiwar movement helped persuade President Johnson not to run for reelection.

As students paged through their texts, Ms. Smart wrote "persuade" and "persuasive" on the blackboard. Jose's hand shot up.

Jose: I think persuasive means that the argument worked.

Teacher: What do you mean, Jose? Can you elaborate on that a little for us?

Jose: Well, it seems like first President Johnson was going to run for reelection, but all the people marching in the streets made him change his mind.

Teacher: What in the world does marching in the streets have to do with an argument?

Jann: People were protesting the war. They wanted it to end. They blamed Johnson for it and didn't want him to be president any more.

Teacher: What was their argument?

Jann: They were saying that the war is morally wrong. They were also saying that we couldn't win the war. And I think they were saying that Johnson couldn't win because too many people were against him. I think that was the most persuasive part. Seeing all the protesters made Johnson decide that he couldn't win. That was probably the reason he decided not to run. He probably figured, why should I waste my time and energy when so many people are against me that I'm not going to be president again anyway.

Teacher: So what can we conclude about the use of the word "persuasive" from this context?

Nancy: An argument is persuasive if it makes you change how you feel or think or act. The argument has to have good reasons for why you should think a particular way.

Teacher: What would be an illustration of a persuasive argument?

Tanya: It's better to eat fruit for dessert than to eat candy. If you eat too much candy, your teeth will fall out. And fruit won't make your teeth fall out, no matter how much you eat.

Teacher: Why is that argument persuasive?

Tanya: Because you really wouldn't want your teeth to fall out.

Teacher: OK. What would be an example of an argument that is not persuasive?

Noah: Don't eat too much candy or you won't have room for dinner—when dinner is going to be (yuk!) liver.

Teacher: Why isn't that argument persuasive?

Noah: How many kids do you know that like liver?

Teacher: You have a point there! OK, so as I suggested earlier, one of the objectives of today's lesson is for you to learn how to develop a persuasive argument. In particular, we will focus on two related objectives: one—planning your argument, and two—giving reasons to support your conclusions or providing evidence.

As the teacher wrote these objectives on the board she asked, "What do we mean by "planning your argument"? Students were silent.

Teacher: What do you do when you plan to solve a math problem? Let's apply what you do there to this situation.

Bob: You decide what to do before actually solving the problem.

Teacher: So how would we plan in writing?

Bob: I guess by deciding what we are going to write before we start writing.

Teacher: And what kinds of things do we have to decide?

Getting no response, the teacher prodded a little harder.

Teacher: Think back to math again. What are some things you decide before solving a word problem?

Denny: What formula to use.

Teacher: What else?
Denny: What all the steps are for solving the problem.
Alicia: What order to do the steps in.
Teacher: OK, and what else?

A third time silence filled the air. But this time it persisted until faces began to show puzzled reflection. Finally one student asked whether they could look at their notebooks. Jennifer remembered a list of planning questions she wrote down to use for solving math problems.

Jeff: Oh, I know! First we have to say what the problem is.
Tanya: And we have to figure out how to write down the important information.
Marika: We're also supposed to think about how we could picture the problem in our minds.
Teacher: OK, now we have a list of the kinds of decisions you have to make when planning to solve a math problem. What does that imply about the planning we have to do in a writing assignment? What are some questions you could ask yourself to help you plan writing a persuasive essay on the Vietnam War?

As the students brainstormed self-questions, the teacher wrote them on the board next to the math planning steps. (See Table 12.2.)

TABLE 12.2   Student-Generated Self-Questions for Planning: Writing

Math	Writing
What formula should I use?	What am I supposed to write about?
What steps do I follow?	Will I have to use my textbook?
In what order do I do these steps?	Will I have to go to the library?
What is the problem?	What steps will I have to take to write the essay?
How do I record the important information?	How will I organize the information?
What would a "mental picture" (image) of the problem look like?	What will the essay look like?
Have I ever solved a problem like this before?	In what order should I do the steps?
	What do I already know about the topic—reasons for America's involvement in the Vietnam War?
	Who am I writing this for?
	What is the purpose of this essay?

Teacher:	Why shouldn't we just start writing? Why should we ask ourselves such questions?
Bob:	You said we should always ask ourselves questions before we do any kind of work.
Teacher:	But why? What is the value of such questions? What is the value of planning?
Bob:	It helps you do a better job.
Teacher:	In what way?
Bob:	So you remember to include all the important information.
Teacher:	And . . .
Nancy:	So you don't forget any steps.
Teacher:	Ok. What else?
Jann:	If you plan, then your essay will sound better.
Teacher:	Why?
Jann:	It helps you figure out what to put first, second, third—like that.
Teacher:	And why is that a good thing to do?
Nancy:	Well, if you're trying to convince somebody of something, then it's important to figure out your list of reasons and put them in a place where they'll have the best chance of changing somebody's mind—like at the very beginning or the very end.
Teacher:	How can learning how to develop a persuasive argument help you in your everyday life?
Sean:	I hope it will help me convince my parents to allow me to ride my bike alone to the park and to stay up later at night.
Shannon:	I want it to help me persuade my sister to share her clothes with me.
Serge:	Maybe I'll be able to convince my parents to let me go to a sleepaway camp next summer!
Tanya:	It could help me write better in general.
Noah:	It could help us write better letters like to our friends who live far away.
Alicia:	It could help us write better letters when applying for a job.
Teacher:	Yesterday when we studied the Vietnam War, we learned that a lot of young people were opposed to the war. What did some of these people do?
Denny:	Some of them burned their draft cards.
Jann:	Some went to jail.
Jeff:	Some left their families and moved to Canada.
Marika:	Some of them became "conscientious objectors."
Teacher:	What does that mean?
Marika:	Some men were excused from serving in the war because of their religious beliefs and said "Thou shall not kill" is in the Ten Commandments.
Teacher:	Um hum. Did everybody who wanted to become a "conscientious objector" in fact become one?
Alicia:	No—Some people were turned down.

Teacher:	Why?
Alicia:	Some places had a limit on the number of people who were allowed to be conscientious objectors.
Teacher:	Why else?
Bob:	Some people only said they had religious reasons for not wanting to go, but they really weren't religious.
Teacher:	Right. And another way of looking at it is to say that these men did not convince the authorities that their "conscientious objector" claim was valid.

The teacher made a semantic web of a variety of reasons people gave about why they should be granted "conscientious objector" status. (See Figure 12.1.)

The teacher asked the class to examine the reasons on the board in regard to two things: 1) Which reasons are the most effective? 2) What are the characteristics of good reasons? After considerable discussion the class brainstormed these guidelines.

1. There should be logic or evidence to support reasons.
2. Good reasons are justified based on facts and logic rather than emotions and biases.
3. Opinions that are based on fact or expertise are more influential than those based on emotion.

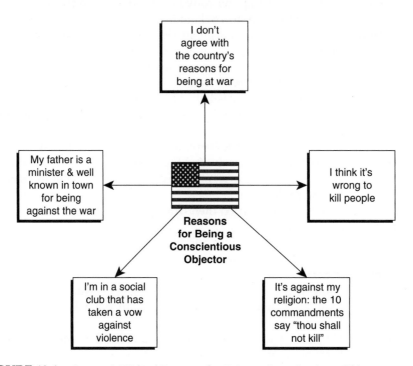

FIGURE 12.1   *Semantic Web of Reasons for Being a Conscientious Objector*

4. Personal bias distorts reasons and makes them hard to believe or accept.
5. Reasons are sometimes good because they are presented in combination with other reasons.

Then the teacher made an assignment.

Teacher: You are to interview two people in this class about their views on the Vietnam War. Find one person who will argue that the United States should have fought and one who will argue that we should not have fought. You are to present both arguments. Then you should analyze each argument and decide which is better and why. Then you will develop an argument in which you will try to persuade the reader that the argument you selected is the more convincing of the two. Each person in the class must take two turns being interviewed. One time you must argue in favor of the war. One time you must argue against it.

As the students began working, the teacher wrote the following homework assignment on the board.

Homework Assignment

Find at least one newspaper or magazine article and show how in real life the journalist cites reasons and provides evidence for the arguments made.

1. Identify the arguments and then look at how they are constructed.
2. Show how the author supports the argument.
3. Evaluate the author's reasons and evidence. Decide whether the arguments are persuasive and explain why or why not.

To begin the in-class assignment, Marika reviewed the poster on the wall, "Thinking Tools for Reading and Writing" (see Tables 12.3 and 12.4). Although most of the time she remembered what to do, why, and how, sometimes she checked the chart just to make sure. She remembered how she used to look at it all the time before she started using these strategies on a regular basis. Gradually they became hers. "I'm going to make up a list of all the questions I can think of that I might want to ask the people I interview. Then I'll pick the best ones, put them in groups, and decide what order to ask them in. I also better think about how long each interview will take so I make sure I have enough time to do a good job on everything."

Writing Problems

What types of writing problems, other than grammar and spelling, are typical of your students? Which problems are most serious in terms of interfering with students expressing their ideas? For example, common important problems include sentence structure and word usage. Sentence fragments can convey incomplete thoughts. Word usage problems can convey wrong ideas. Another type of problem is resistance to revising.

TABLE 12.3   Thinking Tools for Reading and Writing: Guidelines for Strategies

Strategy	What	When	Why
Reading			
	Generate schema	Before	Activate existing relevant knowledge
	Skim	Before	Get initial understanding
	Self-question	During	Test understanding and memory
	Clarify	During	Repair breakdown of understanding
	Image	During	Aid and enrich comprehension and memory
	Predict Outcome	During	Show purpose in reading
	Review	After	Consolidate and remember
	Summarize	After	Establish main idea
Writing			
	Pre-write	Before	Generate general ideas
	Pre-compose	Before	Generate task-specific ideas
	Write	During	Change thoughts into print
	Share	After write	Get and give feedback
	Revise	After feedback	To improve
	Edit	After revise	Make refinements
	Proofread	After revise	Ensure accuracy
	Evaluate	After graded	Assess extent to which standard was met
	Plan	After graded	Figure out how to improve future writing

TABLE 12.4   Thinking Tools for Reading and Writing: Constraints

Reading	Writing
Native language literacy	Knowledge to construct and express ideas
Text language: native/foreign	Writer's language: native/foreign Vocabulary for communication
Text difficulty	Audience and purpose
Strategy use	Context

Often students resist getting critical feedback and/or using feedback to improve their writing, even when problems limit the ability of a reader to understand their ideas. How good are your students at organizing ideas according to their relevance to the specific topic? Do they present ideas using an appropriate sequence? Do they make overgeneralizations or uncritically include cultural myths or stereotypes? Consider the ideas and strategies in this lesson that you could apply to your own teaching to help students express themselves more fully and accurately.

Research shows that expert and novice writers differ in the thinking processes they use while writing. The three major processes needed for writing are planning, sentence generation, and revising. Experts and novices engage in these processes differently. Unlike novices, who tend to be rigid and linear in their thinking, experts are flexible and recursively shift between planning, translating, and reviewing. For example, while they are planning, expert writers review and revise their plans, while at the same time transforming the ideas in their plans into text. They think about the big picture of what they are writing (persuading a reader to accept their arguments), but also think about mid-level goals, such as having an intriguing title, and lower-level goals such as writing the first sentence.

Extensive writing experience helps writers put important writing skills, such as planning and revising, on automatic pilot so that they don't put a burden on short-term memory. Novice writers often have preconceptions or misconceptions about writing. One is that the ability to write is innate—either you have it or you don't. Another preconception is that writing involves communicating everything you know about a topic instead of being selective. A third is that writing is easy for good writers, that they record their ideas the best way on their first try and don't have to make revisions. Computer-based writing tools can help novices learn to write more like experts. Such tools include word processors, idea organizers, process prompts, and text analyzers.

Teaching students to manage their work by planning, monitoring, and evaluating helps them to develop critical thinking skills so they can analyze their own work, make use of feedback from others, determine when and how to revise and improve what they have written, and write more proficiently in the future. Such management strategies for academic work are discussed in Chapter 6 on Students' Reflective and Critical Thinking. What are your own strengths and weaknesses as a writer and as a writing teacher?

I DREAM of A

There is a very helpful tool that has been developed to help students plan, monitor, and evaluate their work in writing. It also makes them aware of their attitudes toward the writing assignment. It is called "I DREAM of A." It uses strategies of questioning and thinking out loud. A math/science version is described in Chapter 10 on Mathematics.

I DREAM of A expands on and integrates a general problem solving model with specific focus on the writing process. It includes consideration of students' attitudes toward the writing task and prescribes instructional techniques (questioning and thinking aloud). The I DREAM of A process is not a rigid, cookbook formula. It is intended to be personally transformed by each person who uses it, each time it is used. It is meant to be adapted to each unique situation.

I DREAM of A is an acronym for a systematic approach to thinking about the processes involved in writing. Its purpose is to increase students' awareness of how they write, and help them take control over their own performance, helping them to become better writers. The first four letters, I, D, R, and E, are all planning steps that may be accomplished in any order. **Planning** is often described as the thinking that is done before actually beginning to write. Students often err by jumping in and trying to write before they understand the specific topic or assignment. **Monitoring** has at least three aspects: checking up on students' understanding of the content covered in the specific writing assignment, checking up on their understanding of procedures to follow so they may successfully fulfill the assignment, and checking up while work is in progress to make sure they are headed in the right direction. Students seek clarifying information or change approaches as needed. **Evaluating** involves judging both the finished work product and the process of how it was completed. Planning, monitoring, and evaluating are recursive, not linear processes. Sometimes they occur simultaneously. Teach students to apply these thinking processes to practically everything they do until the processes become automatic. Also teach students to be selective when applying these forms of thinking. Not all are needed all the time.

I = identify and define the task; establish positive attitudes
D = diagram or outline
R = recall relevant content, vocabulary, grammar, syntax rules, spelling, punctuation, definitions, prior writing assignments and feedback on types of errors.
E = examine alternative methods for approaching the topic or expressing an idea
A = apply the results of the planning process, developing a draft of the writing assignment
M = monitor progress on the task. Make revisions as needed. The student's attitude is also monitored. If the attitude is negative, strategies should be used to change it.
A = assess the final product based on feedback, determine what and how to improve for the next task, and reward successful performance

The questions and suggestions in Table 12.5 illustrate the types of questions that can guide a writer in the process of a writing assignment such as an essay. Questions should be **generated by the writer for each specific writing task.** They are not generic questions that are always asked regardless of what is being written. These questions are intended to stimulate thinking about the types of questions to ask during each phase of the writing process. Questions are more effective when they are self-generated by the writer than when they come from an external source such as a teacher.

TABLE 12.5   I DREAM of A in Writing

Component of "I DREAM of A" Writing Process	Sample Questions and Tasks
I Identify	• What is the general topic of your essay? • What are some points you would like to make? Why? • Think out loud about the topic. • What is your topic sentence? • Which points support your topic? How good are they? • How would you clearly state your thesis? • How could you elaborate on/clarify that? • How do you feel about your ability to write on this topic? • How can you benefit from this writing assignment?
D Diagram	• Make a web or sketch of the main points and other important ideas. • How could the ideas be connected and organized effectively? • Create a mental picture of what your paper will look like. • What might be included in the introductory paragraph? • What could be included in the developmental paragraphs? • Do an outline or web of what each paragraph might look like. • Are the parts in a logical sequence? • Make a tree diagram to show your topics, main points, and the supporting examples.
R Recall	• What content needs to be incorporated? • What verb tenses will you use? • What types of grammatical problems have you had in the past? • What needs to be reviewed before writing begins?
E Explore	• Think out loud about what might be put into an introductory paragraph. • What are some good examples to choose from? • Are there other points that might go in the introductory paragraph? • How could the situation be viewed from a different perspective? • What might be a better way of saying that? • How might the whole paper be reorganized?

(*continued*)

TABLE 12.5 (*Continued*)	
Component of "I DREAM of A" Writing Process	Sample Questions and Tasks
A Apply	• Take the plan and write a draft. • Look back at notes to remember key points. • Don't worry about grammar or spelling now. • Get out your ideas first and take care of the rest later. • Talk out loud to hear what is being written. • Maintain a positive outlook.
M Monitor	• How is the writing going so far? • Reread aloud what has been written. • How do you feel about what you've written so far? • Are your ideas flowing smoothly? • How could it be better? • Are you developing all your main points sufficiently? • Is the path of your thinking clear? • How well is it organized? • Is there anything important that's missing?
A Assess	• What did the teacher think about your essay/paper? • What did you do well? • How could you do better next time? • Did you revise your paper before word processing it? • Did you and someone else carefully proofread the final copy before turning it in? • Should you reward yourself for a job well done?

There are at least four ways to use the model in Table 12.5. The first way is for you to model your own processes as a writer, using self-questioning and thinking aloud strategies so students can see how you think through the writing process. The second way is for you to ask students such questions when guiding them through the writing process. The third way is for you to teach students to use the model as a guide for questioning each other as they collaborate in guiding each other's writing. Students can take turns alternating between question asker and question answerer. The fourth way is for students to use the model when working on their writing alone.

The questions in Table 12.5 are phrased as a teacher would ask a student, or a student would ask another student. Following are examples of self-questions students can learn to ask themselves:

• Did I express my ideas clearly?
• Do my examples support my thesis?
• Are my conclusions logical?
• Am I varying my vocabulary enough?

- How well am I avoiding repetition?
- Do I have any irrelevant examples?
- Do I have run-on sentences?

Use questioning and thinking aloud as techniques to guide students through a systematic approach to writing. This will help them internalize the processes and be able to use them in the future. With practice, students learn to automatically self-question and guide their own writing through the stages of the writing process.

What *Is* the Topic?

Sometimes students go in the wrong direction when completing an assignment. Misinterpretation is a prevalent problem in practically all subjects, from determining a specific essay topic, to understanding what's being asked on a multiple-choice item, to identifying a math problem to be solved. Students can learn techniques that will help them correctly identify the specific topic they need to address when writing. These techniques require students to carefully analyze the information provided, ask and answer appropriate questions about it to clarify the meaning, and integrate this information with their prior knowledge. Students should know that there are just a few different basic types of essays, and should know the characteristics of each. Record your thoughts about these characteristics in Table 12.6 and compare your responses with others.

The following are sample self-questions students should learn to ask to help them clarify the writing task:

- What is the topic?
- What do I know about this topic?
- What are the most important parts?
- Does this all make sense?
- How do the parts fit together?
- What other self-questions might be useful?

There are several strategies you can use to help students learn to analyze a topic. They can paraphrase the topic to clarify its meaning and compare their paraphrase to the original topic statement. Show them how to break a complex topic into parts, determine the relationships between the parts, and understand how the parts relate to the whole. Demonstrate, by thinking aloud, how to

TABLE 12.6 Characteristics of Essays	
Type of Essay	**Characteristics of This Type of Essay**
Descriptive	
Persuasive	
Narrative	
Explanatory point of view	

differentiate relevant from irrelevant information, and major ideas from minor ones. Give them prompts or clues to help them do this on their own. Keywords and phrases can be used as clues. Examples include words and phrases such as *compare and contrast, explain,* and *synthesize.* Students should form initial hypotheses about the meaning, but avoid jumping to conclusions. They should not simply "assume" they are right, but should continually verify, revise, or reject initial interpretations.

Types and Levels of Writing Questions

Various other types of questions can help your students write more effectively, such as those in Table 12.7.

TABLE 12.7 Low-, Intermediate-, and High-Level Questions: Writing	
Question Level and Type	**Example of Question Type**
LOW LEVEL	
Label	What is it called when you rewrite a paper in order to improve it?
Define	What is a metaphor?
Describe	What is the topic of your paper?
INTERMEDIATE	
Sequence	In what order will you present those ideas?
Reproduce	How could you express that same idea using other words?
Describe Similarities/ Differences	How does the point you're making in the third paragraph differ from the point you made in the second paragraph?
Estimate	About how long do you expect your paper to be?
Enumerate	What points do you want to make in your paper?
Infer Similarities/ Differences	How is the reader supposed to interpret your phrase, "my head was like an erupting volcano"?
Classify	Which point in your paper does that example illustrate?
Synthesize	Thinking of all your main points together, what might be a good title for your paper?
Apply	How could you use an outline to plan your paper?
Analyze	How could you break down this very long paragraph into three or four shorter ones?

TABLE 12.7 *(Continued)*	
Question Level and Type	**Example of Question Type**
HIGH	
Evaluate	What do you think are the strongest and weakest parts of your paper? Why?
Causal Relation	Why did you decide to put that point at the end of your paper instead of at the beginning?
Infer Affect	How do you think the reader will feel while reading your essay?
Generalize	What do you usually include in an opening paragraph?
Predict Outcome	If you turn in your paper as it is now, what grade do you think you'll get?
Transform	How could you change this paragraph to make your argument more convincing?
Plan	How will you show the connections between the points you are making?
Verify	How can you make sure that the main points of your essay really come through to the reader?
Conclude	What conclusions should the reader draw from your paper?
Propose Alternatives	What other ways could you illustrate that point?
Resolve Conflict	Why did you argue in favor of drug searches in the second paragraph and argue against them in the third paragraph?

Graphic Representations

Graphic representations of information to be included in an essay, paper, or report can be excellent alternatives to the more traditional method of outlining. One advantage is providing a visual summary of the writer's ideas. A second advantage is that it helps students see relationships between ideas. A third is that it is not linear, so students are able to see more options for organizing the information. You can show students how to develop and connect ideas by drawing a graphic organizer, such as a semantic web, on the blackboard, as illustrated earlier in this chapter in Figure 12.1, Reasons for Being a Conscientious Objector. Then you can have students draw their own graphic organizers to develop and organize their ideas for a writing assignment. CMAP, discussed later in this chapter in the section on Technology, is an online graphic organizer tool that can help students with writing. Chapter 9 on Reading has more detailed discussion of the various types of graphic organizers. See information on Inspiration Software in the Technology section of this chapter.

✵ Grammar

How would you characterize your students' knowledge of and skills in the proper use of grammar when they speak and write? What are your goals for them?

How do you conceptualize grammar teaching? How much time do you spend on it? What methods do you use? How do you select and use examples when teaching grammar? How do your students view learning grammar? How did you learn grammar?

There are two major sets of extreme views about teaching grammar. Both are misconceptions. One, the traditional view, is that grammar instruction is teaching a set of rules and forms that students should practice and memorize. The other, a more recent view, is that grammar shouldn't be explicitly taught at all; students will learn it automatically and implicitly by listening, speaking, reading, and writing in a language.

What is grammar and why is it important for students to learn? Grammar is an important communication tool. When students understand it, grammar can help them communicate by effectively constructing and interpreting messages. The communication competence model of grammar instruction synthesizes the two misconceived extreme views of grammar by combining the explicit teaching of grammar with teaching language in a naturalistic context.

Teaching grammar reflectively involves careful selection of examples to make sure they are culturally appropriate and accurate. It also emphasizes examples as tools for understanding the specific grammar issue focused on in the lesson. Finally, it views grammar structures, forms, and rules as guides for meaningful communication in specific situations.

Three strategies that are effective for teaching grammar reflectively are questioning, error analysis, and contrastive analysis. While reading about them, think about which of these techniques you already apply and which you might try.

Types and Levels of Grammar Questions

Asking questions is important for helping students think reflectively and critically about their grammar use. Table 12.8 illustrates low-, intermediate-, and high-level questions on grammar.

Grammar Errors

What grammar errors are common in your students? How aware are students of their mistakes? What strategies do you use for correcting students' grammar?

TABLE 12.8   Low-, Intermediate-, and High-Level Questions: Grammar

Question Level and Type	Example of Question Type
LOW LEVEL	
Label	What is the term for when a verb matches the subject, as in "Her greatest need is friends"?
Define	What is a gerund?
Describe	How do you form possessive nouns in these cases: employee and boss?
INTERMEDIATE	
Sequence	What is the correct order of the object, subject, and verb when asking a question in English?
Reproduce	How could you rewrite that sentence so that it says the same thing in the active voice instead of the passive voice?
Describe Similarities/ Differences	How do plurals compare to and differ from possessives?
Estimate	About how many times do you think you made subject–verb agreement mistakes in your paper?
Enumerate	What are all the grammar rules we learned today?
Infer Similarities/ Differences	How did your grammar usage here compare to your last paper?
Classify	What type of error did you make in that sentence?
Synthesize	Looking at all the examples, how would you formulate a rule for punctuating sentences with independent and dependent clauses?
Apply	How would you apply that grammar rule to this paragraph?
Analyze	Which sentences contain no grammar errors?
HIGH	
Evaluate	What areas of grammar do you think you should concentrate on most? Why?
Causal Relation	Why did you use an analogy in that sentence?

(continued)

TABLE 12.8 *(Continued)*	
Question Level and Type	**Example of Question Type**
Infer Affect	What are you trying to convey by your use of the subjunctive?
Generalize	When are semicolons usually used?
Predict Outcome	What would happen to the reader's interpretation of the story if it were written in the past tense instead of the present?
Transform	How would you change this sentence to achieve subject–verb agreement?
Plan	What tense will you use in writing this story?
Verify	How can you make sure that you didn't make any grammar mistakes?
Conclude	What would you conclude about the relationship between mastery of grammar and effective writing?
Propose Alternatives	What are different ways you could change that sentence so that it isn't a "run on"?
Resolve Conflict	Why did you refer to "students" in the first part of the sentence and "student" in the second part of the sentence?

Technology can offer students some assistance with grammar. Most word processing programs have grammar and spelling checkers built into them, which identify actual or possible errors and make recommendations for changes. In Microsoft Word this option is found in the Tools menu, called "Spelling and Grammar." Although it is important for students to know about this possible form of assistance, they should be aware that sometimes the checkers don't understand what the writer is trying to say. They may misidentify correct spelling or grammar as incorrect and may make inappropriate recommendations.

However, when there isn't another person around to provide feedback, the advantages are likely to outweigh the disadvantages. It's not good enough to simply tell students this option is available. Give them explicit information on when and why to use the grammar and spelling checkers in their word processing software. Demonstrate how to use them, thinking out loud to explain your actions as you proceed.

Teaching grammar reflectively includes error analysis, which involves identifying patterns in students' errors. Patterns of grammar mistakes are common on the individual student level, the class level, grade level, school-wide, and in the larger community. For example, common patterns of grammar errors include confusing the formation of plurals with the formation of possessives, subject–verb agreement, tense shifts, and split infinitives. Some of these errors are more serious than others in their impact on clear communication.

One strategy for helping students become more reflective about their grammar usage is having them keep a list of their common grammar mistakes inside the front cover of their English notebook. Students can then be prompted and encouraged to look at this list after they have written a first draft of an essay or paper and check to see if they have made any of the identified types of errors. The list and self-checking process helps students become more aware of their grammar usage and more in control of the quality of their work. If they have trouble identifying these mistakes, they can show their writing and list of common errors to someone with better grammar knowledge and skills to get feedback. Help students establish priorities on which errors merit the most attention.

Make sure not to overwhelm students with negative feedback on their grammar. Remember to focus mostly on the bigger picture of the content conveyed in the communication. Excessive criticism can undermine language learning by discouraging students, increasing the likelihood that they dread language learning rather than appreciate it as an important and precious tool for communicating, both orally and in writing, in all of the school subjects and in everyday life.

Another good strategy for promoting reflective thinking about grammar is **contrastive analysis,** also discussed in the chapter on foreign language learning. Contrastive analysis uses charts to highlight proper and improper language use. By seeing the incorrect and correct grammar examples next to each other, students have a better perspective on what they tend to do incorrectly versus what they should do. Table 12.9 is an example.

TABLE 12.9   Contrastive Analysis in Grammar

Grammar Error Category	Common Grammar Error	Proper Grammar Use
plurals vs. possessives	Her books' were in her backpack.	Her books were in her backpack.
Subject–verb agreement	The books in her backpack was for history and science.	The books in her backpack were for history and science.
verb tense shift	She studied for her chemistry test for three hours after dinner. After she finished studying she calls her best friend to talk about plans for the weekend.	She studied for her chemistry test for three hours after dinner. After she finished studying she called her best friend to talk about plans for the weekend.
split infinitive	Her backpack contained notes to carefully study for the upcoming tests.	Her backpack contained notes to study carefully for the upcoming tests.

⚹ Standard English and Code Switching

A common issue in urban classrooms is that many students are accustomed to using informal language appropriate in their community, but not in school or the workplace. It is important not to devalue students' culture and make them feel that the language they use at home is "wrong." Instead, students should learn the concept of "code switching" so they understand when is the appropriate time and situation for using informal versus formal versions of English. Contrastive analysis between standard English and urban variants can help students learn to differentiate between the two. An online resource for using contrastive analysis to teach code switching is available at http://faculty.users .cnu.edu/rwheeler/wheeler swords_chapter_4.pdf. Through contrastive analysis, students learn the unique characteristics of languages. They can use this knowledge to reflect on and critically evaluate which language forms they are using and self-correct their language use so that it is appropriate for the specific context. They can learn to track their own code-switching strengths and weaknesses.

In a publication sponsored by the National Council of Teachers of English, Wheeler and Swords have a Code-Switching Shopping List Checklist using contrastive analysis. The abbreviated version of it in Table 12.10 can help middle school students keep records of their language use on different papers they write.

TABLE 12.10   Code-Switching Shopping List Checklist

Name _____

Do any of the top 10 or 12 informal English patterns appear in your paper? If so, put a check in the corresponding box and the code-switch to formal English! Put a smiley face to show when you use formal patterns in your writing.

Informal vs. Formal English Patterns	Paper 1	Paper 2	Paper 3	Paper 4
1. Subject–verb agreement She walk_ v. She walk<u>s</u>				
2. Showing past time I finish__ v. I finish<u>ed</u>				
5. Making negatives She <u>won't never</u> v. She won't <u>ever</u>				
7. Plurality: "Showing more than one" Three cat_ v. Three cat<u>s</u>				
8. Possessive: Singular The dog_ tail v. The dog<u>'s</u> tail.				

⚔ Technology

Numerous resources for teaching English are available online and can help you think reflectively about what you teach and how to do it more effectively and reflectively. Comprehensive sites for teaching literature include those that address many different genres of literature, such as http://www.teachingliterature.org/teachingliterature/ and http://teacher2b.com/literature/literature.htm., which also includes lesson plans. Some sites, including http://thwt.org/writingandlit.htm, focus on using technology to teach writing and literature. One of the most comprehensive and diverse teacher resource sites on children's literature and literacy is http://www.childrenslit.com/sites_teacherres.html, which also includes teacher guides and lesson plans.

The National Council of Teachers of English (NCTE) sponsors a site called The Assembly for the Teaching of English Grammar (http://www.ateg.org), which is described as a national forum for grammar instruction. NCTE also has an online position paper on teaching writing

The National Writing Project has links to a PDF version and a printable version of its publication "30 Ideas for Teaching Writing" at http://www.writingproject.org/cs/nwpp/print/nwpr/922.

Computer-based writing tools can help novices learn to write more like experts. Such tools include word processors, idea organizers, process prompts, and text analyzers. See Kozma in the resources at the end of this chapter.

Two different technologies can help students apply graphic organizers to their writing. CMAP, the online concept mapping software mentioned earlier in this chapter, is available free online to educators (http://cmap.ihmc.us/); however, only concept maps are available. Sponsored by the Institute for Human and Machine Cognition, it allows the user to make links to videos, images, and web pages, thereby increasing the modalities and depth of written communications.

Inspiration is another graphic organizer software application; it has many different graphic organizer structures for representing information. Most of the graphic organizers in this book were created with Inspiration. It also includes modifiable templates so that the writer doesn't have to build the structure from scratch. There are seven different Language Arts specific templates:

1. Characteristics of the primary character
2. Comparison and contrast
3. Literary web
4. Mythic journey
5. Persuasive
6. Poetic analysis
7. Vocabulary

Figure 12.2 shows the basic outline of the Literary Web template. Although the software is not free, the price is reasonable and a free 30-day trial version can be downloaded at the company's Web site. See Chapter 9, Figure 9.1 for the poetic analysis template. Recognizing the power and value of this software, many school districts have opted to get a site license for all their schools.

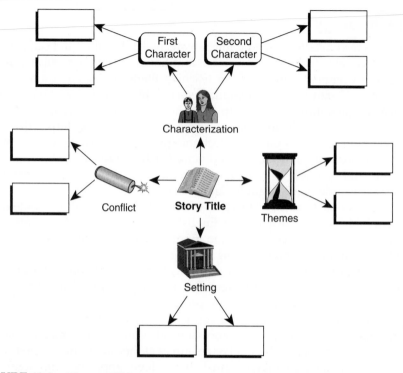

FIGURE 12.2 *Literary Web*

Summary

Teaching English is so multifaceted and fundamental that this chapter focuses on the aspects of literature, writing and grammar, and teaching reading and English as a Second Language are addressed in separate chapters. Students tend to have preconceptions about each of these topics, so it is important for teachers to become aware of and help students overcome their wrong ideas. Questioning can be a powerful tool to help students think reflectively and critically about literary content as well as how they write and use grammar. Other techniques promoting reflective thinking, including graphic organizers, error analysis, contrastive analysis, and code switching, can improve writing. Various forms of technology can aid reflective and critical thinking in English.

Resources

Appleman, D.; R. Beach; S. Hynds; and J. Wilhelm. Teaching Literature. Retrieved July 23, 2007 from http://www.teachingliterature.org/teachingliterature/.

Children's Literature Teaching Materials. (n.d.). Retrieved August 6, 2007 from http://www.childrenslit.com/sites_teacherres.html.

Hayes, J. R.; and L. Flower. "Identifying the Organization of Writing and Processes," in *Cognitive Processes in Writing*, ed. Lee W. Gregg and Erwin R. Steinberg. Hillsdale, NJ: Lawrence Erlbaum Associates, 1980.

Halliday, M. *Introduction to Functional Grammar*. London, New York: Arnold, 1994.

The National Capital Language Resource Center. Washington, D.C. Retrieved June 7, 2006 from http://www.nclrc.org/essentials/grammar/grindex.htm.

Inspiration (n.d.). Retrieved August 6, 2007 from http://www.inspiration.com/.

Institute for Human and Machine Cognition. (n.d.). IHMC CMAP Tools. Retrieved August 6, 2007 from http://cmap.ihmc.us/.

Karolides, Nicholas. "Teaching Literature as a Reflective Practitioner: Script and Spontaneity." *The Wisconsin English Journal* 32, no. 2 (Fall 2001), pp. 16–19. Retrieved October 24, 2006 from http://www.uwrf.edu/wej/Fall2001.pdf.

Kozma, R. "Computer-Based Writing Tools and the Cognitive Needs of Novice Writers." *Computers and Composition* 8, no. 2 (1991), pp. 31–45. Retrieved September 1, 2006 from http://computersandcomposition.osu.edu/archives/v8/8_2.

National Council of Teachers of English. 2007. Retrieved July 23, 2007 from http://www.ncte.org/.

National Writing Project. 30 Ideas for Teaching Writing. 2007. Retrieved July 23, 2007 from http://www.writingproject.org/cs/nwpp/print/nwpr/922.

Paul, R.; A. J. A. Binker; D. Martin; C. Vetrano; and H. Kreklan. *Critical Thinking Handbook: 6th–9th Grades. A Guide for Remodelling Lesson Plans in Language Arts, Social Studies, & Science*. Rohnert Park, CA: Center for Critical Thinking & Moral Critique, 1989.

The National Capital Language Resource Center. Teaching Grammar. 2004. Retrieved August 6, 2007 from http://www.nclrc.org/essentials/grammar/grindex.htm.

Wheeler, R. S.; and R. Swords. (n.d.). Code Switching: Teaching Standard English in Urban Classrooms. Retrieved July 24, 2007 from http://faculty.users.cnu.edu/rwheeler/wheeler_swords_chapter_4pdf.

Learning Foreign Languages Reflectively

One of the most important considerations for foreign language instruction involves reflecting on the prior knowledge students bring to the classroom from their native language. Literacy in one's native language (L1) is an important precursor to acquiring literacy in another language (L2). Some cultures rely on oral language traditions so reading and writing are not considered basic skills. Students who are not literate in their native language usually have difficulty becoming literate in a foreign language. However, literacy in L1 can interfere with learning L2. You and your students need to apply strategies for reflecting on and addressing the relationships between L1 and L2.

✵ Forces Influencing Foreign Language Instruction

According to the Association for Supervision and Curriculum Development's Web site, K–12 foreign language instruction is being shaped by the following forces:

1. The new national standards for foreign language learning were developed by a collaboration between The American Council on the Teaching for Foreign Languages (ACTFL), the American Association of Teachers of French (AATF), the American Association of Teachers of Spanish and Portuguese (AATSP), and the American Association of Teachers of German (AATG). The standards embrace five broad goal areas for designing state and local curricula, the "five Cs of foreign language education": communication, cultures, connections, comparisons, and communities. Eleven standards were derived from these goals.

2. The critical need to participate in global events. A language program's design is shaped by its intended purposes, which will influence decisions about which languages to learn, the onset and duration of instruction, the instructional delivery system, and assessment practices.

3. An emphasis on communication in course outcomes, instructional tasks, and assessment. To be competent communicators in real-life situations, students need instruction to emphasize authentic cultural contexts. The goal of effectively using a foreign language requires class sizes to be small enough for students to have sufficient time to practice speaking.

4. The shift toward cognitive constructivism as the dominant learning theory guiding instruction, which is supported by recent research on the brain and how children learn. Constructivism emphasizes students making meaning and approximating a norm, rather than mastery, or producing perfect utterances at the outset. Research on learning styles calls for adapting content, pacing, and instructional methods to meet the needs of individual learners.

⚔ Goals

An important consideration in foreign language teaching is why each student is studying the language. Are your students required to take a foreign language to graduate from high school or to get into college? Students who are just fulfilling a requirement and are not particularly interested in the language they're studying may need special attention to their motivation. Some schools require students to study two foreign languages. However, even given foreign language requirements, there are usually several languages students can choose from. Ask students why they are studying the particular foreign language you are teaching. Are your students studying a foreign language because they plan to visit a country where this language is spoken, as an exchange student, or for a family vacation? If so, they may be highly motivated to learn it.

For immigrants who plan to make their home in the United States of America, learning English as a foreign language is usually vital for succeeding in the culture. These students are likely to be intrinsically motivated to learn to read, write, speak, and listen in English effectively. To understand these students, it is helpful to know what language is spoken at home and whether the parents and other family members speak English. It is also helpful to know whether the students' parents are literate in their native language, and how their family feels about literacy in general and English in particular. A student's family background and cultural values and practices can have important impacts on the student's success in developing English literacy.

What are your goals for your students' foreign language learning? What do you expect them to be able to do after studying the language with you? How do you assess their progress? Do your students know what you expect? Do they know how they'll be assessed?

One set of foreign language learning goals is

1. Apply vocabulary effectively in oral and written communication.
2. Produce proficient speech in the foreign language.
3. Accurately interpret reading the foreign language.
4. Write effectively in the foreign language.

Table 13.1 is a simple rubric for evaluating oral communication in a foreign language from the Internet (http://www.cathedralhigh.org/foreign_scaffold .htm). Students are rated from a low of 0 to a high of 5.

To what extent do your classroom activities reflect your academic goals? Reflective foreign language teaching can help align your teaching goals with

TABLE 13.1 Oral Communication Rubric

Score	0	1	2	3	4	5
Pronunciation	no response	barely intelligible	numerous errors, difficult to understand	understandable, much native language interference	understandable, minimum native language interference	no conspicuous mispronunciations
Structure	no response	many errors, little sentence structure	numerous errors interfere with communication	frequent errors do not hinder communication	good, several errors	excellent, very few or no errors
Vocabulary	no response	inadequate	limited to basic words, often inaccurate	functional, fails to communicate complete meaning	adequate	precise, varied
Listening Comprehension	no response	recognize simple memorized phrases	comprehends slow or directed speech	comprehends simplified speech	understands speech well, requires some repetition	understands nearly everything
Speaking/Fluency	no response	fragmented, barely intelligible	able to use routine expressions	incomplete sentences, communicates meaning with frequent errors	adequately conveys meaning, several errors	natural, very few errors or no errors

the time students are engaged in class activities. For example, if one of your goals is to develop students' vocabulary in the foreign language, how much class time is devoted to this objective? To what extent do you assign homework with the objective in mind? If another goal is to improve students' grammar in the foreign language, how much time is spent on grammar in class or on out-of-class assignments? Ask yourself similar questions about speaking, reading, and writing in the foreign language. Which of these are your highest priorities? Why? Then modify in-class and out-of-class assignments according to answers so that students' engaged time is consistent with your teaching goals.

⚔ Prior Knowledge

Prior knowledge is often a double-edged sword in foreign language learning. In some cases it facilitates learning, in some cases it has no effect on learning, and in other cases it inhibits learning. For example, if you know the Spanish word "educación" from your native language, then its similarity to the English word "education" makes the English word easier to learn, and vice versa. However, knowing the Spanish word "queso" is too different from the English word "cheese" to facilitate learning in either direction. Knowing the Spanish word "futball," which equates with soccer in the U.S.A., can inhibit learning English because of its similarity with "football."

Reflective foreign language teachers can ask self-questions such as

- What words are similar in my students' native languages to words they will be learning in their foreign language? Recognizing similarities can facilitate making connections between L1 and L2.
- To what extent do students recognize the similarities?
- How can I help students become more aware of the similarities?
- What words from my students' native languages are so different from words in their foreign languages that students won't make connections facilitating learning, or connections might actually cause interference?
- What strategies can I use to help students learn these words?

In some situations, prior knowledge of one's native language can interfere with learning the foreign language because students make connections when they shouldn't. Interference can occur with words, as in the example of "futball" already described, or with sounds. In addition, it is common for native speakers of English to have difficulty learning Spanish vowels (and vice versa) because the letters are the same but the pronunciations are different: "e" in English corresponds to "i" in Spanish; "j" in Spanish corresponds to "h" in English; "y" in Spanish corresponds to "j" or "g" in English. Therefore reflective foreign language teachers can ask self-questions such as

1. How might characteristics of students' native languages make it harder for them to learn characteristics of foreign languages?
2. What strategies can I use to help students recognize and remember the differences between characteristics of L1 and L2?

Students vary in the ease with which they learn foreign languages. What did you find easiest and most difficult when learning a foreign language? Foreign language learning can be difficult because of discrepant patterns of syntax and different grammar rules. For example, Chinese students learning English often have trouble with sentence structure because of a discrepancy in use of definite and indefinite articles, such as "the" and "a." Chinese students often omit "the" and "a" in speaking and writing English because there are no corresponding articles in Chinese.

✴ Contrastive Analysis

ESL and other foreign language teachers can benefit by increasing their awareness of patterns of students' English usage errors that result from the influence of their native language. Reflective foreign language teachers can ask self-questions such as "How do sentence structures in the students' native languages compare with sentence structures in their foreign language?"

An effective strategy for helping students identify, understand, and remember differences between L1 and L2 characteristics is contrastive analysis, which systematically and explicitly focuses on language discrepancies. One Web site defines contrastive analysis as "an inductive investigative approach based on the distinctive elements in a language." Contrastive analysis is useful for helping understand how L1 can interfere with learning L2. By reflecting on L1/L2 differences, second language learners can become aware of common language learning problems and use this awareness to self-check and self-correct their own language usage. Contrastive analysis is often combined with error analysis to identify mistakes in language learning and use.

Lay's (1991) *Contrastive Guide to Teach English to Chinese Students* describes such differences and how to address them. As previously mentioned, in Chinese, both definite and indefinite articles are nonexistent so Chinese students may have trouble learning to use them. Articles may be omitted when they are needed and inserted when they aren't. Based on analyses of Chinese students' writing in English, Lay developed a composition checklist to help address such problems. The section of the checklist that deals with articles identifies several aspects of a paper to check for definite and indefinite articles, including whether they are missing in front of concrete nouns, abstract nouns, and before adjectives. Consider your own writing checklist. How might it differ depending on the student's native language?

Contrastive analysis can be performed within a language as well as across languages. Within a language, it involves looking at similarities and differences between features including phonemes, morphemes, lexemes, semantics, and translational equivalences.

Another example of sentence structure difficulties of students applying knowledge from L1 to L2 involves word order. For example, native speakers of English often make sequence errors in Spanish, Italian, and French because in English the adjective comes before the noun it modifies, as in "beautiful lake," whereas in the other three languages the adjective comes after the noun it modifies, as in "lago bonito."

Another difficulty in foreign language learning is the issue of gender ascription. Most native English speakers tend to view language as gender neutral, with a few exceptions such as referring to boats in the feminine. However, in the Romance languages such as Spanish, French, and Italian, there are male and female words and male and female endings to words. This gender specificity is a whole new linguistic concept for most native speakers of English and may be hard for them to learn.

⚔ Questioning

Teaching reflectively, ask self-questions such as "To what extent are my students aware of and experienced with gender ascription in language? What other languages might they know that could help them learn this foreign language?"

Students whose native language is Spanish tend to find it easier to learn Italian than a native English speaker learning to speak Italian because the grammar and syntax rules are more similar to each other in Spanish and Italian than they are in English and Italian. However, once a native English speaker learns Italian, it will be easier to learn Spanish (L3) because of having acquired knowledge and experience with these new linguistic structures such as word order and gender ascription.

In some cases foreign language learning is especially difficult because of linguistic unit differences. For example, when learning Russian, a native English language learner will find that some of the Russian alphabet is similar to English but some is different. When trying to learn Chinese, Korean, Hebrew, or Arabic, native English learners will discover different linguistic units, such as characters and different alphabets. In these cases, prior knowledge that the reflective foreign language student can utilize to facilitate learning is much more limited. What questions might you ask yourself and your students to guide their learning these types of languages? What strategies might you use to help?

Teaching a classroom with diverse students is especially challenging, because of its complexity. English as a Second Language (ESL) or English as a Foreign Language (EFL) classes typically have students who not only speak a range of different native languages, but also come from a wide range of cultural backgrounds. Consider, for example, a classroom with twenty students who speak just two native languages: Spanish and French. Native Spanish speakers may come from a very wide range of countries including Mexico, Dominican Republic, Ecuador, Spain, Cuba, Colombia, Bolivia, Chile, Argentina, Puerto Rico, Peru, and Venezuela. Native French speakers may come from countries including Haiti, Canada, Martinique, Morocco, Belgium, Switzerland, Algeria, Cambodia, or France. In this example, a classroom with twenty students having only two different native languages could reflect twenty different countries of origin, each with its own distinctive cultural mores and practices, as well as variations in language use! What questions could you and your students ask to investigate the similarities and differences in their language use?

Reflective teaching can be helpful for ensuring effective communication in such a complex classroom. Self-questions could include Am I speaking slowly enough? How clearly am I pronouncing the words? Is my sentence structure too complex for now? What sentence lengths are best to use for this class? Do I have an accent that might confuse students about standard pronunciation? How and to what extent does my nonverbal communication help students understand what I'm saying? What discrepant cultural factors, like the appropriateness of eye contact between student and teacher, might affect students' communication and comprehension? How comfortable are my students questioning me when they don't understand something I've said? To what extent are students used to interacting with the teacher and other students during class rather than passively listening and writing?

Types and Levels for Foreign Language Questioning

Questioning can be a powerful tool for foreign language learning. Questioning strategies include teachers' questions to students, teachers' self-questions, students' questions to teachers, students' questions to each other, and students' self-questions.

To think reflectively about your use of questions in foreign language teaching, consider the following: What types of questions do you tend to ask most often? What types of questions do your students ask most frequently? To help students learn to think effectively in their new language, ask different levels and types of questions. Try to spend most of your time beyond the lowest level of questioning so that students can think more deeply and critically in the foreign language. Table 13.2 illustrates foreign language questions at low, intermediate, and high levels.

TABLE 13.2   Low-, Intermediate-, and High-Level Questions: Foreign Language

Question Level and Type	Example of Question Type
LOW LEVEL	
Label	What is your native language?
Define	What does "literacy" mean?
Describe	How would you characterize some of the cultural values in a country where this language predominates?
INTERMEDIATE	
Sequence	What was the sequence of events that led you to study this language?
Reproduce	How would you paraphrase that idea in your own words using the new language you are studying?
Describe Similarities/ Differences	How does the new language you are learning compare and contrast with your native language?

TABLE 13.2   *(Continued)*

Question Level and Type	Example of Question Type
Estimate	About how long have you been studying the new language?
Enumerate	Who else do you know who speaks your new language?
Infer Similarities/ Differences	What are some similarities and differences between the cultures of two countries where this language predominates?
Classify	What type of language is this?
Synthesize	If you combine what you know about characteristics of the new language you are learning, how would you describe it to someone who has never heard it spoken?
Apply	How could you use your new language to communicate with someone in another part of the world via the Internet?
Analyze	What features of the new language are most confusing?
HIGH	
Evaluate	What are your strengths and weaknesses in this language?
Causal Relation	Why are some vocabulary words harder than others to learn?
Infer Affect	How can you identify someone's emotions by listening to them speak in this language?
Generalize	What mistakes do you usually make when writing in this language?
Predict Outcome	If you wrote a letter to someone today using your new language, how successful do you think you'd be conveying your thoughts?
Transform	How has your learning of the new language changed your understanding of the cultures where it predominates?
Plan	How will you continue to learn this language when you're done with school?
Verify	How can you make sure that your accent is accurate?
Conclude	What conclusions can you draw about how your knowledge of your native language affected your learning the new one?
Propose Alternatives	What are at least three ways you could improve your use of the new language?
Resolve Conflict	How can you make sure that habits from your native language don't interfere with learning the new language?

✶ Teaching Writing to ESL Students

Research shows that not all writing problems are a result of the influence of the first language transferring over to learning the second. Cognitive development, prior language, and/or writing instruction and experience are also important factors. ESL teachers need to remember that not all problems are a result of the native language interfering with learning English and that not all students from the same background will have the same problems or cultural preferences associated with their group.

Research on ESL writers suggests teachers can help students with the composing process by using the following strategies, which increase reflection on writing:

1. include more work on planning, such as generating ideas and figuring out how to structure the text to make writing more manageable;
2. have students write in stages, with each draft having a different focus, such as content and organization in one, and linguistic issues in another;
3. provide realistic strategies for revising and editing, and keep these two processes separate.

Whereas native speakers of a language have intuition about "what sounds good," often second language learners, especially those with lower levels of proficiency, do not have this intuition. As a result, they may be interested in learning explicit grammar rules. Many ESL teachers do not have enough background in grammar to clearly explain rules regarding verbs, nouns, articles, and prepositions, which are common ESL writing errors. You may find it more useful to emphasize teaching students how to communicate clearly and de-emphasize specific rules. If students argue about this approach, you can try to *adjust their expectations* and help them understand that it is *unrealistic* to expect them to write like native speakers of English, with all grammar correct.

Many students resist proofreading their papers, hoping teachers will do that for them. Encourage students to proofread their own papers. Resist student pressure to find and fix all their mistakes. Teaching writing is intended to make better writers, not to make better papers! You can help students more if they are aware of their own strengths and weaknesses in English and are willing to admit when they need more information. Be prepared for occasional resistance. Not all students are in ESL willingly. Some have little if any desire to improve their English. Some have no opportunity to practice English once they return home.

Improving writing in a foreign language is hard work. How do you motivate your students to improve their writing? To what extent are your students aware of what motivates them to learn? A Framework for Culturally Responsive Teaching emphasizes the importance of intrinsic motivation, based on a personal desire to learn, rather than relying on extrinsic (external) rewards such as praise, grades, class rank, and pizza parties. This framework has four components, which were described in Chapter 4 on Emotional Aspects of Thinking and Learning. Reflect on how you might adapt this framework to your classroom to better meet the needs of your culturally diverse students.

ESL teachers should know the academic priorities of their school's ESL program. Is the program more concerned with writing than speaking? Does the program emphasize the development of all language skills? How are students supposed to acquire them all? In writing, is the program more concerned with fluency and clarity or with grammatical correctness? What types of reading and writing assignments are students expected to have?

Research suggests that teachers are often unprepared to deal with their students' different patterns of grammatical errors and rhetoric. You can help students most by prioritizing among students' errors and focusing on one or two at a time. It helps to set specific goals for each class. Establish a hierarchy to select the most important areas to focus on in a session. For example, errors that interfere with the reader's understanding (global errors) are more serious than minor grammatical errors (local errors). Start from students' strengths, find and acknowledge what they did well in writing their paper, and move on from there.

Speaking a Foreign Language

In **Conversation Circles**, students in informal settings get exposed to native speakers of the language and have opportunities for meaningful discussions with them. How might you recruit participants for a conversation circle?

Immersion in the culture where the foreign language predominates is the best way to learn it. Knowing one is going to have that experience can be a powerful motivator for foreign language acquisition. Students can become very excited about learning Spanish if they know they are going to a Spanish-speaking country, either on a visit or as an exchange to live with a Spanish-speaking family. Mastery of the language is usually accelerated by experiences living in the culture. Immersion experiences help foreign language learners reflect on action as they prepare to communicate with others in the language they are learning, and help them reflect in action as they assess the effectiveness of their actual, real-time communications.

Not everyone can go abroad, so such opportunities should be cultivated here. How might you help your students become immersed in the foreign language they're learning? Some online travel organizations provide virtual language immersion opportunities such as online access to museums and radio stations where second language learners can listen to authentic use of the language they are studying. One such site is World Class Tours, which includes resources for studying German, French, Spanish, Italian, and Greek. Active Worlds Educational Universe is a 3D multi-user virtual environment (MUVE) where participants choose an avatar and can interact with people in real time around the world through chat and instant messaging. It has over 1,000 worlds to explore. Visit http://www.activeworlds.com/edu/awedu.asp and examine the possibilities!

Additional Foreign Language Teaching Strategies

Collaborative action research has been recommended for reflective foreign language teaching because it helps teachers make better instructional decisions and solve their own problems by sharing common classroom problems, thinking critically about these classroom situations and their complexities, generating alternative approaches, monitoring and evaluating their effectiveness, and using feedback to plan for future improvements in teaching. The collaborative dimension involves several people collecting classroom data, sharing perspectives and interpretations, and helping each other reach new conclusions about causes and solutions. Books such as Beaumont and O'Brien (2000) and online resources such as those from the Center for Applied Linguistics can help you learn more about the use of collaborative action research in foreign language teaching.

Journals and audio and video recording can help you as a teacher share your experiences with other teachers and better understand yourself and your students. Journal entries serve no meaningful function if you don't review them, which you can do individually and collaboratively. Benefits of teacher journals for reflection on foreign language teaching have been identified as including a first-hand account of what occurs in the classroom, which can increase awareness of interrelationships between classroom events and patterns or trends.

Reflective teaching of foreign language requires careful observation of yourself and the impact you and instructional activities have on your students. That's why videotapes are especially useful. Too much happens during class to take in everything that is going on. A video record of the classroom allows you to take your time examining both events you know you want to study in more detail and things that occurred that you didn't know about at the time. You might miss what is going on with one student, such as head scratching and a puzzled expression on his face, because you are engaged in a discussion with another student. Analyzing videotapes can help you not only identify strengths and weaknesses in teaching and learning, but also develop and refine your observational skills so that you become more aware of events as they occur during class.

Student journals can have dual benefits: helping students become reflective learners, and providing teachers with feedback on instructional activities from the students' perspective. Teaching does not equal learning, and student journals can help bridge the gaps between teaching and learning and provide teachers with insights they can't obtain otherwise. When using student journals, one of the things to request is for students to check up on their comprehension of what happens in class by answering self-questions such as What wasn't clear to me? What was most difficult to understand? What questions do I have about today's class?

Periodically collect these journals to obtain feedback from students and provide students with feedback. The results can be surprising. Sometimes lessons that you thought were clear have left students confused and struggling to understand. Sometimes the reverse occurs: lessons that you think are more complex or difficult are perceived as less difficult than anticipated. Even if you explicitly ask, many students are reluctant to tell you they don't understand something while class is going on or even afterward. English as a foreign language students are often insecure or embarrassed about their lack of proficiency in speaking English. Journals can provide a more comfortable environment for communicating learning problems.

You might also have a discussion and/or take a survey of what your students like to do outside the classroom and integrate related topics and activities into your curriculum and instruction. You can use a questionnaire to find out what types of instructional activities and learning strategies are preferred and considered most useful to your students. Some students prefer reading the foreign language whereas others prefer listening to it. Research suggests that it's best for teachers to present material in multiple modalities to broaden and deepen encoding of the new language and to accommodate learner preferences.

✕ Parent Involvement

Parent involvement in education can be a major factor in students' academic success. In many cases, students studying English as a Foreign Language come from immigrant families that are not involved with their children's schools. What special challenges do these parents face? How do these challenges affect their children academically? To what extent do these parents help their children with their schoolwork? To what extent do they participate in school activities and events such as parent–teacher conferences and Parent-Teacher Associations? If your students' parents aren't very involved with their education, what are the reasons? What can you do to bridge the chasm?

By asking such questions, reflective foreign language teachers can be instrumental in getting immigrant parents more involved with their children's education and bridging the gaps between home and school environments and between native and foreign cultures.

One of the major reasons immigrant parents are often not involved in their children's education has to do with weak or nonexistent English literacy skills. Reflective teaching of English as a Foreign Language can include reaching out to parents and bringing them into the school and educational process. Because language barriers are often a major reason for lack of parental involvement, you may want to consider a variety of approaches to breaking down these barriers. One method involves inviting parents to the school for an after-school program designed to improve their English literacy skills. Start with speaking and listening. After developing some proficiency in these areas, move on to reading. Finally tackle writing. Another approach involves sending bilingual or multilingual parent volunteers into students' homes to work with parents. A third option involves translating school documents into parents' native languages. Each of these approaches can be structured to show parents that you value and respect them and their culture.

Another common problem limiting immigrants' parental involvement with their children's education is lack of their own formal schooling with a resultant sense that they don't have much to contribute to their children's academic success. A reflective question to ask is "How can I help such parents be educational assets to their children regardless of their own level of schooling?" One answer to this question focuses on the distinction between parent as educator, which requires subject matter knowledge, and parent as educational manager, which does not. Parents with no formal schooling of their own who have little or no English language skills can be educational resources for their children even if they are not literate in their own native language. See Figure 13.1.

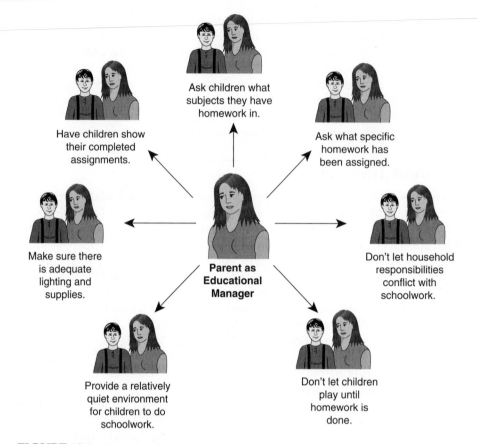

FIGURE 13.1   *Parent as Educational Manager*

Developing parents' educational management skills can have several bene-fits, including increasing their self-confidence about their ability to contribute to their children's education, demonstrating to their children that their education is taken seriously, and lessening parents' intimidation about school-related activities.

In some cases parents' concerns about economically supporting their fam-ilies may be a higher priority to them than providing academic support. Visiting the school might mean reducing their paycheck. How could you familiarize working parents with the school environment and inform them about school procedures without adversely affecting their income? Often immigrants aren't aware of all the available strategies and resources for assisting them to pay their bills. How might you inform them of such opportunities?

Some teachers (and schools) have found it useful to create a Web site for their students and their families to keep them informed of students' assign-ments and school policies and school events. You could even post materials in students' native languages to better meet their families' individual needs. Free online translation software makes this approach quite accessible. (One such site is http://www.freetranslation.com/.) However, given the digital divide, a class or school Web site is not likely to meet the needs of all your students' parents.

❈ Technology

Following are some foreign language teaching reflective questions related to technology: To what extent are you experienced with online communication experiences? Do you use e-mail? Have you visited chat rooms? Have you seen or participated in a teleconference? Have you ever visited online foreign language resource sites and explored the options? How did you feel about each of these technology experiences? To what extent do you use modern technologies in your foreign language instruction? To what extent and how might you make more use of technology in your teaching?

There are many excellent foreign language teaching resources available online, in addition to the Active Worlds site discussed earlier in the chapter. One site, http://www.csun.edu/~hcedu013/eslsp.html, has links to over 600 mini lesson plans, an online Spanish workbook, virtual picture books that include tales from India and Argentina, and links to materials for teaching Spanish, French, German, Latin, English, and other languages.

Another site, Teaching Ideas for Foreign Language Teaching (http://www.teachingideas.co.uk/foreignlanguages/contents.htm), includes activities such as vocabulary, learning names, revising words, and games such as Living Bingo, volleyball, hot potato, and ideas for using music in teaching foreign languages. Although many of the ideas are designed for young children, they can easily be adapted for use with middle and high school students.

Principles of and methods for second language teaching are available at http://coe.sdsu.edu/people/jmora/ALMMethods.htm. Approaches to foreign language teaching discussed at this site include grammar-translation, reading, audio-lingual, total physical response, and communicative. One communicative approach discussed is functional-notational, which emphasizes the importance of the context in which a language is used and the concept of "code switching," so that students understand the situational appropriateness of using different languages, language forms, and dialects.

A very comprehensive and detailed set of rubrics for evaluating foreign language learning at different levels is available from the Fairfax County Public Schools at http://www.fcps.k12.va.us/DIS/OHSICS/forlang/PALS/rubrics/index.htm.

The InTime resource Web site for K–12 teachers, with lesson plans and videotapes of technology rich, pedagogically sound lessons, pays special attention to multicultural education and culturally responsive teaching. Two lessons focus specifically on foreign language/ESL teaching. The lesson for upper elementary grades, 4–6, is for ESL students. The high school lesson is for students studying French and focuses on the famous bicycle race, Le Tour de France. You can visit the site and watch these lessons in action. The high school lesson has the following Activity Overview at the Web site:

> The project is entitled "Le Tour de France." The French IV students follow the route of the current year's "Tour de France" bicycle race. They search for information about the cities along the course. Specifically, they need to know tourism information and the history of each area. The students imagine that they are a tour company that is trying to promote the trip to prospective

customers. They are asked to make a travel brochure and a PowerPoint presentation in French. They gather information by contacting tourism offices (via e-mail) in France, by using the Internet to search sites, and by using other printed and on-line materials.

The National K–12 Foreign Language Resource Center (NFLRC) has many online resources for language learning. One set of projects focuses on assessment and evaluation, which promote reflection on action. There are additional projects on language teaching and language learning and on distance education. LearningLanguages.net is a portal that brings together foreign language resources for English-speaking K–12 teachers and students. It includes video lessons, a foreign language word of the day, grammar games and exercises, and cultural information. Foreign Language Home is another online resource, unique in offering specific foreign language teaching tips and access to specific language learning courses and software.

One option is to meet online, which can be done with or without teleconferencing, and can occur synchronously or asynchronously. Teleconferencing has the added benefits of enabling nonverbal communication and feeling a more personal connection to participants, but this requires synchronous communication. Many teenagers today enjoy the synchronous experience of visiting chat rooms on the Internet and meeting new people. This motivation and experience can be used to facilitate foreign language learning. To what extent do your students have online experience in general? To what extent do they have experience with chat rooms in particular? To what extent have they had positive and negative experiences conversing with people online? To what extent do they get frustrated from having bad connections, or getting cut off? To ensure positive, safe experiences, some teachers make formal arrangements with classrooms in other countries so the chatting experience is an official, sanctioned, and supervised instructional activity. Chats occur during school time with school equipment and technological support.

Asynchronous conversations have the advantage of communicating with someone in a different part of the world without having to worry about time differences. They also have the advantage of allowing students to get help with spelling and grammar before sending a communication. What technology equipment does your school have? What technological support is available?

There are also foreign language learning labs, centers, and tutorials online, which can supplement what occurs in the classroom. They have resources such as audio- and videotapes. Foreign language radio and TV can also be retrieved on the web. How might you use such resources? Why might they be beneficial for your students?

Summary

Students learn foreign languages for various reasons. Consider the different reasons when establishing and prioritizing instructional goals. Many students in the U.S.A. are not native speakers of English and have to learn it because it's the dominant language and consequently is important for succeeding in the culture.

A student's native language can aid or inhibit learning a foreign language. Help students see similarities and differences between their native and foreign languages. Identify and address recurring errors and patterns through techniques such as Contrastive Analysis. Questioning can help both teachers and students to think reflectively and critically about the new language they are learning. Reaching out to immigrant parents whose native language isn't English can help them and their children. A variety of technology-based resources can help students learn foreign languages and help you assess their progress.

Resources

Active Worlds Educational Universe. 2007. Retrieved August 17, 2007 from http://www.activeworlds.com/edu/awedu.asp.

American Council on the Teaching of Foreign Languages (ACTFL). Discover Languages: Discover the World. 2005. Retrieved September 24, 2006 from http://www.actfl.org.

Bartlett, L. "Teacher Development through Reflective Teaching." In *Second Language Teacher Education*, ed. Jack C. Richards and D. Nunan. New York: Cambridge University Press, 1990.

Beaumont, M.; and T. Obrien, eds. *Collaborative Research in Second Language Teaching*. Trent, U.K. and Sterling U.S.: Trentham Books, 2000.

Davis, R. Randall's ESL Cyber Listening Lab. 2007. Retrieved August 6, 2007 from http://www.esl-lab.com/.

Donato, R. Action Research. *Digest*. Center for Applied Linguistics. 2003. Retrieved August 17, 2007 from http://www.cal.org/resources/digest/0308donato.html.

Foreign Language Home (n.d.). Retrieved September 24, 2006 from http://www.foreignlanguagehome.com/.

French, K.; and J. Harris. "Opening Doors to the World: Using Activity Structures to Design Foreign Language Instruction: A Note from Judi Harris," *Learning and Leading with Technology* 29, December 2001.

Graham, L.; S. Lee; M. Liu; and Z. Moore. "A Look at the Research on Computer-Based Technology Use in Second Language Learning: A Review of the Literature from 1990–2000." *Journal of Research on Technology in Education* 34, 2002.

Holman, Linda J. "Meeting the Needs of Hispanic Immigrants." *Educational Leadership*. April 1997, pp. 37–38.

Indiana University. Language Learning Resources. 2005. Retrieved September 24, 2006 from http://languagelab.bh.indiana.edu/call/langlinks.html.

InTime. Foreign Language/ESL Videos. 2001. Retrieved September 24, 2006 from http://www.intime.uni.edu.

Internet Scout Project. LearningLanguages.net. College of Letters and Sciences. 2003. Retrieved August 6, 2007 from http://www.learninglanguages.net.

Iowa State University. National K–12 Foreign Language Resource Center (NFLRC). 2003. Retrieved September 24, 2006 from http://nflrc.iastate.edu.

Linguascope. Foreign Language Lesson Plans and Resources. 2007. Retrieved August 6, 2007 from http://www.csun.edu/~hcedu013/eslsp.html.

Loos, E. U.; J. D. H. Day; P. C. Jordan; and J. D. Wingate, eds. What Is Contrastive Analysis? LinguaLinks Library. SIL International. 2004. Retrieved August 6, 2007 from http://www.sil.org/LINGUISTICS/GlossaryOfLinguisticTerms/WhatIsContrastiveAnalysis.htm.

Pachero, Allen Quesada. Reflective Teaching and Its Impact on Foreign Language Teaching. *Revista Electrónica "Actualidades Investigatives en Educación" V. 5 Numero Extraordinario*. 2005. Retrieved September 24, 2006 from http://www.revista.inie .ucr.ac.cr/articulos/extra-2005/archivos/reflective.pdf.

Paulson, J. B. New Era Trends and Technologies in Foreign Language Learning: An Annotated Bibliography, *Interactive Multimedia Electronic Journal of Computer-Enhanced Learning*. 2001. Retrieved September 10, 2006 from http://www.imej .wfu.edu/articles/2001/1/05/printver.asp.

Richards, J. C.; and C. Lockhart. *Reflective Teaching in Second Language Classrooms*. New York: Cambridge University Press, 1994.

Wallace, M. J. *Training Foreign Language Teachers: A Reflective Approach*. New York: Cambridge University Press, 1991.

Wallace, M. J. *Action Research for Language Teachers*. Cambridge: Cambridge University Press, 1998.

Warner, M. Foreign Languages: General Ideas. 2007. Retrieved August 6, 2007 from http://www.teachingideas.co.uk/foreignlanguages/contents.htm.

Wlodkowski, R. J.; and M. B. Ginsberg. "A Framework or Culturally Responsive Teaching." *Educational Leadership*. September 1995, pp. 17–21.

World Class Tours. (n.d.) Retrieved September 24, 2006 from http://www.wctours.ca/ links/index.html#spain.

Reflective Teaching of History

What is your conception of the nature and purpose of history as a field of study? How do your students view their study of history (or social studies)? When you think about historians, how do you conceptualize them? How do your students conceptualize historians? To what extent do your students learn about and reflect on multiple perspectives in history and social studies rather than considering only a U.S.A. or Euro-centric perspective? In this chapter, all of the ideas presented in the context of teaching history are also assumed to apply to teaching social studies, and vice versa.

Many people have preconceptions or naïve theories of what history is all about. Often, based on their own experiences in elementary school social studies and/or high school (and even college) history classes, they believe that learning history is all just a matter of memorizing dates, such as the Battle of Hastings, 1066, and facts, such as the Spanish American War involved President McKinley's efforts to help secure Cuba's independence from Spain.

However, historians view history very differently. Learning dates and facts is just a part of the larger and more important picture of using rules of evidence, interpreting, analyzing, and making sense of events, and using this information to better understand events and people's behavior in everyday life. Historians focus more on big ideas and concepts than facts and dates. Their goals are to help students become critical thinkers about historical conclusions and to become competent citizens. In today's world, many historians view competent citizenship on local, regional, national, and global scales.

✛ History/Social Studies Goals and Competencies

What are your goals when teaching history? What is your view of the competencies students need to achieve your goals? Reflective teaching of history requires recognition that the social problems addressed tend to be multifaceted, complex, and usually controversial. There is usually no single right solution to these problems. In order to solve social problems, students need to consider a combination of logical approaches and multiple, often conflicting perspectives.

Students need to engage in disciplined inquiry about a problem or issue, including genuine openness to considering viewpoints different from their own, to reach a reasoned decision. Then they can take an informed stand on an issue and provide a convincing defense of their position.

To achieve this goal, students need more than the ability to engage in persuasive reasoning, or the skillful justification of their position. Five competencies have been identified as vital components of higher-order critical reasoning in social studies.

1. Having empathy: the ability to view the world from another's perspective. For example, educators in the Middle East have brought Palestinian and Israeli high school students together in order to promote peace and positive social change by meeting and communicating online working on a collaborative project. This project, MEET (Middle East Education through Technology), is intended to help students understand each others' viewpoints.

2. Applying abstract concepts to specific situations. For example, students apply the abstract concept of democracy by analyzing voting patterns in different states within the United States of America, where there are different candidates representing different political parties, and comparing these patterns to voting patterns in other countries, where there is only one candidate and party to vote for.

3. Inferring beyond limited data to draw conclusions. For example, after collecting data on voting patterns in the U.S.A. and other countries, students draw conclusions about which countries are democratic and which are not.

4. Clarifying comprehension of an issue by engaging in critical discourse. For example, students debate the issue of whether African Americans have overcome the consequences of the decades of slavery using the structured controversy approach. As a consequence, they have a broader and deeper perspective on the legacy of slavery and its implications for African Americans in society today.

5. Developing defensible decisions about a problem by applying evaluative criteria. For example, students conduct research on the history of gender equality in the workplace and make a judgment about whether it exists, or the extent to which it exists, by using objective criteria such as salaries for comparable work and the number of high-level management positions in major corporations.

To what extent do you incorporate these five competencies in your teaching? What methods do you use to develop these competencies in your students? How important are these competencies in your and your school's philosophies of teaching? To what extent do your students acquire these competencies? How do you assess students' progress in developing them?

To what extent do your students think critically about history? Are they aware of issues such as Eurocentric vs. Afrocentric perspectives on it? To what extent are they aware of the implications of and limitations of white middle-class males writing history for white middle-class students? In science textbooks, the history of women's contributions to discoveries such as the double helix structure of DNA are often shortchanged. How can you make sure that your students aren't shortchanged and develop a broader and more critical view of the history they read about in their textbooks and see in the media?

Students need to have a substantial knowledge base in order to engage in critical reasoning about complex problems. However, it is often difficult to get students to persist sufficiently for them to acquire depth and breadth of knowledge about history, sometimes because they find it boring or irrelevant and resist studying it. Engaging students with content, such as the civil rights movement, through problem-based, authentic learning experiences that include multimedia learning environments, helps motivate students to persist in learning and to develop deeper, more complex understanding and perspectives on social problems or issues.

What topics, issues, or social problems do your students need to learn and understand in depth? How might you structure problem-based, authentic learning experiences around them? What multimedia resources are available and appropriate for your use?

⋈ Experts' versus Novices' Conceptions of History

Research comparing experts with novices in history shows that novices generally focus on surface or superficial features of a situation. They tend to view history as a direct record of events and get confused by multiple perspectives or conflicting accounts. In contrast, history experts look more deeply into social problem situations to make judgments about events and evidence. They use abstract concepts such as equality and justice to structure, organize, analyze, and interpret information and to reason through an issue. They identify and discuss meaningful issues in an authentic context. They challenge explanations and conclusions to make sure they are based on sound knowledge and reasoning. How well does your view of history match this perspective?

To help students become more like history experts who think more deeply about social problems and develop their own interpretations of evidence, have them create their own historical narratives and confront them with conflicting viewpoints. Expert history teachers are very aware of problems of interpreting historical evidence, and help students understand the complexity of the subject and of historical analysis. Expert history teachers also emphasize "big ideas" instead of details, and try to make sure their students understand the implications of history for everyday life experience. What strategies do you use to emphasize "big ideas"? To what extent and how do you connect history to everyday life? How might you guide students in using abstract concepts as reasoning tools for analyzing situations, genuinely considering alternative perspectives, evaluating evidence, making inferences, and drawing conclusions?

Experts and novices in history differ in how they read the same text. Experts have greater awareness of the structure of historical knowledge, are more aware of differences in interpretations of historical events, and are more adept at integrating many different pieces of historical evidence into a coherent whole. (For more information on differences between experts and novices in their reading of history texts, visit the Web site "Different Sides of the Same Coin." Also see the section "Reading Textbooks" later in this chapter.)

Students tend to think of history as **static** and having **only one** correct view of what took place. Even some novice history teachers might share these perspectives. However, expert history teachers, who reflect on both history and how history is taught, realize that history is a **dynamic** subject and that sometimes there are **multiple** correct views of what took place. How do you view history in relationship to the static/dynamic distinction?

Expert history teachers also know that sometimes what is commonly believed to be true in history is not accurate. For example, President Lincoln is commonly credited with ending slavery, but he didn't completely abolish it. How could you help your students appreciate history as dynamic and characterized by alternative correct perspectives?

Another common naïve belief is that historians are academics who teach students about what happened in the past. But there are also public historians whose mission is to relate what is learned by scholars (often in academia) to people who are not in school environments. Museum directors, tour guides at historical monuments, documentary filmmakers, authors of historical novels, writers for the History Channel, and members of various advocacy groups come under this umbrella. How could you help your students develop a bigger and more accurate picture of who historians are in actuality?

The view of history as memorizing dates and facts has different implications for using instructional strategies and assessing students' learning than the more complex and deeper view of history by historians. The former emphasizes use of passive instructional strategies such as reading and lecturing, where students simply take in information and assessment generally involves reporting back the dates and facts acquired.

In stark contrast, the latter emphasizes use of active instructional strategies such as debating and role playing, where students evaluate and apply information, and assessment involves explaining reasons and providing evidence for conclusions. In this approach, facts and dates are learned and applied in a meaningful context and multiple perspectives are considered. To what extent do your teaching and assessment strategies reflect the former and the latter?

⚔ Instructional Strategies

What lessons have you taught that stand out in your mind either because they were successful experiences in helping students think like historians or because they were unsuccessful in this regard?

One especially useful strategy for becoming more reflective about your history teaching is to keep a written record of such **"critical incidents"** so that you can examine them and gain insights that improve your teaching and your students' learning.

As a history teacher, in comparison with many other teachers, you might have a special appreciation of your own history as a teacher and your students' histories as learners. Ask your students to keep their own written records of critical incidents in their learning of history so that they can gain insights into their own learning experiences—what works and what doesn't work for them individually.

Scaffolding, or providing students with temporary support, for inquiry into complex problems so that they think more like experts, has been described as including four types of guidance.

1. Conceptual: what knowledge should be considered. Novices tend to treat all information as equally important, whereas experts are better at differentiating

important ideas from details. How can you help your students distinguish between relevant and irrelevant information so that they focus on key points instead of treating all information as being of equal value? What cues can you tell them to look for so that they don't always need your guidance to steer them in the right directions?

2. Reflective: how to think during learning. Analysis of evidence and the sources of the evidence are very important in history, so students should ask themselves questions such as "What information or documents provide support for this report or for this interpretation of events? Who is the source of this document or report? How credible is this source? What do other sources say about this event or interpretation?" Model this type of self-questioning for students. To scaffold, provide prompts or cues to encourage them to ask themselves appropriate questions. Remove this support as students begin to ask themselves similar questions while reading their history texts and examining historical documents.

3. Procedural: how to use available resources. Show students how to read historical documents and their history textbooks by thinking aloud as you read them, thereby modeling how an expert reads history. Think aloud while conducting historical research to externalize for students the steps you take to answer historical questions. For example, where on the Internet would you look for information? If you are using the National Archives, what sequence of activities would you engage in to answer your questions? How would you use the school or a local library? What steps would you take to find the information you are looking for? How would you record important information once you found it?

4. Strategic: alternative approaches to facilitate decision making. For example, suppose your students had to conduct research on causes of the fall of the Roman Empire. To strategically address this issue, students need to consult a variety of sources that represent different points of view. For example, Italians may have different explanations than other Europeans. Americans, Asians, and Africans might have different perspectives than Italians or other Europeans. Within Italy, Europe, America, Asia, and Africa there are likely to be various alternative interpretations.

Researching and reflecting on alternative approaches can help students synthesize diverse perspectives and formulate their own, carefully considered conclusions. To accomplish this complex goal, show students how you and other experts in history synthesize disparate information from a variety of sources. What types of scaffolds or temporary supports might you provide so your students think more like social studies experts? What are specific scaffolds you could use for examining alternative approaches to historical content, deciding how to interpret it, and synthesizing the disparate data?

How and to what extent does your teaching of history help students break down stereotypes, overcome problematic conceptions, prejudice, and racism, and build positive relationships with culturally diverse students so that they can be good citizens? One strategy is to help them understand history by **connecting it to their own use of history in their everyday lives.** For example, when meeting new friends, it's common to tell them about yourself and your background, your personal history. Have students write about their own histories and share them with others in the class. Have them reflect on the similarities and differences between personal history and history as a school subject in terms of what they are, when and why they're used, and how they're developed and communicated.

Connecting history with everyday life can be especially useful to help students reflect on, understand, appreciate, critically evaluate, and effectively use maps. Ask questions such as "What are maps?" "What are some different types of maps?" "Why are they used?" "How do you read them?" "What do the symbols on them mean?" "Why do you think those symbols were chosen?" "How does a good map differ from a poor one?" "Why are maps important in history?" Individually or collaboratively, students can create maps of their route to school, their neighborhood, a farm, a mall, their city center, and the surrounding community.

Often students have learned something about the history or social studies you are covering from other teachers in previous grades. To activate their prior knowledge, so they can connect it to the new material thereby making learning meaningful, and so that you can identify and prepare to overcome their naïve conceptions, when first beginning a topic regularly ask questions such as "Who has heard about this topic before coming to this class? What do you know about it?" Put their answers on the blackboard in a graphic organizer so that everyone gets a big picture of the class's starting point on the topic.

Debating

Debating is another good teaching method for helping students learn to think like historians. Debates help students see historical interpretation as a dynamic process of amassing, analyzing, and interpreting evidence and drawing conclusions. It also increases their awareness of controversies in how historical events are interpreted by people from different backgrounds and perspectives. Have your students debate whether we should have gone to war in Iraq in 2003 from the perspectives of a variety of people such as people who served in Iraq, family members of soldiers killed or injured in Iraq, President Barack Obama, Senators John McCain and Russ Feingold, and Secretary of State Hillary Clinton. Have them consider how the issue of the existence or absence of weapons of mass destruction the economy, and the issue of Al Qaeda's role in Iraq enter into the debate.

These issues are selected to help students see how our understanding of history changes with the discovery of new information, thereby making the study of history a dynamic process. Once students have researched and debated their position on an issue, have them reverse roles and develop and make arguments from an opposing perspective. This is part of the **structured controversy** method, which culminates in students synthesizing information from different perspectives, forcing reflection on discrepancies, and leading to students forming new, more well-reasoned conclusions.

An alternative to doing this type of debate in the classroom is to have it occur online in a discussion forum. Such an environment has the advantage of students being able to conduct research and write their positions at their own pace and on their own schedules. It also provides more opportunities for students to reflect on, evaluate, and revise their thinking and how they communicate their ideas.

Role Playing

Role playing or dramatizations of history can be especially useful methods of promoting reflection about history. On reenacting Rosa Parks' refusal to move to the back of the bus, my students had a deeper appreciation of the courage she needed to take such a controversial position, especially at that point in American history. It also helped students analyze the situation from the perspectives of the bus driver, other passengers on the bus, the police who came on the bus to move her out of the front of the bus, and members of the civil rights movement at that time. That learning experience was a critical incident for both me and many of my students because it demonstrated how role playing can have transformative effects on students' understanding of historical events and their abilities to examine them from multiple perspectives. Students' understanding of this important event in American History was deepened not only by the role play itself, but also by the research each of the students had to conduct in order to successfully perform their roles. Reflection on learning history was enhanced by having students write about their experiences preparing for and participating in the role play.

Classmates who observed this role play reflected on and wrote about their experiences watching the reenactment. They reported that it increased their understanding of this famous historical event because seeing their peers act it out heightened their awareness, increased their engagement, and gave them different perspectives on what actually had occurred and its significance. All learners realized from the role play that previously they had invalid assumptions about the event. There is a pervasive naïve belief that Rosa Parks' decision not to move to the back of the bus was a spontaneous occurrence, rather than a planned act of civil disobedience!

One of the most common complaints about learning history is that it's boring, which is often due to the emphasis many teachers place on memorizing dates and facts about what was taking place during important periods of time. Experiences like the one just described demonstrate how exciting and meaningful it can be to study history. Dates and facts are embedded into a larger social context, which reveals their significance.

Questioning

Teachers often talk about "covering" the history curriculum, but what does this mean? Covering history content by telling students important information doesn't guarantee learning. Asking about students' prior knowledge of a topic is an excellent way to begin any history lesson and make it more meaningful. Questioning is also a good method of helping students learn to think critically about the nature of historical evidence and how to evaluate it.

A Web site called "Learn to Question" emphasizes questioning as a strategy for promoting critical thinking and discusses the value of questioning for students learning how to follow rules of evidence so that it is clear how they reach their conclusions.

To help students become and stay interested in a topic it's useful to ask a variety of questions, such as those in Table 14.1. What thinking skills are needed to be good history teachers and learners? Research suggests it's best for promoting breadth and depth of learning if you minimize the number of low-level questions

TABLE 14.1   Low-, Intermediate-, and High-Level Questions: History

Question Level and Type	Example of Question Type
LOW LEVEL	
Label	What was the name of one of the important pieces of legislation that Truman got passed?
Define	What is the "stinking weed"?
Describe	What was the role of the "stinking weed" in Virginia?
INTERMEDIATE	
Sequence	What was the sequence of events that led to the American Revolution?
Reproduce	What would a map of the New England colonies during 1650 look like?
Describe Similarities/ Differences	How was Harry Truman like Andrew Jackson?
Estimate	Approximately how long did it take for Massachusetts and Rhode Island to agree on a common boundary?
Enumerate	What were the American Colonies during the 17th century?
Infer Similarities/ Differences	How did the 1980s compare with the 1950s?
Classify	How would you categorize American women's roles during the postwar years?
Synthesize	Overall, what was the financial impact of World War II on the United States? Why?
Apply	How does your understanding of the 1960s Civil Rights Movement affect your perspective on race relations today?
Analyze	How could you break down the 1960s Civil Rights Movement into stages?
HIGH	
Evaluate	How would you assess the impact of the McCarthy era on American society? Why?
Causal Relation	Why was there so much diversity in the English colonies during the 17th century?
Infer Affect	How do you think Rosa Parks felt when she was removed from the bus and arrested?
Generalize	What generalizations could you make about the causes of immigration?
Predict Outcome	What do you think would have happened to the U.S. if the Allies had lost World War II?

Question Level and Type	Example of Question Type
Transform	How did the English colonies alter the maps of North America?
Plan	What steps would you take if you were to write a research paper on racial segregation in the U.S.A.?
Verify	How can we determine whether Alger Hiss was really a Soviet spy?
Conclude	What can you conclude about the impact of William Penn's "Holy Experiment"?
Propose Alternatives	What are some tactics Americans could have used to decrease Joe McCarthy's impact during the 1950s?
Resolve Conflict	How can we celebrate Columbus' "discovery of America" when Native Americans were here long before him?

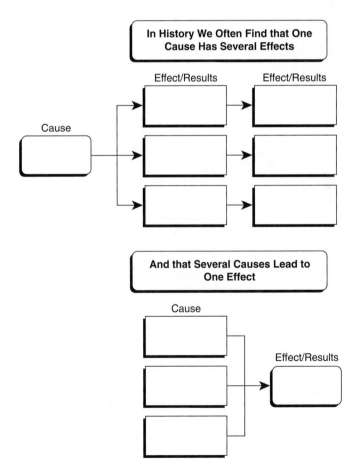

FIGURE 14.1   *Causes and Effects in History*

and have students spend most of the time thinking at the intermediate and high levels. Which of these types and levels of questions are most typical of you? Which might you ask more of?

Graphic Organizers

Teachers and students can draw their own graphic organizers and/or use software-provided tools, including templates. Flow charts and/or timelines drawn on the blackboard can help students to conceptualize a sequence of actions associated with important historical events such as the Civil War. For example, when did abolition, Lincoln's election, Harriet Tubman's escape from slavery, and the Dred Scott decision occur in relation to the Civil War? To assess students' understanding of the sequence of events, ask them to draw their own flow charts or timelines of these incidents.

The graphic organizer software, Inspiration, has five social studies-specific templates for teachers and students to adapt as needed (see Figures 14.1–14.3). The templates are:

1. Cause and Effect
2. Events
3. Historic Period
4. History Web 1
5. History Web 2

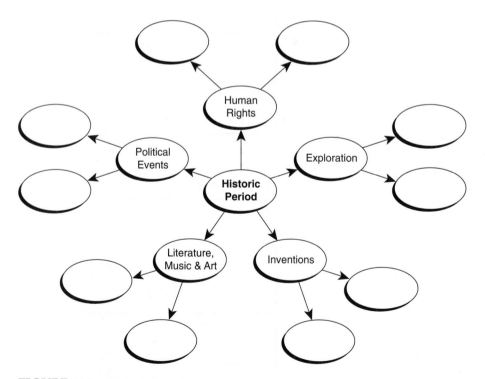

FIGURE 14.2   *Historic Period*

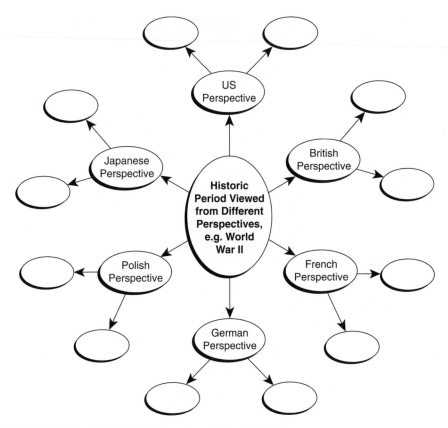

FIGURE 14.3   *Multiple Perspectives of World War II*

The historic period template could be easily modified to focus on different perspectives on the same event, as in the example of World War II in Figure 14.3.

School districts can purchase a site license so the software can be used in all their schools. Before recommending this software to your school district, test it out with the 30-day free trial at their Web site.

⚹ Reading Textbooks

How do your students read their history or social studies textbooks? The National Council for the Social Studies (NCSS) identifies eight different organizational patterns or text structures for thinking about social studies while reading. They are description, compare/contrast, cause and effect, concept definition, sequence, problem/solution, proposition/support, and goal/action/outcome (see Table 14.2). How can you help your students read with these text structures in mind? How can you assess their effectiveness in reading for these text structures? These are important issues for the reflective social studies/history teacher to consider and struggle with.

TABLE 14.2   Reading History

Organizational Structures for Reading History	Examples
Description	In the Boston Tea Party, colonialists in America protested against the British policy of taxation without representation by destroying crates of tea in the Boston Harbor.
Compare/Contrast	World War I and World War II had some commonalities, such as the involvement of several countries, and some differences, such as the precipitating causes.
Cause and Effect	The Watergate scandal is generally considered to be responsible for bringing down Richard Nixon's presidency, more because of the cover-up than due to the break-in itself.
Concept Definition	Civil disobedience involves following one's conscience and disobeying laws to protest nonviolently against something one believes the government is doing that is morally wrong.
Sequence	After the Supreme Court decision *Brown vs. the Board of Education* in 1954, schools throughout the south and in other parts of the country began the process of desegregation.
Problem/Solution	The problem of Europe's repeated colonizing the American continents and extending Old World influence to the New World was solved by the Monroe Doctrine whereby it was declared the United States would no longer tolerate such interference in American affairs.
Proposition/Support	Most modern historians view the Renaissance as more of a cultural than historical era because most of the changes that occurred were in knowledge, like mathematics, the arts, such as painting, and literature, such as poetry.
Goal/Action/Outcome	The Declaration of Independence was drafted and signed when there were massive uprisings of colonists against Britain for the purpose of formally separating the American colonies from British rule. The result was that the individual colonies began creating their own governments, which were later united in a General Congress.

In addition to reading with these eight text structures in mind, the NCSS recommends that social studies teachers help students learn the subject by engaging them in activities that include using strategies for learning vocabulary; making inferences and predictions; and summarizing, synthesizing, and evaluating information. To what extent do your instructional materials and activities engage students in these types of learning experiences? The Reciprocal Teaching method described in Chapter 9 is an effective approach for engaging students in some of these text comprehension activities. Part of being a reflective social studies teacher includes selecting materials and designing activities like these, which help students learn to think like historians.

By teaching students to use social studies-specific text structures when reading and by using teaching methods that engage students in the above types of activities, you can help students achieve civic competence, which NCSS defines as "the ability to make informed decisions for the public good as citizens of a culturally diverse, democratic society in an interdependent world." To what extent have your students achieved civic competence? Research suggests that an important component of making competent civic decisions is being able to critically reason about social problems. Problem-based learning is a good strategy for achieving this objective.

⚔ Primary Sources

Responsibilities of historians include determining the origin of primary sources and assessing whether or not a source is biased. Do your students know the differences between primary and secondary sources? Do they understand why it's an important distinction? A Web site called "Historical Primary Sources: A Guide" includes information defining primary and secondary sources and describing various types of primary sources. It also includes questions such as the following to ask about primary sources in order to properly evaluate their quality.

1. Who created the source and why? Was it created through a spur-of-the-moment act, a routine transaction, or a thoughtful, deliberate process?
2. Did the recorder have firsthand knowledge of the event? Or, did the recorder report what others saw and heard?
3. Was the recorder a neutral party, or did the recorder have opinions or interests that might have influenced what was recorded?
4. Did the recorder produce the source for personal use, for one or more individuals, or for a large audience?
5. Was the source meant to he public or private?
6. Did the recorder wish to inform or persuade others? (Check the words in the source. The words may tell you whether the recorder was trying to be objective or persuasive.) Did the recorder have reasons to be honest or dishonest?
7. Was the information recorded during the event, immediately after the event, or after some lapse of time? How large a lapse of time?

How might you incorporate these questions into your history teaching?

Sample Lesson: Critical Thinking and Transfer in History

Below is a sample lesson and dialogue designed to promote critical thinking in history and to help students transfer what they learned to other subjects. The lesson is based on the Rich Instruction Model described in Chapter 2, Managing Teaching Reflectively.

Mr. Wise was busily writing today's objectives on the board as the ninth graders entered his American History class.

> **Objectives**
>
> Students will make inferences and draw conclusions based on their analysis of raw data in a chart of facts about early European explorers.
>
> Students will compare and contrast facts about early European explorers/exploring with their knowledge of modern-day explorers/exploring and appreciate risk-taking.

As usual, history class started with a discussion of what objectives were to be achieved in this lesson and why. Mr. Wise always made a distinction between the immediate purpose of the lesson and its long-term benefits. Rather than tell students what he expected the benefits to be, he usually elicited these ideas from the students based on their reflective analysis of the explicit objectives.

Teacher: What do you think you might learn of value from today's lesson?

Jessica: (after examining the objectives outlined on the blackboard) We might have a better understanding of why some people today choose to become astronauts, since they're modern explorers of space.

Shakira: And we may learn about the kinds of risks people take when they are explorers. Before learning about the space shuttle, *Challenger,* exploding, I never thought about the dangers of exploring space. I only thought about how exciting it must be to explore the unknown.

Several students in the class nodded in accord. Studying the tragic death of the teacher, Christa McAuliffe, in the 1986 chilled many students' enthusiasm about possibly becoming an astronaut. As sophisticated as our technology is, there are no guarantees. Even McAuliffe herself appeared to have been naïve about the risks of her exploration.

Teacher: Okay. What else might we get out of this class?

Phil: We could learn how to get more meaning out of charts.

Juan: And to draw better conclusions. And make inferences when we read in other subjects—not just history.

Michael: Some day we may have jobs in which we have to group together things that are alike and keep them away from things that are different.

Teacher: What would be an example?

Michael: Well, like a lawyer who keeps all his murder cases in one drawer and all his aggravated assault cases in another.

Teacher: Sounds like you've been watching too much television!

Everyone laughed while nodding in agreement.

Teacher: Anything else?

There was no response. Mr. Wise provided the class with ample time for reflection but ultimately determined that the class had finished generating ideas on this topic.

Teacher: One final benefit might be some self-knowledge about your own likelihood to take risks.

Mr. Wise passed out a "data chart" describing early European explorers, what they sought, and what happened to them. At the bottom of the page under the heading "Think About It" was a series of questions. He tried to emphasize intermediate and higher-level questions, using lower-level questions as building blocks. (See examples of levels and types of history questions earlier in this chapter.)

Teacher: Read the data chart and write answers to the questions at the bottom. Afterward we will share and discuss your answers.

Lenny took out his pen and began to write.

Teacher: Hold on a minute, Lenny. What are you doing?

It really irked him when students impulsively began to work, without taking thinking time or following directions.

Lenny: I'm answering the last question first. Is that OK?

Teacher: The order you answer the questions in isn't as important as what you do to prepare for your answer.

Blood rushed to Lenny's face as the heat of embarrassment made him realize once again he was being "impulsive" instead of "reflective."

Lenny: I guess you mean I should read the chart first, before I answer the questions.

Teacher: Good. You realized it yourself, without me having to tell you.

Mr. Wise wanted to bridge his criticism with praise for student self-awareness and correction.

While reading, several students raised their hands asking for clarification of something on the chart they didn't understand. Mr. Wise's first approach always was to turn the question around back on the student, to try to get him or her to figure out the meaning on his/her own.

Because a number of students were raising their hands, Mr. Wise decided to modify his original lesson plan and discuss the chart itself before students finished preparing their answers. He thought to himself, "By allowing them to ask their questions before the planned discussion, I can accomplish two things at once. Not only can I make sure students in fact understood what they read, so they give better interpretations of the data, but I can use the opportunity to further develop their thinking skills of inference, comparison/contrast, and drawing conclusions."

After the students had finished writing and were waiting for the next phase of the lesson, Mr. Wise took a moment of "wait time" himself to think about which type of questions to ask the class. He pictured the chart of higher-, intermediate-, and lower-level questions shown at an in-service workshop.

He decided to start at the intermediate level and then move up to the high level. First he asked students to describe similarities between early exploration and today. His next question required inferring similarities between the past and present. Then he moved to the high level.

Teacher: How do you think Vasco de Gama became a wealthy merchant through exploring the Indies?

His following question, also high level, involved inferring affect or emotion.

Teacher: How do you think Vasco de Gama felt about exploration toward the end of his life, when he realized it was responsible for his wealth, his illness, and impending death?

After a series of questions, which indicated students did, in fact, comprehend the material, Mr. Wise returned to the lesson as planned.

Teacher: Before we share and discuss your answers, who can tell me what steps you've been taking in doing this assignment?

Dennis: First I skimmed the questions, so I had an idea what would be important to understand and remember while reading. Then I read the chart. Next I went to the first question. It was hard because it's so general. So I had to look back at the chart and think about what conclusions I could draw from the data. I noticed some relationships between what happened to the explorers. I decided that one thing I could say about the business of exploring based on the chart was that it was a pretty dangerous business in the past. So I wrote that on my paper.

Teacher: And how did you reach that conclusion? What evidence supports it?

Dennis: A lot of the explorers died because of their exploration. Some were murdered and some got sick, the chart says.

The next phase of the lesson was a cooperative learning activity in which students worked in one of three "Transfer Groups." The purpose of each group was to identify ways of applying what was learned in the lesson. One group's context was "Within the same subject, to another topic," another was "Across subjects, i.e., to a different curricular area," and the third group's context was "Everyday life, outside of school."

Mr. Wise tried to conduct transfer groups as a regular part of his lessons. Students rotated groups each time, so that all students would have multiple experiences making connections in all three contexts. Sometimes Mr. Wise gave each group a question to help them focus their thinking about transfer. Other times students within each group provided their own structure. After generating connections, the groups shared their transfer strategies with the rest of the class so all students could learn about transferring in each context.

Today Mr. Wise wrote each group's task on the blackboard.

Transfer Group Tasks

Group 1: Within History
     How did these explorers influence our culture? What kind of legacy did they leave us? For example, what were some of the political and economic consequences of exploration?
Group 2: Across Subjects
     How could you apply the thinking skills focused on today to other school subjects? For example, how could you use the skills of drawing conclusions and projecting patterns in data in science, and in math?
Group 3: Everyday Life
     How does modern-day exploration affect our lives? For example, how does space exploration affect technology?

During the group discussion, Marika's eyes wandered to the corner of the board where the night's homework assignment was usually posted. It read, "Design two advertisements to attract explorers: one from the past and one from the present." A kaleidoscope of images danced through her mind. She preferred tasks that had her create information to those that had her reproduce the ideas of others.

Mr. Wise had a couple of other activities planned to follow up on this lesson. One required students to go out on the school's nature trail and "explore," keeping an explorer's journal of what was discovered. For the other, students had to go to town hall to get longitudinal data charts from the town's annual report and/or other documents and see what predictions could be made or what conclusions drawn for the community.

TABLE 14.3   Early American Explorers Data Chart

Explorers	What They Sought	What Happened to Them
Vasco de Gama	Trade route to riches of Indies	He found it. Became wealthy merchant but got sick and died on his third voyage.
Marco Polo	Trade route to riches of China	He found it. Found wealth and adventure. Died of old age, a successful merchant, but also spent three years in jail.
Christopher Columbus	Trade route to riches of Indies	Kept bumping into unknown continent. Died of old age after spending time in prison, neglected and in poverty; he never knew what he had found.
John Cabot	Northwest passage to riches of Indies	Unknowingly found Newfoundland. Lost at sea on his second voyage.

(continued)

TABLE 14.3 (Continued)

Explorers	What They Sought	What Happened to Them
Francisco de Coronado	Fabled cities of gold in area presently covering southwestern USA	No luck. Died in poverty in Mexico. Considered by all as a failure.
Ponce de Leon	Fountain of youth and gold in Florida	No luck with either. Killed by Indians in Florida.
Hernando de Soto	Gold in areas presently ranging from Georgia to Texas	No luck. Became sick and died on his way back to Cuba.
Vasco de Balboa	Personal wealth in New World	Discovered the Pacific Ocean. Became very wealthy but was beheaded by the Governor of Panama for treason.
Ferdinand Magellan	To be the first to sail around the world	Killed by a tribe of natives in the Philippines. Some members of his crew did make it.
Amerigo Vespucci	To explore region around Columbus' Indies for merchant and banking interests	Became famous as first to realize what America was. Died of old age, cartographer to King of Spain.
Jacques Cartier	Northwest passage to riches of Indies	Discovered St. Lawrence River. Died of old age on his country estate in France.
Samuel de Champlain	Northwest passage to riches of Indies	Opened Great Lakes region to fur trade. Died of old age after successfully establishing a colony at Quebec.
Rev. Jacques Marquette	To convert the Indians to Christianity	Explored upper Mississippi River for French. Became sick and died on the shores of Lake Michigan.
Louis Joliet	To open new lands for France	Explored Mississippi River with Marquette. Died of old age, a successful businessman.
Robert de la Salle	To open new lands for France	Explored Mississippi River to its mouth. Assassinated by his own men in area now Texas.
Henry Hudson	Northwest passage to riches of Indies	Discovered Hudson River and Hudson Bay. Set adrift in a small boat in Hudson Bay by his mutinous crew.

Think About It!

What can you say about the business of exploring based on the facts presented here? What about exploring is so appealing that people are willing to risk their lives? What kinds of persons would want to be explorers? Who are today's explorers? What risks do they take? What rewards do they seek? What, if anything, is different about the business of exploring today as compared to the days of the early explorers? Would you like to be an explorer? If so, why?

Reflecting on this lesson, what do you see as its strengths and weaknesses? What ideas might you apply to your own teaching?

Technology

How and to what extent can technology improve students' learning of history? How and to what extent do you use technology in your own teaching? How else might you use it?

A potentially major resource for history teachers, which can help students learn to think like historians, is computer-based archives. Some are available on CD-ROM for purchase, such as The Valley of the Shadow, on the Civil War, which includes detailed timelines and copies of newspaper articles from the 1860s for students to analyze. Some are available online, such as those on American History from The Library of Congress.

One example is The Veterans History Project, where students can see and hear veterans' own stories to develop perspectives on war. In addition to document archives, it has photographs, exhibitions, multicultural resources, and sponsors Webcasts. It even has a special area for teachers, which includes lesson plans for classroom activities based on primary sources. Visit the site and ask yourself reflective teaching questions about its potential use, such as "How might my students engage in guided inquiry with some of these primary sources to answer questions that will give them insight into current events?"

An archive that focuses on World History has a search engine built into it so you can look for specific topics or documents. It is designed to provide a working-class, non-Euro-centric view of history. It is organized into these categories: The World, Asia and Oceana, The Americas, Africa, and Europe.

The American Memory Project is another history resource available at the Library of Congress. It includes sections on African-American History, Native American History, Women's History, presidents, government and law, war and military, immigration, and other topics. For a comprehensive view of the resources in the American Memory Project, click on "List All Collections." How might you use these resources in your teaching?

History Matters is an outstanding and unique online multimedia resource for high school and college teachers teaching U.S. and World history. One unusual component is "Making Sense of Documentary Photography," which can help students think reflectively and critically about visual history sources. Another is "video oral histories." The Web site also includes an annotated guide to the most useful Web sites for teaching social studies and U.S. and World history.

River City is a student-oriented, graphic interface, multi-user virtual environment modeled after Active Worlds and its subcomponent, Virtual High School, and gaming environments where many students spend their spare time. It's a simulated city environment, digitized from the Smithsonian Museum's rich collection of visual objects that were historically found in cities at the times targeted in the curriculum. The middle school standards-based curriculum enables different types and levels of inquiry about authentic problems in the context of a realistic historical, immersive, virtual environment. River City teaches students about the history of the Industrial Revolution and its impact on the culture and environment in the 1800s. In an animated, online, game-like environment, students collect water samples, identify incidences of disease, analyze the relationships between pollution and illness, and write letters to the mayor of River City with recommendations based on their conclusions. As is apparent, this lesson is multidisciplinary, including history, science, and English composition.

WebQuests are another excellent way of using technology to promote reflective learning in history. Through structured inquiry experiences, students conduct their own historical research online, accessing a variety of resources such as documents, databases, and archives. The emphasis is not just on looking for information, but also on using it to support analysis, synthesis, and evaluation. These higher-level thinking strategies are important components of reflective thinking. There are 138 WebQuests with the word "history" in the title or description, ranging from grades 3 to 12. There are six WebQuests on immigration. One focuses on Chinese immigration to California during the Gold Rush. Another involves research on Mexican immigration. A third is a problem-solving exercise about immigration to Idaho.

One of the most innovative and motivating ways for students to learn history is through computer-simulated gaming types of environments, such as the well-known Oregon Trail. The Oregon Trail simulation software involves students in a role-playing environment where they travel 2000 miles and encounter obstacles comparable to the actual pioneers in the 1840s such as diseases, drowning, and snakebites. The goal is to reach Willamette Valley by making sensible decisions that require reflective thinking. Students learn history by experiencing it in an enjoyable computer environment where they have to think like the pioneers.

At my school in fifth grade, everyone took part in a dramatization of the Oregon Trail. In groups, some of us built our own covered wagons, dressed like pioneers, and took our "families" on the Oregon Trail, where we encountered other students who were native Americans, with beautiful headdresses and exciting dances that helped us learn about their culture and about conflicts over the land. Over 40 years later I have vivid memories of this adventure and remember it as my favorite experience learning history. Which, if any, of your history lessons will students find most memorable? Why?

WebQuests are another way students can use technology to learn about the Oregon Trail. A multidisciplinary project for middle school students (grades 6–8) is described on the WebQuest Web site as follows:

Westward Expansion 1801–1861 Focuses on the period of Expansion and Reform from 1801–1861. This is done by exploring the following. The history of Louisiana Purchase, the state and federal policies that influenced the Cherokee tribe, social and political impact of the idea of Manifest Destiny pertaining to the Oregon Trail, the significance of Lewis and Clark expedition and its contributions to friendly relations with Native Americans, and the importance of the Monroe Doctrine and War of 1812 during the 19th Century.

The InTime Web site, a database of technology-rich, student-centered lessons across subjects and grade levels, has online videotapes of lessons, along with lesson plans, probing questions, and links to Internet resources, including national content and technology standards. There are 18 social studies lessons ranging from lower elementary school through high school. One of these lessons designed for students in 8th grade is "A Walk Through History." Another is "Introduction to Black Studies" for students in grades 9–12. Both lessons have sets of probing questions to help teachers think reflectively about the lessons: a set of multicultural pre-video viewing and post-video viewing questions, and ten other categories of pre- and post-video viewing questions: teacher interview, lesson overview, principles of learning, information processing, content standards, tenets of democracy, technology, teacher knowledge, and teacher behavior.

Sample questions are in Table 14.4.

TABLE 14.4 InTime History Questions				
Lesson	Multicultural Pre-Video Viewing Questions	Multicultural Post-Video Viewing Questions	Tenets of Democracy Pre-Video Viewing Questions	Tenets of Democracy Post-Video Viewing Questions
A Walk Through History	How can history classes be structured so that lesson content and strategies promote cultural pluralism in society or intergroup harmony in the classroom?	How could this lesson be changed in order to encourage students to view history through the eyes of other cultural groups besides white, middle-class perspective?	What situations are teachers most likely to face in terms of intolerance in the classroom? What can they do to prevent this from happening?	What other tenets of democracy that are not displayed in the video could have been introduced in the lesson? Explain how their integration would have affected the structure of the lesson.

(*continued*)

TABLE 14.4 *(Continued)*

Lesson	Multicultural Pre-Video Viewing Questions	Multicultural Post-Video Viewing Questions	Tenets of Democracy Pre-Video Viewing Questions	Tenets of Democracy Post-Video Viewing Questions
Introduction to Black Studies	Was Black history ever discussed in your high school experiences? Should history classes include Black history curriculum? Explain.	Which key concepts to guide the study of ethnic and cultural groups did Dial utilize in this lesson? How could more be incorporated?	Callahan (1998) described some common problems in critical thinking. One instance is when students try to win an argument by ignoring the issue and attacking the other person. Callahan coined this as "getting personal." As a teacher, how will you help your students avoid this problem that may arise when thinking critically with others?	The teacher engages the students in making meaning by involving them in a dialogue about race relations. What are the beliefs expressed by students regarding this subject?

Summary

It's common for students to have naïve theories or preconceptions regarding what history is all about. Teaching them how historians view history can give them a new perspective on the subject and help them develop reflective, critical thinking skills. Various strategies can be used to help students understand the complexities of history and to recognize and appreciate that historical events can be viewed from multiple and diverse perspectives. Reflective thinking about history can also help students understand how it relates to their every-day life experiences. Knowing the structure of history texts can improve students' reading comprehension. Numerous technology-based resources including primary source materials and exciting instructional methods are available online.

Resources

Alu, J. African American History in the Language Arts Curriculum. American Memory Project. 2002. Retrieved August 6, 2007 from http://www.chatham.edu/pti/African%20American%20History%2002/Alu_02.htm.

Calder, Lendol; and Melissa Beaver. (n.d.) A Worse Result. *Journal of American History.* Retrieved June 9, 2006 from http://www.indiana.edu/~jah/textbooks/2006/calder/pr_worse.html.

Cohen, A. Peace Via Technology. 2005. Retrieved August 19, 2006 from http://www.boloji.com/wfs4/wfs496.htm.

Dede, C.; and D. J. Ketelhut. River City Views. 2003. Retrieved August 19, 2006 from http://muve.gse.harvard.edu/muvees2003/prior_research.htm.

Developing History Teaching through Reflective Practice. 2006. Retrieved June 7, 2007 from http://www.hca.heacademy.ac.uk/resources/guides/refl_prac.php?id=126.

Dodge, B. WebQuest. 2007. Retrieved July 5, 2006 from http://webquest.org/.

Historical Primary Sources: A Guide. (n.d.) Retrieved August 20, 2006 from http://www.library.auckland.ac.nz/subjects/hist/primsources.htm.

History Matters: The U.S. Survey Course on the Web. 2006. Retrieved July 24, 2007 from www.historymatters.gmu.edu/.

Hockwald, H. Different Sides of the Same Coin: How Experts and Novices Use Tacit Knowledge to Understand History from Text. 2002. Retrieved August 19, 2007 from http://www.gse.harvard.edu/~t656_web/Spring_2002_students/hochwald_hilde_history_experts_notices_tk.htm.

Inspiration Software (n.d.). Retrieved July 24, 2007 from http://www.inspiration.com/.

InTime. 2001. Retrieved July 24, 2007 from http://www.intime.uni.edu.

Knowplay. History Software. Your Guide to History Learning Software on the Web. 2004. Retrieved August 19, 2006 from http://www.educational-software-directory.net/social-studies/history.html.

Leinhardt, G.; I. L. Beck; and C. Stainton. *Teaching and Learning in History*, Hillsdale, NJ: Lawrence Erlbaum Associates, 1994.

Library of Congress. Retrieved July 18, 2006 from http://www.loc.gov/index.html.

Library of Congress. Retrieved September 10, 2006 from http://memory.loc.gov/ammem/index.html.

National Council for the Social Sciences. Retrieved July 5, 2006 from http://www.ncss.org/.

Oregon Trail Simulation Software. Retrieved August 9, 2006 from http://www.academicsuperstore.com/market/marketdisp.html?PartNo=564916.

Schon, D. *Educating the Reflective Practitioner.* San Francisco: Jossey-Bass, 1987.

Shopes, L.; and D. A. Doyle. The Task Force on Public History: An Update. American Historical Association. 2003. Retrieved June 9, 2006 from http://www.historians.org./Perspectives/Issues/2003/0309/0309aha3.cfm.

Structured Controversy. Retrieved July 5, 2006 from http://olc.spsd.sk.ca/DE/PD/instr/strats/structuredcon/index.html.

U.S. History.org. Retrieved August 19, 2006 from http://www.ushistory.org/.

Virtual Classroom. Thinking about History. Learn to Question. (n.d.) Retrieved August 20, 2006 from http://www.learntoquestion.com/resources/lessons/intro/text/1.html.

World History Archives. Retrieved July 18, 2006 from http://www.hartford-hwp.com/archives/.

Index